1,001 Things You Always Wanted to Know About the Holy Spirit

J. Stephen Lang

THOMAS NELSON PUBLISHERS
Nashville

Also by J. Stephen Lang
from Thomas Nelson Publishers

*1,001 Things You Always Wanted to Know About the Bible
But Never Thought to Ask*

Published in Nashville, Tennessee, by Thomas Nelson, Inc.

Unless otherwise noted, the Scripture quotations in this publication are from THE NEW KING JAMES VERSION. Copyright © 1979, 1980, 1982, Thomas Nelson, Inc., Publishers.

Scripture quotations noted KJV are from the KING JAMES VERSION of the Bible.

Scripture quotations noted NASB are taken from the NEW AMERICAN STANDARD BIBLE ®. © Copyright The Lockman Foundation 1960, 1962, 1963, 1968, 1971, 1972, 1973, 1975, 1977. Used by permission.

Scripture quotations noted NIV are from the HOLY BIBLE: NEW INTERNATIONAL VERSION®. Copyright © 1973, 1978, 1984 by International Bible Society. Used by permission of Zondervan Publishing House. All rights reserved.

Library of Congress Cataloging-in-Publication Data

Lang, J. Stephen.
   1,001 things you always wanted to know about the Holy Spirit /
  J. Stephen Lang.
     p. cm.
   ISBN 0-7852-7046-9
   1. Holy Spirit Miscellanea. I. Title.
BT121.2.L24 1999
231'.3—dc21   99-15323
                                                   CIP

Printed in the United States of America.
2 3 4 5 6 QPK 04 03 02 01 00 99

Contents

1

Gifts and Fruits of the Spirit

1. fruits of the Spirit

"The fruit of the Spirit is love, joy, peace, longsuffering, kindness, goodness, faithfulness, gentleness, self-control" (Gal. 5:22–23). These admirable qualities are listed by Paul—following a quite different list of qualities of people who follow their sinful natures.

Fruits of the Spirit are different from the spiritual gifts found in 1 Corinthians 12. (See 11 [lists of gifts of the Spirit].)

Christians disagree over the nature of spiritual gifts today, but all agree that the fruits of the Spirit are to be desired by every believer.

2. love

There are many kinds of love: love for friends or family; sexual or romantic love; spiritual love. The Bible shows God's love for man as the greatest love—selfless, forgiving, merciful, at times tough, but strong and durable. That sort of love appears in the New Testament, and the Greek word is *agape*, a love described in Paul's famous Love Chapter, 1 Corinthians 13. The message is to love the way that God does, unselfishly, seeking the other's welfare. *Agape* is difficult to translate, since "love" for many people means the love found in romance novels, rock songs, or pornography. The King James translators understood this and translated *agape* as "charity," but most modern translations have "love."

3. joy

People think of Christians as being anti-sin. True, but a life built on being "anti" is not much of a life. It is amazing how many times the word *joy* occurs in the New Testament. Christians are to find joy in God, in the forgiveness of their sins, in fellowship, in the anticipation of heaven, even in difficulties. The Bible says relatively little about happiness but much about joy.

4. peace

To us, *peace* means "no war." In the Bible it meant more: the state of well-being, security, the condition of being in a right relation with both God and man. The Greek *eirene* conveys this rich meaning. One with faith in God can have this type of peace even if war is raging. Christ the Savior is referred to as "our peace" (Eph. 2:14). The Bible's view of peace is summarized in Isaiah 26:3: "You will keep him in perfect peace, whose mind is stayed on You, because he trusts in You."

5. longsuffering

Older versions of the Bible, including the King James, use this word to refer to God's patience in dealing with humanity. The word was coined by Tyndale in the 1500s, and even though most modern versions don't use it, it is an excellent word. The Bible continually stresses that God is slow to anger, patient—holding off punishment when, by rights, it is long overdue. Paul insisted that Christians should also be longsuffering toward one another.

6. kindness

The Bible speaks constantly of God's kindness toward sinners, a kindness that forgiven sinners are expected to extend toward others. Paul used the Greek word *chrestotes*, based on the root word *chrestos*, "kind." The early Christians noticed the resemblance of *chrestos* and the Greek name for Christ, *Christos*.

7. goodness

This term sounds generic. It refers to a kind of overall moral excellence. The Greek word here, *agathosune*, suggests something like "generosity." Paul said in 2 Corinthians 9:7 that God loves a cheerful giver. You cannot be good unless you are good in relation to others.

8. faithfulness

The word occurs hundreds of times in the Bible. It refers to man's spiritual trust in God, in Christ, in the divine commandments. Paul wrote often about faith in his epistles. For him it was the submissive trust in Christ (1 Cor. 15:1–3). To be a Christian meant not just saying yes to a set of beliefs but also trusting that Christ the Savior restored man's broken relationship with God. As believers trust God as reliable, so we should be reliable in our own relations.

9. gentleness

The whole Bible is anti-pride—if pride means being arrogant, thinking too highly of oneself, making oneself a god. Gentleness is praised—not the meekness of milksops or people harping on their own faults, but a meekness rooted in love for others. Paul told the Christians, "Let nothing be done through selfish ambition or conceit, but in lowliness of mind let each esteem others better than himself" (Phil. 2:3).

10. self-control

The Greek word *akrasia* means something like "self-indulgence" (which means we are living in an *akrasia*-filled age). The word Paul used in his list of fruits of the Spirit is just the opposite: *enkrateia* means "power over the self." For the Christian, of course, the ultimate Power over the self is God. Paul no doubt used *enkrateia* to mean that Christians are not a self-indulgent people. Galatians 5:19–21 lists the sinful indulgences that the Spirit-led person would avoid.

11. lists of gifts of the Spirit

In 1 Corinthians 12, the apostle Paul listed various "gifts of the Spirit," or "spiritual gifts." They include wisdom, knowledge, faith, healing, miracles, prophecy, distinguishing between spirits, speaking in tongues, and interpretation of tongues: "One and the same Spirit works all these things [gifts], distributing to each one individually as He wills" (12:11). Paul emphasized that all Christians are members of one body and all should not expect to have the same gifts. He also stressed in 1 Corinthians 13 that self-giving love is more important than the more demonstrative gifts.

Romans 12:3–8 also refers to spiritual gifts. Paul's list here includes prophesying, teaching, serving, encouraging, contributing to the needs of others, leading, and showing mercy. The Romans list is somewhat more down to earth than the 1 Corinthians list (since it doesn't include healing, miracles, or speaking in tongues), but both lists emphasize the use of gifts to benefit others. There is a mini list of gifts in Ephesians 4:11. The various gifts are explained in the following entries.

12. Paul's "body" chapters

Romans 12 and 1 Corinthians 12 contain Paul's teaching on spiritual gifts. In both places he emphasized that the Christian fellowship is a body, with Christ as the head and each member having an important (though different) role to play. Paul was telling the early Christians—and Christians today—that there is no place for either envy or pride in the church, for "there are diversities of gifts, but the same Spirit . . . And there are diversities of activities, but it the same God who works all in all" (1 Cor. 12:4, 6).

13. miracles (1 Cor. 12:10, 28–29)

The Greek word is *dynameis,* literally "powers." In the book of Acts this word referred to casting out evil spirits and healing sickness (Acts 8:6–7; 19:11–12). (Healing was also listed as a separate gift. See 14.) It probably included the rare instances of raising the dead (Acts 9:36–40; 20:9). Paul the apostle exercised the gift of miracles and put it forward as proof of his apostleship (2 Cor. 12:12).

14. healing (1 Cor. 12:9, 28, 30)

Jesus and His apostles performed many acts of healing, as seen again and again in the Gospels and in Acts. Jesus promised His followers that this would be so. Both the person healing and the person healed had to express faith in God (except, of course, in the case of an unconscious person). As the age of the apostles passed, the gift of healing did not, and it still continues, though there always will be skeptics. Skepticism is probably inevitable, given that there are indeed some shysters operating as faith-healers. Luke, the "beloved physician," was a friend of Paul, so apparently the early Christians accepted that some healing occurred via medical science, while some healing occurred miraculously.

15. helpers (1 Cor. 12:28)

Our word *helper* is so vague that we don't immediately know what this gift meant to the early Christians. Based on Acts 20:35, in which Paul exhorted elders to "help the weak" (NASB), we can assume that it refers to helping the needy. The early Christians inherited from the Jews a concern for poor and oppressed people. Not all Christians enter gladly into this ministry, so it seems appropriate that certain people would be described as having a special gift for being helpers.

16. government administrations (1 Cor. 12:28; Rom. 12:8)

Churches in the sense of buildings or denominations did not exist in the New Testament period, and there was no standard way of organizing the Christian communities. The gift of "governments" or "administrations" may refer to the Spirit-given ability to organize and administer rightly. This is indeed a rare and valuable gift (not one that every pastor or church leader possesses!). In the early church the leaders would have been people who earned their living through a trade. There was no professional, full-time clergy in our modern sense. In some ways that was a blessing. The only way to be a leader was by showing ability (as opposed to graduating from a seminary or passing an exam from a denominational board).

17. faith (1 Cor. 12:9)

Jesus had told His followers that faith could accomplish amazing things (Matt. 17:19–20). This mountain-moving faith seems to be what Paul had in mind here. All believers have faith, but the special kind of *charisma* faith mentioned here is a gift of the Spirit, not given to every believer. There is no doubt that in times of persecution, then and now, this kind of faith is a valuable gift to exercise.

18. apostleship (1 Cor. 12:28)

Originally, the title *apostle* applied only to Jesus' inner circle of twelve disciples. But as Paul's writings made clear, he definitely considered himself an apostle, though he was not one of the original twelve. So did Paul's missionary companion Barnabas, and so did James, head of the Christian community in Jerusalem. The title was limited to those who had a clear mission to preach the gospel widely. Over the centuries, various Christian heroes have made such a name for themselves that they became known as apostles (such as the "apostle to the Irish," the renowned St. Patrick).

19. prophets (1 Cor. 12:10)

These were not fortune-tellers but, as the Old Testament prophets, "forth-tellers"—telling the word of God forth in the world. Some prophets did actually foretell future events (Acts 11:28; 21:10–11), but mostly, the prophet's mission was edifying and instructing the local churches. The New Testament gives the impression that they were itinerant preachers. As the church became more ritualized and institutionalized over the centuries, its organization had no place for these people.

20. discerning of spirits (1 Cor. 12:10)

Some parts of the New Testament state that all believers are to exercise their God-given wisdom in discerning between true and false spirits (1 Thess. 5:20–21; 1 John 4:1). But Paul's listing of discernment as a spiritual gift indicates that some believers are especially gifted in this matter. When Christianity was in its infancy, there were many false prophets, especially traveling ones, and it helped that some believers were better than others at discerning just which people were true prophets of God.

21. teaching (Rom. 12:7; 1 Cor. 12:28–29)

What was the difference between a prophet and a teacher? At times, not much. But it appears that a prophet proclaimed the word of God and that a teacher was adept at explaining the prophet's meaning. To use a modern analogy, the prophet was the dramatic guest speaker, and the teacher was the leader of the Bible study class, engaged in diligent study. Not all speakers make good teachers, and not all teachers are good speakers.

22. exhortation (Rom. 12:8)

The apostle Barnabas, friend and fellow missionary of Paul, was originally named Joseph. Barnabas, actually a nickname, means "son of encouragement" or "son of exhortation." One who exhorted could be a prophet or teacher, but the gift of exhortation suggests a more personal role of love and sympathy. Personal charm and grace might be part of the gift of exhortation.

23. the word of wisdom (1 Cor. 12:8)

Wisdom is mentioned many, many times in connection with the Spirit. In some ways the Spirit imparts wisdom to all believers, but not all believers grasp easily certain "deep things of God" (1 Cor. 2:10). Most Christians, regardless of their worldly wisdom, have trouble understanding the ways of God. So a person with the special gift of wisdom would have a better grasp of such things and perhaps the ability to explain them to others.

24. the word of knowledge (1 Cor. 12:8)

How is this different from a "word of wisdom" mentioned in the same verse? We can't be sure. "Knowledge" suggests a basic grasp of key Christian principles or facts, while "wisdom" suggests something that can be applied to life. "Word of knowledge" may also refer to being receptive to divinely revealed secrets about another person's need.

25. tongues (1 Cor. 12:10, 28)

This gift, apparently common in New Testament times, has been the subject of endless controversy (and was so in Paul's day, as 1 Cor. 14 indicates). When someone speaks in tongues, he addresses himself to God in prayer and praise, edifying himself (and, with the aid of an interpreter, others). One who speaks in tongues speaks forth in ecstasy, a distinctive prayer language. Some Christians today and in earlier times have attributed tongues to fakery or even to the work of demons. The renewal movement has opened the mainline denominations, and the church in general, to the possibility (and desirability) of speaking in tongues.

26. interpretation of tongues (1 Cor. 12:10, 30)

Paul spent a great deal of time in 1 Corinthians 14 explaining the importance of interpreting tongues. Clearly, many Christians did and do experience the joy of speaking in tongues, speaking their distinctive prayer language to the Lord. But Paul indicated that it does not edify other Christians unless an interpreter is present. Paul seemed to suggest that there are more tongues speakers than there are interpreters.

27. evangelist (Eph. 4:11)

All Christians are expected to be witnesses to the gospel, but just as clearly, being an evangelist is a special gift and task of some people. Only a few times is anyone in the New Testament referred to with this term. Paul called Timothy an evangelist (2 Tim. 4:5), and one of the seven deacons was known as Philip the evangelist (Acts 21:8). The word comes from the Greek word *euangelion,* meaning "good news" but usually translated "gospel." So an evangelist is one who spreads the gospel.

28. service (Rom. 12:7 NASB)

Jesus, the Lord but also the servant, emphasized to His disciples that greatness came from serving, not from lording it over others (Matt. 20:26). The Greek word here is *diakonia* (from which we get our word *deacon*). The early Christians in Jerusalem chose seven men (known generally as the deacons) to serve in various ways. It is possible that Paul was referring to people who are especially good at this office.

29. contributing (Rom. 12:8)

Jesus was especially kind in His words about the poor widow who nonetheless gave generously (Mark 12:41–43). A willingness to be generous is expected to be a mark of all Christian believers (2 Cor. 9:6; 1 Tim. 6:18). But some people seem especially suited to works of generosity, even giving till it hurts.

30. giving aid (Rom. 12:8)

Perhaps this doesn't differ much, or any, from the gift of being a helper (see 15) or from acts of mercy. If this work does not seem particularly gift related, consider this: aiding a criminal or suspected criminal is usually a crime in itself. Time and time again throughout history Christians have been persecuted, often to the point of death, and aiding them could bring persecution to the person giving aid.

31. xenolalia

The word *glossolalia* refers to speaking in an unknown tongue, a private praise language. But Acts 2 points to something different: speaking in a foreign language that one has not learned. Acts records that the apostles "began to speak with other tongues, as the Spirit gave them utterance," and the amazed listeners observed that "we hear them speaking in our own tongues the wonderful works of God" (Acts 2:4, 11). This is *xenolalia*—literally translated "foreign speaking." Like glossolalia, it occurs under the power of the Spirit. It occurred not only at the Pentecost gathering in Acts 2 but also many times throughout history when missionaries proclaimed the gospel in languages they had not learned. The Catholic missionary Francis Xavier (see 390) was one example.

Charles Parham, a key figure in the history of Pentecostalism, originally believed that all the Bible's references to tongues were referring to xenolalia. That delighted him because he believed the gift would make any preacher into an "instant missionary" when sent abroad. (In other words, why learn a foreign language when the Spirit can endow you with the gift?) What Parham himself eventually experienced was glossolalia, not xenolalia.

32. no tongues, no baptism

Put another way, if you have not spoken in tongues, you have not been baptized in the Spirit. Most charismatics today do not take this position, though it is the classic Pentecostal position, and quite a few Pentecostals still believe it. As there is more and more interaction among various groups of people in the movements, this attitude will likely be less common than it once was.

33. indisputable proof

The historic Pentecostal revival in 1901 at Charles F. Parham's Topeka Bible school began (on the human level, anyway) with Parham's students. Parham claimed that he assigned his students to study the book of Acts, and they reached the consensus that speaking in tongues was "indisputable proof" of the baptism of the Holy Spirit. (See 476 [Parham].)

34. biblical sign

Agnes Ozman (see 477) spoke in tongues on January 1, 1901—a historic day in the renewal movement. A student of Charles Parham at his Topeka Bible school, Ozman asked Parham to lay hands on her and pray that she would be baptized in the Spirit, as evidenced by a "biblical sign." Ozman then spoke in tongues (Chinese, according to Parham) and did not speak English for three days. Ozman later claimed that she had not expected the tongues episode but accepted it as the "biblical sign."

35. initial evidence

These two words have caused a lot of discussion among Pentecostals and charismatics. In essence, they mean that speaking in tongues is *the* evidence of having received the baptism of the Spirit. But this first experience of speaking in tongues is *not* the same as having the gift of tongues, since the gift is permanent. In other words, for those who believe in initial evidence, everyone baptized in the Spirit will speak in tongues, though not all of those people will continue to do so afterward.

Several major denominations, including the Assemblies of God, the Church of God (Cleveland, Tennessee), and the International Church of the Foursquare Gospel, officially teach the doctrine of initial evidence. Not every person in these denominations accepts this, nor do many other people who would describe themselves as charismatics or Pentecostals. Many people in the renewal movement accept that tongues could be one evidence of baptism in the Spirit—but not necessarily the *only* one.

36. cessationism

This is the belief that the gifts of the Spirit ceased with the age of the apostles. While the history of the church shows that this is not the case, it is clear that when the church became established as the official religion of the Roman Empire, fewer people exercised spiritual gifts. Augustine (see 362), one of the most influential theologians, held to cessationism, and at the time of the Reformation, so did the great theologian John Calvin (see 380). Regrettably, it is the position of many Christians today. Logically, people who see no evidence of spiritual gifts will cease to believe in them.

37. "seek not, forbid not"

The Christian and Missionary Alliance (CMA) took this official position on the subject of speaking in tongues. The CMA struggled with how to deal with the rising Pentecostal movement, and devotional writer A. W. Tozer may have been the source of the phrase "seek not, forbid not." It embodies a fairly tolerant attitude toward tongues: they are not to be prohibited in the church, but also not to be particularly sought out. This is not the position of most Pentecostal churches (which do believe in seeking the gift of tongues), but it is an attitude that most Pentecostals and charismatics can live with.

38. the dispensational view

Several paragraphs would be needed to do justice to the Christian view known as dispensationalism. In brief, it divides history into several eras, or dispensations, during which God deals with mankind in different ways. The view claims to be based on the Bible, and its most famous advocate was C. I. Scofield, famed for his popular *Scofield Reference Bible* and its explanatory notes (see 942). Dispensationalists in general take a dim view of the gifts of the Spirit, many of them believing that the gifts ended with the New Testament period. One dispensational scholar, Merrill Unger, claimed to base this belief on Paul's words in 1 Corinthians 13:10: "When that which is perfect has come, then that which is in part will be done away." According to Unger, the "perfect" thing is the completed New Testament. In other words, now that we have the Bible, we need no longer look for the spiritual gifts.

39. the deaf

People who are deaf—even deaf from birth—have spoken in tongues. How can they do that unless the Spirit genuinely moved them? The phenomenon puzzles skeptics, who like to believe that tongues speakers are faking the experience by imitating other people who claim to have spoken in tongues.

40. an end of prophecy?

In Paul's lists of gifts of the Spirit (found in 1 Cor. 12 and Rom. 12), prophesying is one of the gifts. It is clear from the book of Acts that there were prophets in the early church. But not long after the New Testament period, the idea crept in that prophecy had ended; that is, instead of giving heed to Spirit-led prophets, Christians should be content with the revelation found in the Bible. Hippolytus, an early Christian author, stated that "prophet" applied only to the prophets in the Bible. By the fourth century or so, official Christian teaching was that the spiritual gift of prophecy belonged to the past—a contradiction of Paul's letters. But various groups throughout Christian history have found that the gift of prophecy is still to be found wherever people allow the Spirit to move.

41. Vatican II Council on spiritual gifts

Before the beginning of the Catholic charismatic renewal, the historic Vatican II Council (1962–65) had prepared the way by issuing a statement on spiritual gifts: "These charismatic gifts, whether they be the most outstanding or the more simple and widely diffused, are to be received with thanksgiving and consolation, for they are exceedingly suitable and useful for the needs of the church." When various spiritual gifts were seen in the churches following the council, the church stuck by its statement and gave them a warm reception.

42. "silver and gold have I none"

Acts 3 tells the story of a disabled beggar who asked the apostle Peter for money. Peter replied, "Silver and gold have I none; but such as I have give I thee: In the name of Jesus Christ of Nazareth rise up and walk" (v. 6 KJV). The beggar was healed and began to praise God.

Fast-forward to the 1500s: Pope Leo X reigned from 1513 to 1521. Leo was worldly and loved to spend money on art and music. A cardinal, observing a lavish cathedral, said to Leo, "Truly, the church can no longer say, 'Silver and gold have I none.'" Leo replied, "Neither can it say, 'Rise up and walk.'" A sad truth: when the church increases in wealth and worldly power, the spiritual gifts such as healing are seldom seen.

43. talent or gift?

Believers frequently debate the spiritual gifts described in the New Testament, wondering about the difference (if any) between natural talents and gifts of the Spirit. We often refer to a talented artist or musician as a gifted person, and it is true that any human ability is, in some way, a gift from God. But the specific gifts that Paul refers to are different in a crucial way: *they are for building up the church in its worship and witness to the world.* That is, the gifts meet a deep need of the church. They may not have any connection with the person's natural abilities—a person with a low IQ might receive a word of knowledge from the Lord, and a prophecy might come from someone with no talent for speaking.

44. *Sounds of Wonder*

Jubilation is the word author Eddie Ensley uses to describe what we call speaking in tongues or singing in tongues. In his 1977 book he claims that the "wordless vocalized entrance into the mystery of God's love" is found in the New Testament and in the church today. *Sounds of Wonder* was published by Paulist Press, a Catholic publisher, one of many examples of the Catholic church's openness to the charismatic movement.

45. what of the pre-Pentecostal Christians?

Speaking in tongues has occurred throughout Christian history, but between the book of Acts and the early 1900s, it was rare. When it became common with the Pentecostal revival in the 1900s, some sensitive people asked an obvious question: Were all the great Christians of the past lacking the Spirit? Did the fact that men such as Martin Luther and John Wesley never spoke in tongues mean that the Spirit's power was not on them? A few Pentecostals said yes, but more than a few said no. Many did, and do, say that when Christians of the past clearly showed the fruits of the Spirit (see 1), then obviously, they had the Spirit's power.

46. *The Third Force in Missions*

Evangelicals, said Paul Pomerville in this 1985 book, are gung ho on missions but tend to stress the Bible and correct belief at the expense of experiencing the work of the Spirit. In other words, evangelicals stress the mind at the expense of the heart, while both are essential. More than that, evangelicals typically downplay the sign gifts (tongues, healing, miracles), which are so evident in growing churches.

47. reincarnated missionaries?

Xenolalia (see 31) refers to the Spirit-given ability to speak in a language that one has never learned. This has occurred many times on the mission field (more often than skeptics would like to believe). Among Buddhists and Hindus there is an explanation for xenolalia: the ability to speak in the local language means that the missionary had lived there in a previous lifetime and the language had carried over. In other words, Missionary Joe from Cincinnati speaks only English, but in India finds himself speaking the Tamil language. Joe knows this was by the power of the Spirit, but some of his Tamil listeners believe his soul must have lived among them in a previous life.

Not

2

Churches of Note

48. Church on the Way

The popular song "Majesty" is only one of the more than three hundred songs that Jack Hayford (b. 1941) has written, but his ministry reaches far beyond songwriting. He is pastor of the Church on the Way in Van Nuys, California, affiliated with the International Church of the Foursquare Gospel. The Church on the Way has become one of the most noted American churches, growing from less than twenty members to more than six thousand, and opening the King's College and the King's Seminary. The songwriter and pastor is also a noted conference speaker and author of such books as *Moments with Majesty.*

49. Yoido Full Gospel Church, the world's largest

Paul (David) Yonggi Cho (b. 1936) is pastor of the world's largest Christian congregation, which is not in the U.S. or Europe but—surprise!—in Korea. Cho was raised as a Buddhist in a Buddhist land. He relates that Jesus appeared to him in the middle of the night, called him to the ministry, and filled him with the Holy Spirit. Cho graduated from an Assemblies of God Bible school and began a tent church in Seoul, South Korea's capital, in 1958. The church grew so that he built a 1,500-seat revival center in downtown Seoul, naming it Full Gospel Central Church. At its dedication there were divine healings, and membership grew even more. In 1973 Billy Graham was host at the dedication of the new 10,000-seat building, home to 100,000 members by 1979 and more than 700,000 (yes, that's correct) by 1998. Huge as the church is, its focus is on small group fellowship, with literally thousands of leaders of home cell groups. Cho officially changed his first name from Paul to David in the 1990s.

50. the Toronto Blessing

One of the more amazing outpourings of the Spirit in the 1990s began at a Vineyard Fellowship near Toronto's airport. The Toronto Airport Christian Fellowship, thanks in part to its location, has attracted thousands of international visitors each year, and thanks to the Britain-Canada connection, the Toronto Blessing spread to Great Britain. Thousands and thousands more are turning to Christ at the amazing church.

51. World Harvest Church

Located near Columbus, Ohio, and pastored by Rod Parsley, this church grew out of a backyard Bible study group. The huge multiracial congregation has a noted healing ministry, and Parsley hosts the *Breakthrough* TV program.

52. Angelus Temple

The huge church in Los Angeles is the headquarters of the International Church of the Foursquare Gospel (see 151), founded by evangelist Aimee Semple McPherson (see 474). Sister Aimee dedicated the church in 1923 and pastored it until her death in 1944. In large part the church, which seated 5,300 people, was designed by Aimee herself. Made of steel-reinforced concrete, the temple had a Watch Tower, in which volunteers prayed around the clock. The church had its own radio station, KFSG (Kall Four Square Gospel).

It was not a "Sundays only" church. There were various prayer and Bible study services almost every night and regularly scheduled healing services. The church also helped poor and unemployed people, and it established the L.I.F.E. (Lighthouse of International Foursquare Evangelism) Bible College. Presently the temple, somewhat redesigned, seats 3,300 and has Hispanic and Korean services as well as English services.

53. Bethel AME

Bethel African Methodist Episcopal Church in Baltimore, founded in the 1700s, is one of the oldest black churches in the U.S. Its pastor beginning in 1975 was John Bryant, Baltimore native and son of an AME bishop. Bryant (who later became an AME bishop) experienced the power of the Spirit and took the historic church in a charismatic direction. Bethel, with more than twelve thousand members, emphasizes not only the gifts of the Spirit but also social concern, reaching out to the community in the areas of employment, education, and food and shelter. It broadcasts *Outreach of Love* on television.

54. Glad Tidings Tabernacle

Marie Burgess, an associate of Charles Parham, was told by Parham to take the message of Spirit-led Christianity to New York. She responded in 1907 by establishing the Glad Tidings Tabernacle. Small at first, the congregation purchased a large church structure on Thirty-third Street, Manhattan. By that time Marie had married Irish preacher Robert Brown (see 542), and the two affiliated their church with the Assemblies of God. The church broadcast Sunday afternoon services across metropolitan New York and was, through the 1940s, New York's center for Pentecostals.

55. Rock Church

John Gimenez (b. 1931) and Anne Gimenez (b. 1932) were the well-known pastor and copastor of the Rock

Church in Virginia Beach, Virginia. John's early life hardly looked promising—dropping out of school in the eighth grade, then doing time in reform school and prison. But he was converted and became involved in a ministry with drug addicts. His wife, Anne, had been converted at a tent crusade in 1949, and the two were married in 1967. The Rock Church was established a year later and grew by leaps and bounds. The five-thousand-member church is, in effect, the mother church of a denomination, since there are branch Rock Churches in many locations. The couple departed Rock Church in 1995.

56. Garr Memorial Church

Charlotte, North Carolina, was the final stop for globe-trotting evangelist A. G. Garr (see 505), who had ministered in India and other Asian nations. In 1930 Garr and his wife conducted a popular tent revival in Charlotte, and response was so good that they remained there, establishing an independent church. It grew so that the congregation renovated an old city auditorium, first called Garr Auditorium, later Garr Memorial Church. When Garr died in 1944, his wife, Hanna, became pastor. For many years Hanna had a daily radio broadcast, *Morning Thought*.

57. Evangelical Cathedral of Jotabeche

The world's second-largest church is this Pentecostal giant in Santiago, Chile. Its central worship space seats 16,000, but with more than 300,000 members, it is not possible to seat everyone in the cathedral each Sunday. Members are allowed to attend worship in the cathedral one Sunday per month, meeting the other Sundays in one of the 325 *templos* or 60 *locales,* all within ten miles of the cathedral.

58. Miracle Center of Nigeria

An independent charismatic church in Benin City, Nigeria, the Miracle Center has a sanctuary seating twenty thousand. Its pastor, Benson Idahosa (who died in 1998), had seen many miracles, including, so it is said, several people raised from the dead.

59. Vision of the Future Church

Argentina is home to this independent charismatic congregation—and a *grande* congregation it is, with about ninety thousand members. Its senior pastor, Omar Cabrera, travels thousands of miles each month to minister to this church, which holds its meetings in forty-five different sites in central Argentina.

60. Mekane Yesus Church

Signs and wonders are alive and well in this large and growing Lutheran church of Ethiopia. Mekane Yesus Church has witnessed numerous healings, exorcism of evil spirits, and other manifestations of the Spirit. The estimate of its membership is 750,000.

61. Zion Christian Church, South Africa

This massive and still-growing denomination hosts an annual Easter gathering near Pietersburg, where more than a million people gather to celebrate their faith.

62. Rhema Church of Johannesburg

South Africa is home to many large independent charismatic churches, one of the largest being the Rhema Church in Johannesburg. Its sanctuary holds five thousand, and church membership is estimated at ten thousand.

63. Sung Rak Baptist Church

David Cho's church in Seoul, South Korea, is the world's largest, but the country is home to another vibrant megachurch, the Sung Rak Baptist, pastored by Ki Dong Kim. Kim has participated in healing, casting out demons, and even raising the dead. It is a curiosity that the Southern Baptists, the largest Protestant denomination in the U.S., have their largest church in Korea. Sung Rak has about forty thousand members.

64. Carpenter's Home

A 1985 magazine article on Karl David Strader's ministry was titled "The Pastor Who Built a 10,000-Seat Church in a City of 58,000." Strader (b. 1929), an Assemblies of God pastor, did indeed build a 10,000-seat sanctuary in the city of Lakeland, Florida. At the time it was built it was the largest church in the U.S. It is the First Assembly of God, but also known as the Carpenter's Home Church.

65. Melodyland Christian Center

Located in California's densely populated Orange County, the congregation began in 1961 with only a few members, but under pastor Ralph Wilkerson, it grew steadily and needed larger accommodations. In 1969 the church purchased the Melodyland Theater complex near Disneyland and converted it into a church, holding several Sunday services with sometimes fifteen thousand in attendance. It opened Melodyland School of Theology in 1973 and later added a high school and Christian college. Not ignoring social concern, the church had a Melodyland Hotline for helping troubled teens and other disturbed persons. The megachurch is also noted for its charismatic clinics held annually.

66. Mount Paran Church of God

There are many Churches of God in the U.S., but few are known as megachurches. Mount Paran in Atlanta is one of the biggies. Under the long pastorate of Paul Laverne Walker, Mount Paran grew from about five hundred in 1960 to more than eight thousand at the present time, the largest Church of God congregation in the U.S. Walker is now general overseer of the Church of God, and Mount Paran has spawned a second location north of Atlanta.

67. Pensacola outpouring

In the late 1990s Brownsville Assembly of God, Pensacola, Florida, was the site of an ongoing revival. Pastor John Kilpatrick and evangelist Steve Hill have taken little credit, giving it all to the Spirit. Visitors have arrived at the church at the crack of dawn to be sure of getting a seat, and they have been known to stay through the night, praying, singing, and fellowshipping.

68. Without Walls International Church

Randy and Paula White started this vibrant congregation in 1991 as a storefront church in Tampa, Florida. The nondenominational, multiethnic fellowship has grown to 2,500, with numerous street-level ministries and satellite fellowships.

69. Calvary Chapel

During the 1970s California revival loosely known as the Jesus People (see 143), Calvary Chapel received a lot of media exposure. It was a tiny group until pastor Chuck Smith, called in 1965, began the group's outreach to the counterculture youth of southern California. Bible studies and prayer meetings touched the lives of the dropouts from society (which included drug addicts), and the church adopted pop music for Christian uses. Critics disliked the "hipness," but the church was clearly reaching people who would have been uncomfortable at most churches. As an alternative to the sex-and-drugs communes of that era, the church formed its own Christian communes.

The growing church purchased a ten-acre tract in 1971. The church seats 2,500 in a flexible arrangement that set the precedent for many large and growing churches. The church has its fellowship hall set up as an overflow area with closed-circuit television. The congregation has grown to 25,000 members, among the twenty largest churches in the world. It is so large that even with multiple services, it uses the Anaheim Convention Center at times. The congregation has also spawned many other Calvary Chapels in the U.S.

70. Chapel Hill Harvester Church / Cathedral of the Holy Spirit

With his brother Don, Earl P. Paulk Jr. (b. 1927) founded this congregation in Atlanta's suburbs, a church that grew to more than twelve thousand people with more than twenty full-time pastors. The church was home to the weekly TV program *Harvester Television Network*. Ministering to substance abusers, prisoners, and homosexuals, the church opened Earl Paulk College in 1986. The church publishes the monthly magazine *Thy Kingdom Come,* and Paulk has written such books as *Satan Unmasked, Ultimate Kingdom,* and his autobiography, *The Provoker.*

71. First Assembly, Phoenix

America abounds with megachurches, and one is First Assembly of God in Phoenix, Arizona, with an average Sunday attendance of 14,000. Tommy J. Barnett (b. 1937) pastored the Westside Assembly in Davenport, Iowa, and watched its attendance grow from less than 100 to more than 4,000. He went to the Phoenix First Assembly in 1979 and watched it grow like a mushroom. First Assembly is known for its dramatic productions at Christmas, Easter, and other holidays.

3

Worship and Church Life

72. fellowship or church?

Many charismatic or Pentecostal congregations prefer to call themselves fellowships instead of churches. Although the difference is purely one of terminology, the idea of a fellowship does seem closer to the type of Christian community described in the New Testament. The Greek word *koinonia* refers to fellowship, community, a fellow-feeling that many people do not associate with church.

73. laying on of hands

Laying both hands on another person (usually on the head) had serious meanings in Bible times. It could symbolize a parent bestowing an inheritance (Gen. 48:14–20) or an act of blessing (Matt. 19:13). Jesus and the apostles often laid hands on a person asking to be healed (Mark 5:23). Laying on of hands was often associated with conferring the gifts and rights of an office—priest, deacon, pastor, missionary. The ones laying on the hands were respected authority figures who symbolically passed on power and authority to the other person (Acts 6:6; 13:3). The apostles sometimes laid hands on a person who would then receive the Holy Spirit (Acts 8:17; 19:6).

Healing was and is associated with laying on of hands. Jesus and Paul laid hands on people whom they healed (Mark 6:5; Luke 4:40; Acts 28:8). Throughout the centuries and still today, healing prayer is often accompanied by laying on of hands. Laying on of hands is practiced in all charismatic and Pentecostal churches.

74. anointing with oil

In the past, anointing (daubing the forehead or head with a small amount of olive oil) was connected with the Catholic ritual of extreme unction, given only to a person thought to be on the verge of death. Many churches now use it in anointing the sick, as suggested by Mark 6:13 and James 5:14. The early Christians perceived anointing not as last rites (which is how the church had come to perceive it) but as a means to healing, in conjunction with prayer.

75. dancing in the Spirit

Historically, social dancing (especially since the rock 'n' roll era) has been frowned on by Pentecostals and charismatics, but there has long been a tradition of physical movement in worship, unconsciously and sometimes consciously like dancing. Most religions, including early Christianity, have made space for some sort of dancing in worship. Although older believers today often feel uncomfortable as people in their congregations sway or clap in time to music, a younger generation exposed to MTV sees an obvious—and positive—difference between "church dancing" and the lewdness of much contemporary dancing.

76. proxy prayer

A fairly new phenomenon, proxy prayer involves an interested person who sits on a chair in the middle of a small circle of gathered Christians. The persons gathered pray for a person not present, and the person in the chair is the stand-in for that person. The ones praying usually place their hands on the person in the chair. The person being prayed for may be a fellow believer or may be an unbeliever who would not wish to be prayed for. Proxy prayer is fairly common today among charismatics and Pentecostals.

77. touch

Unbelievers, and even some Christians, probably scoff at televangelists who urge viewers to "touch the screen." But as everyone acknowledges today, touch is important in human relations, and charismatic and Pentecostal churches have long been aware of this. Being open to emotion and spontaneity, churches in the renewal movement encourage loosening up, as long as it is kept within the bounds of discretion, of course. Holding hands in a circle of prayer is common, as is touching the shoulder or arm of someone being prayed for. Laying on of hands (see 73) has long been associated with people receiving the gift of the Holy Spirit. Touch is not absolutely essential to Christian worship, but for many believers it adds to the richness of fellowship.

78. Jericho march

The book of Joshua records how the people of Israel walked seven times around the walls of the pagan city of Jericho, after which the city walls fell down. During charismatic worship, an individual worshiper sometimes begins to march around the perimeter of the worship space, with others joining in, sometimes including the whole congregation. The march is accompanied by singing or shouting and might last an hour or more. Often the person initiating the march begins by dancing in the Spirit (see 75). A Jericho march is unplanned and unrehearsed, and can take place only in a church open to such spontaneity.

79. sacred expletives

No, not cursing, but spontaneous outbursts of short phrases during worship. Some familiar ones are "Hallelujah!"; "Thank You, Jesus!"; "Glory to God!"; and the venerable "Amen!" These outbursts are not considered interruptions but are heartfelt affirmations of whatever the speaker has just stated. In churches that allow for spontaneity, they are a welcome addition to worship, enlisting the participation of each person.

80. words of knowledge in worship

Worship and group meetings in renewal churches, being open to interruptions, can involve a person informing the congregation of receiving a "word of knowledge" from the Lord, usually concerning one or several of the people present. The Bible claims that some believers possess this as a spiritual gift (1 Cor. 12:8), but presumably, any believer can, on occasion, utter a divinely received word. Skeptics scoff at this ability, but there is no doubt that some Christians reveal information that they could not possibly have gained through natural means.

81. holy laughter

Not so common today, this occurred fairly often in the early days of Pentecostalism. A person praying at the altar would sometimes begin to laugh and continue for several minutes. Presumably, the laughter was from a sense of release from sin and guilt, a deep and spontaneous expression of joy in the Lord.

82. tent revivals

The *sawdust trail* used to refer to evangelists who held their meetings in large tents (often called tabernacles, from the Bible's word for Israel's sacred tent). The huge tents covered the seating area, which had folding chairs, and on the ground was sawdust or sweet-smelling wood chips. Tent revivals still take place, but over the years they have given way to large, permanent structures (some of them still called tabernacles) with wood or concrete floors. The Ryman Auditorium, Nashville's famous Grand Ole Opry House for many years, was originally built as a revival tabernacle.

83. dress-down Sundays

Our society has become (to state the obvious) more casual and more immodest in dress for both men and women. Not long ago, attending church involved suits and ties for men, neat (and modest) dresses for women, worn with hat and gloves. As society dresses down, so does Christian worship, and many churches allow or even encourage jeans and sometimes shorts. (The shorts would have horrified an earlier generation, assuming they even allowed the person inside.) The New Testament says a great deal about conforming to the world's standards but leaves the particulars to each church and (more to the point) to each individual.

84. high praise

Worship in most Spirit-filled churches is definitely more exuberant than that in the more traditional "stained-glass church." *Praise* is the term used for congregational singing in the usual language, while *high praise* is uttered in unknown tongues, sometimes also called *singing in the Spirit.*

85. ordinances

The Catholic and Orthodox churches have sacraments (seven of them, for the Catholics), meaning certain rituals/acts that are believed to serve as channels of grace. Protestants, if they believe in sacraments, generally believe in two, Communion and water baptism. Most Protestants believe these two are merely symbolic, outward signs of an inward grace, but still just symbols—that is, the acts don't actually cause anything to happen. This is the case in most Pentecostal denominations, which never refer to sacraments; instead, they refer to *ordinances*, meaning the practices are *ordained* by Christ. Many Pentecostal churches also include footwashing among the ordinances.

Charismatics in the Catholic, Orthodox, Episcopal, and some other denominations may hold to their churches' traditional teachings about the sacraments.

86. footwashing

Of the four Gospels, only John's gave the account of Jesus washing His disciples' feet, a symbol of humility and servanthood that He commanded them to follow (John 13). Curiously, John's gospel did not report the Last Supper, even though the footwashing must have occurred just before that. This suggests that John believed footwashing was important—not necessarily that the Lord's Supper is unimportant, but that footwashing should (as Jesus commanded) be part of the church's life. Historically, Pentecostal churches have been faithful in observing this practice, notably the Church of God (Cleveland,

Tennessee). It can be a touching reminder not only of servanthood toward fellow believers but also of a fellowship that knows no barriers of race or class.

87. water baptism

Baptism by water, even in churches that emphasize baptism of the Spirit, is very important and considered essential for anyone joining a congregation. In most Pentecostal churches it is by immersion, either in a baptistery or (still done in country churches) in a lake or stream. Pentecostals insist on believer's baptism—that is, the person has to be of age, willing to testify to having experienced conversion. For this reason Pentecostals do not baptize infants.

All Christian churches, following Jesus' command in Matthew 28:19, baptize in the name of the Father, Son, and Holy Spirit. The exception: the Oneness Pentecostals (see 216), who baptize in the name of Jesus only.

Charismatics in the mainline denominations are more likely to witness baptism of infants, as well as the likelihood of baptism by sprinkling rather than immersion. The mainline churches, particularly Catholics and Episcopalians, view baptism as a *sacrament,* while many other mainliners (as well as Pentecostals) view it as an *ordinance* (see 85).

88. Lord's Supper

Denominations that view the Lord's Supper (also called Communion or the Eucharist) as a *sacrament* celebrate it often, usually every Sunday. This applies to Catholics, Episcopalians, Orthodox, and some others. Most Protestant denominations do it less often, sometimes only quarterly. Pentecostals vary in their frequency. They view the Lord's Supper not as a sacrament but as an *ordinance* (see 85), and it is taken seriously, though not perceived the same way as Catholics and others see it. One notable difference: because of the traditional Pentecostal ban on alcohol, grape juice, not wine, is used in Communion.

89. flame symbol

Charismatics and Pentecostals often use the dove as a symbol since it represents the ascent of the Spirit at Jesus' baptism. They also use the symbol of a flame, basing this on the account of Pentecost in Acts 2. Gathered in Jerusalem, the apostles experienced the sound of a rushing wind, "then there appeared to them divided tongues, as of fire, and one sat upon each of them. And they were all filled with the Holy Spirit" (2:3–4). The flame also harks back to John the Baptist's prophecy that the Christ would baptize not with water but "with the Holy Spirit and fire" (Luke 3:16).

90. prayer towers

One can pray anywhere, of course, but many churches, schools, and ministries set aside special prayer rooms for quietness and privacy. The Bible mentions that the apostles were in an upper room when the Spirit descended upon them (Acts 2), and Elijah also prayed in an upper room (1 Kings 17). From these biblical references comes the idea of an elevated room for prayer. Charles Parham (see 476) converted a dome at his Bible school into a prayer tower, and Aimee Semple McPherson had such a space in her Angelus Temple. PTL had an Upper Room where visitors could pray and receive prayer, and Oral Roberts University in Tulsa has its striking two-hundred-foot-tall prayer tower, staffed twenty-four hours a day by prayer counselors.

91. community fellowships

Pentecostals and charismatics do not usually "leave the world" to join monasteries and convents, but they sometimes form Christian communities. These have arisen partly out of a desire to form close-knit fellowships, partly out of an awareness that modern urban and suburban life tends to isolate people, even when they attend church together on Sunday. Various charismatic communities have sprung up in the U.S. and abroad, often under the guidance of Catholic charismatics, though most groups are interdenominational.

Most groups center on a household of people living under one roof—sometimes a group of singles, but sometimes a family with other community members living with them. Some communities are nonresidential, with members living in their own homes but meeting frequently (that is, more often than on Sunday mornings) for prayer, praise, and fellowship. Most communities have small fellowship groups within the larger group. Unlike the traditional Catholic convents and monasteries, members are not committed for life.

92. "and the fellowship of the Holy Spirit"

Still in use today is a phrase that dates back many hundreds of years: "The grace of our Lord Jesus Christ, and the love of God the Father, and the fellowship of the Holy Spirit be with us all." In one form or another these words, often used as a benediction in ending a worship service, date as far back as the third century. They are a living reminder that the fellowship—community—was intimately connected with belief in the Spirit.

93. church membership

The nation seems to be in an antiauthority, anti-institutional mood, so the idea of full membership in a church has become less meaningful. From the very beginnings some Pentecostal churches had a loose attitude toward membership. This was appropriate, considering that many Spirit-filled clergy and laity had been booted out of their churches because they exercised spiritual gifts. Having been stricken from the rolls, they probably believed that the rolls weren't terribly important, while walking in the Spirit was. This mood prevails today as questions of denominational connection become less and less important.

94. tentmaker ministry

The apostle Paul, like most Jewish men of his time, learned a trade, and even after his life's work became spreading the gospel, he continued the trade of tentmaking. His close friends Priscilla and Aquila, a married couple, engaged in the same trade (Acts 18:3). Today people use the term *tent-maker ministry* to refer to pastors or missionaries who earn their income in a regular job while also working (sometimes for free or for little pay) in their ministry. Pentecostals, particularly in rural and inner-city areas, often rely on tent-makers to serve as ministers and evangelists. The history of the renewal movement would not be the same without the many faithful men and women who worked steady jobs and gave their nonworking hours to working for the Lord.

95. rosary

This refers to the string of beads used, but also to the method of prayer itself. Popular with Catholics, the rosary devotion involves meditating on the fifteen "mysteries" (key events) in the lives of Jesus and His mother. One of the mysteries, however, is the descent of the Spirit at Pentecost. Every time a Catholic "prays the rosary," it brings to mind the Spirit at the first Pentecost.

96. Whitsunday

This is an older name for Pentecost. It comes from "white Sunday," so called because on this day newly baptized persons wore white robes. The Church of England's *Book of Common Prayer* still refers to the day as Whitsunday and the following week as Whitsun Week.

97. Robert Raikes and his progeny

Englishman Robert Raikes (1735–1811) is known as the "father of the Sunday school" because he worked to establish schools in which poor children would learn not only the Bible and Christian doctrine but also job skills. By 1787 such schools enrolled a quarter million students in Britain. Methodist leader John Wesley encouraged his people in the movement, believing they needed classroom instruction as well as good pulpit preaching. The tradition has continued, and most U.S. churches have some sort of Sunday school for both children and adults, usually for an hour or so preceding Sunday morning worship. Note: *teaching* is listed as one of the gifts of the Spirit.

98. Sunday school literature

Most large Pentecostal denominations have their own lines of Sunday school literature. Evangelicals and charismatics in the mainline denominations face a problem because their denominations' publications are thought to be slanted to the liberal side. Independent publishers have filled this gap, offering nondenominational evangelical publications for all age-groups. (In fact, the denominational houses face serious competition from the independents, since it can no longer be assumed that a church of X denomination will want to use the official X publications.) David C. Cook and Scripture Press (which merged in 1997) are two of the best known, and Gospel Light literature is also widely used.

99. praise and worship, or Sunday school?

Charismatic and Pentecostal congregations have grown, but not their Sunday schools. Even though many churches have dynamic praise and worship services *and* active Sunday schools, the trend has been to emphasize the corporate worship and give less attention to what used to be the education hour before Sunday worship. Good preaching (which is easy to find in renewed churches) naturally helps to educate people in the Bible and basic beliefs, but these need to be reinforced and expanded through class study. The decline of Sunday schools in the U.S. is undoubtedly a factor in the appalling ignorance of the Bible and doctrine.

100. cassettes everywhere!

Despite the CD explosion, cassette tapes are still the audio of choice for many people and definitely the most-used means for reproducing sermons and seminars. High-speed duplicators allow churches and ministries to produce tapes cheaply and to minister to millions of people. In an age of illiteracy and semiliteracy, renewal ministries have tapped the potential of audio for people who never read a book or magazine. The spread of the charismatic renewal in the 1960s was in no small part due to the tapes of charismatic conferences being distributed widely.

101. *Thompson Chain-Reference Bible*

F. C. Thompson (1848–1940), a Methodist pastor in New York State, wanted a useful study Bible, so he created his own. Like other study Bibles then and later, his contained footnotes, Bible lands maps, a concordance, and outlines of the Bible's sixty-six books. But it also included the "chains," useful notes that link related verses throughout the Bible. The Kirkbride Bible Company of Indianapolis has sold more than three million copies. It has been a favorite with Pentecostals, being endorsed by Aimee Semple McPherson, among others.

102. King James Version (KJV)

First published in 1611, the beloved KJV was for many years *the* Bible in English, and its phrases have been a rich vein of images and words for English speakers everywhere. Traditional evangelicals and Pentecostals were slow to accept any newer translations, and the Revised Standard Version of 1952, with its connections to the theologically liberal National Council of Churches, was particularly suspect. But as fewer people grasp the beautiful (but archaic) phrasing of the KJV, Christians have come to accept the need for modern versions. The New International Version (1978) has been extremely popular with evangelicals and many charismatics and Pentecostals, as has the New King James Version. These and other versions—some with notes geared toward Spirit-led readers—have opened up the Bible to a new generation of readers. The good news: contemporary Christians have Bibles they can understand. The bad news: there is no longer one version (like the KJV) that unites all readers of the Bible.

103. IHS—"In His Spirit"?

These three letters appear in churches all over the world, usually on pulpit cloths. Does anyone ever explain to the church members what the letters mean? Many people think they mean "In His Spirit" or (for those who know Latin) *Iesus Hominum Salvator* (Jesus, Savior of man). The explanation is simpler. The *H* is actually the capital form of the Greek letter *eta*, an *e. IHS* is, in Greek, the first three letters of Jesus' name. In other words, *IHS* is "Jesus."

104. excommunication

The New Testament lists several reasons for people to be cast out of the church, including sexual immorality and false teaching (1 Cor. 5:1–12; 1 Tim. 6:3–5). Paul had much to say about the subject, concerned as he was for high moral standards and right belief among Christians: "Reject a divisive man after the first and second admonition, knowing that such a person is warped and sinning" (Titus 3:10–11).

Excommunication strikes modern readers as judgmental and mean-spirited. But the early Christians placed a high value on following Christ, and they believed that faith and morals mattered more than tolerance. Regrettably, many Spirit-led believers have found themselves excommunicated because they taught or practiced baptism in the Spirit, healing, speaking in tongues, or other spiritual gifts. This sort of intolerance arises not from the desire to be truly Christian, but from a fear of doing things a new way. But as Acts shows, there is nothing new—and certainly nothing unchristian—about the workings of the Spirit.

105. the doxology

"Praise Father, Son, and Holy Ghost"—in many churches this may be the only mention of the Holy Spirit on an average Sunday. The familiar "Praise God from whom all blessings flow" is actually the last verse of William Kethe's "All People That on Earth Do Dwell," which was his rhymed version of Psalm 100.

106. fasting

Denying oneself food for a certain period is mentioned many times in the Bible. It was connected with consciousness of sin or grief and wanting to obtain the Lord's favor. Jesus did not emphasize fasting, and some of His enemies noticed that, taking it as a sign that He was not spiritual enough (Matt. 11:19; Luke 7:34). In Matthew 6:16–18, He made it clear that fasting is to please God, not to win applause from other people (which He accused the Pharisees of doing). More important, in Matthew 9:14–17, Jesus said that fasting, associated with sadness, was not appropriate for the kingdom of God, which is a kingdom of joy.

The book of Acts shows that some early Christians fasted and prayed (Acts 13:2–3; 14:23), though the apostle Paul never directly mentioned fasting. Many Spirit-led Christians practice it, often accompanying prayer before crucial decisions.

107. tithing

Tithing means giving a tenth of one's income to the Lord—meaning, in practice, to those who minister for the Lord. It goes back a long way, back to Genesis, which shows that Abraham and Jacob tithed (14:20; 28:22). The prophet Malachi emphasized tithing and connected it to God's pouring out His blessing (3:8–10). The New Testament shifted the emphasis: not a mandatory 10 percent, but a cheerful giving of whatever believers can. Historically, Pentecostal churches have stressed tithing, and the people have often given generously.

108. lay preaching

There have always been lay preachers in the church, but often they have been persecuted by the religious establishment, which reserves the right to issue "credentials" to pastors who have "qualified." Too often in Christian history the people with "credentials" have not been particularly saintly, even though they might have had the right education and jumped through all the hoops. A key element in American religious history, particularly among the Pentecostals, has been the trend toward being "ordained by the Spirit"—that is, the person needs no approval other than possessing an obvious gift for preaching. When some churches closed their pulpits to such self-appointed (or Spirit-anointed) preachers, the people often took to preaching in fields, marketplaces, even private homes.

109. prayer cloths

The practice of some healing evangelists, particularly tele-vangelists, of giving out prayer cloths to their contributors is something that unbelievers like to snicker about since it seems slightly superstitious (along the order of a rabbit's foot). The book of Acts mentions that Jesus' apostles healed people, and that handkerchiefs and aprons that had touched Paul brought about healings and exorcisms.

110. Epiphany doves

The liturgical churches (Catholic, Orthodox, Episcopal, and some others) celebrate January 6 as Epiphany, which commemorates Jesus' baptism. Because the Gospels report that the Holy Spirit descended upon Jesus in the form of a dove at the baptism, some Orthodox churches have an Epiphany day ceremony in which a dove is released (some-times over a nearby body of water) as a symbol of the Spirit.

111. Bible readings

The issue of ordaining women as ministers is still being debated, though the general trend seems to favor it. Pentecostal and Holiness churches have generally been fairly open to women as preachers. Even in the churches where women were not technically allowed to preach, there were ways to work around restrictions. One of these was Bible readings, in which a layperson (male or female) would read a passage from the Bible and comment on it—sometimes for several minutes. For all practical purposes the person was giving a sermon based on the text.

112. fivefold ministry

Renewal churches function with all kinds of ministry and government—bishops, elders, deacons, and so on. Some churches claim to have a fivefold ministry, based on Ephesians 4:11, where Paul claimed that Christ "gave some to be apostles, some prophets, some evangelists, and some pastors and teachers."

113. postconversion preaching

Lack of a license to preach has not stopped converts from preaching. One of the hallmarks of the Pentecostal movement has been the urgency of new converts to preach right away—usually just days after their experience with the Spirit. This was true in the early days of the Pentecostals (early 1900s) and is still true today in areas such as Latin America, where people newly baptized in the Spirit hit the streets right away to witness to their faith.

114. "woe is me!"

In 1 Corinthians 9:16, Paul told his readers, "Woe is me if I do not preach the gospel!" Renewed Christians have not been slack about preaching the gospel. Not all the noted evangelists of the last century have identified themselves as Pentecostals or charismatics, but many have. And aside from the stars, thousands of anonymous evangelists across the globe witness to the power of the Spirit in empowering evangelists—not only the tent evangelist, but also the average Joe who has a full-time job and witnesses to his faith whenever possible.

115. *leitourgia*

Our word *liturgy,* meaning "worship," comes from the Greek *leitourgia,* meaning "work of the people." Too often in Christian history it hasn't been the work of the people but the work of the ministers, with the people playing a spectator role. (Strange as it seems, there was not even congregational singing for many centuries.) "Stained-glass religion" involved the minister as "star," preaching, praying, and presiding, with the people contributing only their voices and their money. The renewal movement is a welcome shift back to the work of the people, with laity participation in music, prayer, and testimonies.

116. why write?

Christianity did not begin as the religion of the Bible. It began with the personal witness of people who knew Jesus—word of mouth, not word of book. The faith spread because people personally witnessed to their faith. Only around A.D. 300 was the church pretty much aware of a "New Testament" that set the early reports down on paper (papyrus, rather). In many ways today's renewal movement proceeds by word of mouth. True, modern Pentecostals and charismatics publish books and magazines and also spread the word by TV, radio, and Internet. But as in advertising, word of mouth is most effective, particularly in Third World countries with widespread illiteracy and limited access to broadcasting.

117. experience or doctrine?

In Geoffrey Chaucer's *Canterbury Tales*, one of the characters states that experience is the highest authority. That isn't always wise, since God is the ultimate authority, and our own experiences can lead us down the wrong paths. But the truth is that experience is important in what people put their faith in. In some ways this has been the great divide between evangelicals and Spirit-filled Christians: evangelicals focus on the Bible and doctrine, while Spirit-filled Christians focus on experience. It shouldn't be either/or, and it usually isn't. Spirit-filled Christians measure their experience against the standard of the Bible, and most evangelicals do not cling to the Bible and doctrine without having had some personal experience with God.

118. cell groups

How do you find warm fellowship in the world's largest church? David Cho's megachurch in Seoul, South Korea, pioneered the cell groups—small, intimate fellowships— and the concept has spread to many large and growing churches across the world. (See 49 [Yoido Full Gospel Church].)

119. doves

Doves, which were common in Israel, had a reputation for being gentle, innocent creatures, which lies behind Jesus' words to His disciples to "be wise as serpents and harmless as doves" (Matt. 10:16). The most famous dove of all was the Holy Spirit, who appeared over Jesus in the shape of a dove at His baptism (John 1:32). Based on the story of Jesus' baptism, the Holy Spirit has always been symbolized by a dove. (See 265 [Jesus' baptism].)

120. the Upper Room pattern

Priest, pastor, or people? Traditionally, the priest is in charge (the Catholic pattern), or the pastor, putting forth the Word, is in charge (the Protestant pattern), but what about the entire congregation filled with the Holy Spirit (the Pentecostal pattern)? Some call this the Upper Room pattern, based on the coming of the Spirit on all the apostles who had gathered in the "upper room" in Jerusalem (Acts 2).

121. the church in movement

A German charismatic leader, Heribert Muhlen, has written that the charismatic renewal is "the church in movement, not a movement in the church." This neatly summarizes the renewal: it is not a faction or a fad; it is what the church really should be at all times, a vibrant body set in motion by the Spirit.

122. confirmation

Churches that practice infant baptism usually practice confirmation. The baptized person has come of age (usually twelve or older) and is ready to give his own assent to the faith into which his parents baptized him. In the Catholic church and some other denominations, confirmation involves a ritual in which a bishop lays hands on the person (see 73 [laying on of hands]), and traditionally, this involved the person receiving the Holy Spirit. Most Protestant churches do not accept the idea that the Spirit can be channeled through a mere ritual.

MUSIC, MUSIC, MUSIC

123. musical potpourri

For much of Christian history, an organ was *the* musical instrument for worship, though some smaller churches made do with a piano. Some Spirit-filled churches today have an organ or piano or both, but the trend is toward diversity, with guitars, synthesizers, percussion, brass, string quartets, and the prerecorded sound tracks that surround the singer(s) with studio-quality accompaniment. Music in many churches brings to mind the Psalms with their references to praising God with many kinds of musical instruments. (There were no organs in Bible times.) For many Christians, organs bring to mind the "stained-glass church," boring and ritualistic with no room for emotion or exuberance.

124. Scripture songs

It is impossible to clap your hands while holding a hymnal, and many churches today opt for the clapping and chuck the hymnal. Many churches still use hymns (there is a rich mine of faith in those hymnals!), but words to Scripture songs and choruses are often projected overhead, leaving worshipers free to dance, clap, sway, and lift up the hands. Lifting up your face instead of having to lean into a hymnal also allows for more hearty singing. Some familiar choruses are sung from memory. Songs are often simply passages of Scripture (particularly the Psalms) set to music—a good way of learning the Bible while worshiping at the same time.

125. CCM

It means "contemporary Christian music" and has connections with (but is not the same as) gospel music. Christian music prior to the 1960s tended to be "stained-glass music" (choirs singing formal anthems, either a cappella or with an organ) or real gospel (the bouncy but reverent singing of quartets or choirs, perhaps most vibrant in the choirs of black churches). As American young people latched on to their own music (and rejected the music styles of their parents), many church musicians realized that the old music styles were alienating the younger audience. Renewal churches remedied this with their openness to contemporary instruments (guitars, drums, synthesizers) and a willingness to bring the omnipresent beat of pop music into worship. Taken to extremes, contemporary Christian music has come to include Christian rap and Christian heavy metal—not for everyone's taste certainly, but probably effective in reaching the youth audience. (See 123 [musical potpourri].)

126. fast music

What are the distinguishing marks of the renewal movement? In its early days, some Pentecostals claimed that it was fast music. Pentecostals and their critics had observed that the singing in Spirit-led meetings was usually more vibrant (and faster) than in traditional church music. Things haven't changed much. The music in renewal congregations may not always be fast, but it is almost always more energetic than "stained-glass music."

127. "Veni Sancte Spiritus"

This ancient Latin hymn has been translated into English many times. The basic meaning of the Latin title is "Come, Holy Spirit." It dates from the 1200s and has been attributed to Pope Innocent III and to Stephen Langton, archbishop of Canterbury. The medieval church neglected teaching about the Holy Spirit, but the hymn and many others like it show that the Spirit was never totally forgotten.

128. "Breathe on Me, Breath of God"

Edwin Hatch, author of this hymn, was aware that in the original languages of the Bible, "spirit" and "breath" were represented by the same word. God's "breath" is His Holy Spirit. Hatch's hymn, written around 1878, asks the Spirit to "fill me with life anew" and to breathe "until my heart is pure." The hymn reflects the Bible's teaching of the Spirit as Creator and Sanctifier.

129. "Creator Spirit, by Whose Aid"

John Dryden (1631–1700) was England's poet laureate. He translated an ancient Latin hymn, *"Veni Creator Spiritus"* (literally, "Come, Creator Spirit"). Dryden's translation mirrors the teaching of Genesis 1, showing the Spirit active in creation. Dryden used the New Testament word *Paraklete* for the Spirit, usually translated as "Comforter" or "Counselor."

130. "Spirit Divine, Attend Our Prayers"

This hymn is like a brief course in the Holy Spirit. Its author, Andrew Reed (1787–1862), referred to the Spirit as "fire" and "dove" and as the light that leads into the paths of life. Reed was a London pastor and active in establishing orphanages and other charities.

131. "Come, Holy Spirit, Heavenly Dove"

Isaac Watts (1674–1748) was one of England's best hymn writers, and his songs are still sung around the world. Few of his hymns mention the Spirit, but this one does, referring to the Spirit as the "heavenly Dove" that can "kindle a flame of sacred love in these cold hearts of ours."

132. "There's a Sweet, Sweet Spirit"

Doris Akers's 1963 composition is probably the most-sung song about the Holy Spirit today. As in so many songs about the Spirit, the reference is to the "heavenly Dove," which fills believers with love and leads to inner renewal.

133. "O Spirit of the Living God"

James Montgomery (1771–1854) was an English hymn writer, probably most famous for the Christmas song "Angels from the Realms of Glory." His hymn to the Holy Spirit asks the Spirit to "give tongues of fire and hearts of love" and to give "power and unction from above."

134. "Come, Holy Ghost, Our Hearts Inspire"

Charles Wesley (1707–88) was, with his brother John, founder of Methodism and also one of the world's great hymn writers. Charles had the rare knack of penning poetic words that taught Christian doctrine. In this hymn to the Spirit, he spoke of Him as "celestial Dove" and the "Source of the old prophetic fire." He wrote several other hymns to the Spirit, including "Spirit of Faith, Come Down."

135. "Gracious Spirit, Holy Ghost"

Christopher Wordsworth (1807–85) was a nephew of the great English poet William Wordsworth and was a talented poet—or, more precisely, a hymn writer. In his collection *The Holy Year* are hymns for every occasion, including

Pentecost. His "Gracious Spirit, Holy Ghost" is found in many hymnals and is interesting because every stanza mentions "love, heavenly love" as the greatest gift. The hymn echoes Paul's words in 1 Corinthians 13, in which he said that the spiritual gifts will someday pass but love will always remain.

136. *Church Hymnal*

Not a very catchy title, but this 1951 hymnbook published by the Church of God (Cleveland, Tennessee) has been extremely popular, selling several million copies, not only to the Church of God but to many other Pentecostal and independent churches. In 1969 the Church of God published another popular collection, *Hymns of the Spirit*.

137. *Praise Hymns and Choruses*

This has been one of the biggies of recent years among hymnals, having gone through several revisions already. The publisher, Maranatha, is a key provider of music among renewal churches.

4

Groups
Large and Small

138. Promise Keepers

If you gather 48,000 men together, a place named Thunderdome seems the right spot. The huge stadium in St. Petersburg, Florida, was the gathering place for this Christian men's movement founded by Coach Bill McCartney. Although not specifically geared toward charismatics and Pentecostals, Promise Keepers (PK) draws plenty of both. Essentially, PK asks men to be men—faithful and loving to their wives, caring and moral as role models for their children. So why did the media make PK out to be controversial? Beyond Thunderdome, PK gathered in the thousands on Washington's Mall for "Stand in the Gap: A Sacred Assembly of Men" in October 1997.

139. Assemblies of God

America's largest Pentecostal denomination, the Assemblies of God (AG) has experienced phenomenal growth in recent years. The AG established its headquarters at Springfield, Missouri, in 1918 and has grown steadily since then. To the surprise of many intellectuals and liberal Christians, the AG has not only grown but has become amazingly respectable in America. Like all Pentecostal denominations, the AG emphasizes baptism in the Spirit, with the evidence of speaking in tongues. Pentecostals have traditionally been distrustful of denominations and for good reason: mainline denominations often took a dim view of Pentecostal activity. The AG has managed to work around this obstacle and not only grow in numbers but maintain the respect of other Pentecostal bodies. The AG has about 2.3 million members in the U.S. and about 22 million worldwide. Numerically, it is larger than many of the so-called mainline denominations in the U.S.

Regarding the name: the Greek New Testament word that we translate "church" is *ekklesia,* which means "assembly." When the AG named itself Assemblies of God, it started a trend among Spirit-led Christians toward calling the congregations something besides churches, as seen in the many "fellowships" and "Christian centers" abounding today.

Giving a compressed history of the AG is impossible in this short space. Many of its key figures are discussed elsewhere in this book.

140. Full Gospel Business Men's Fellowship International (FGBMFI)

Some people's first introduction to the full gospel of the Spirit-filled life has been through a dinner meeting of the FGBMFI. Often held in hotel ballrooms, the Fellowship's meetings center on the testimonies of men who have experienced joy and release from anxiety following the baptism of the Spirit. The Fellowship, founded in 1951 by Demos Shakarian (see 578), is an interdenominational group with 3,000 local chapters and more than 300,000 members in 87 countries. Being composed of businessmen, many of whom are very successful, the FGBMFI has done a lot to make the renewal movement respectable in the United States, in addition to reaching thousands of people with the gospel.

141. Chi Alpha

College campuses usually have fraternities with Greek letters as their names. Chi Alpha comes from the first letters of *Christou Apostoloi*—Christ's Ambassadors. It is the name of the campus ministry of the Assemblies of God, founded in 1953, with its first chapter at Southwest Missouri State College. Many other chapters have been established.

142. Vineyard Churches

This association of churches began with the original Vineyard founded by Kenn Gulliksen in West Los Angeles in 1974. But it sprang to prominence when John Wimber's home prayer group affiliated with the Vineyard. Wimber founded the Anaheim unit of the Vineyard Christian Fellowship in 1983, and it is now the "mother church" of the Association of Vineyard Churches, established in 1985. With more than 250 churches in the association, Wimber's messages of power evangelism and power healing have spread across the country. Vineyard Ministries International coordinates the various ministries, including seminars, books, and tapes.

143. Jesus People

One author described them as "fundamentalists theologically and hippies socially." The Jesus People were the counterculture youth of the late 1960s who—much to America's surprise—"turned on" to Christianity instead of drugs. Beginning about 1967 in California (where else?), New York's Greenwich Village, and other counterculture centers, the experience-oriented movement was noted for its music (usually guitars), warmth, communal living, divine healing, and speaking in tongues. Some of the Jesus People were going through a phase in a lifetime of varied spiritual experiences, but many converts were sincere. Many found among the Jesus People a warmth and a richness of experience that were lacking in most churches.

144. Charismatic Episcopal Church (CEC)

Its name would suggest that it split from the Episcopal church, but not so. It was founded in 1992 by three pastors from Pentecostal/charismatic backgrounds who studied the early church and came to believe that the best way to worship was with the Episcopal *Book of Common Prayer* (but *not* within the Episcopal church). The CEC ordains its ministers on the principle of apostolic succession (see 795), does not ordain women (as the Episcopal church does), and emphasizes the sacraments *and* the gifts of the Spirit. Headquarters are in San Clemente, California, and the fellowship has about five hundred churches in the U.S. (See 802 [convergence movement].)

145. barbell boys

Would a man with a five-foot chest get your attention? John Jacobs has one. He is head of the Dallas-based Power Team, musclemen who take their antidrug, proabstinence message to public schools and, in auditoriums and churches, witness to their faith in God. One of the Power Team hulks can bench-press 744 pounds.

146. Church of God (Cleveland, Tennessee)

There are probably a dozen or more denominations named "Church of God," but the one with its headquarters in Cleveland, Tennessee, is the best known. In spite of its southern roots, the denomination now has churches in all 50 states and more than 100 countries, with a total membership of nearly 2 million (about 750,000 in the U.S.). The church began as the Christian Union in 1886 under two Baptist pastors, Richard G. Spurling Sr. and Jr. They stated that they wanted to "restore primitive Christianity," a key goal of all Pentecostal groups.

In 1902, under the leadership of A. J. Tomlinson, it was renamed the Church of God, making its permanent headquarters in Cleveland. From that time on the Church of God (CG) emphasized the baptism of the Spirit. Tomlinson, the first general overseer, helped the denomination spread across the Southeast. Tomlinson's leadership style did not please everyone, and in 1923 he was replaced as overseer and left to form a separate denomination. The CG opened its Church of God School of Theology (in Cleveland, of course) in 1975, with an adjoining Pentecostal Resource Center.

147. The Evangelization Society (TES)

A spin-off from the Pittsburgh Bible Institute, TES was founded by Charles Pridgeon in 1920 for the purpose of evangelism at home and abroad. TES has five missionary outreach churches in the U.S. and numerous churches and ministries in Taiwan, India, and Zaire. TES is completely supported by unsolicited donations. It is both evangelical and Pentecostal.

148. Fire-Baptized Holiness Church

According to Matthew 3:11, John the Baptist prophesied that believers would be baptized with the Holy Spirit and with fire. B. H. Irwin, a Holiness pastor in Nebraska, taught that the baptism of fire was a third blessing beyond justification and sanctification. This fire baptism would usually be accompanied by such phenomena as shouting and/or moving, and the recipients would feel fire inside them or actually see balls of fire. The Fire-Baptized Holiness Church was founded by Irwin in 1895 and accepted this teaching. Irwin spread his message in revivals in the South and the Midwest. He became eccentric, claiming there was not only fire baptism, but also baptisms by dynamite, lyddite, and oxidite. Distancing himself from most Holiness churches (as they did from him), Irwin taught a strict dress code, including, for some reason, prohibiting men from wearing ties. He also prohibited pork so that his members became known as "no-necktie, no-hogmeat people."

149. Anglican Renewal Ministries

The Church of England seems to be declining in numbers, although the percentage of its people who are charismatic is growing considerably. Anglican Renewal Ministries publishes a newsletter and sponsors renewal conferences for clergy and laity.

150. Free Will Baptist Church of the Pentecostal Faith

Many Baptist groups take a dim view of charismatics. This is true of the Free Will Baptists, which is why in 1923 some Free Will Baptists in South Carolina formed an association of members who had experienced the working of the Spirit. Later these Free Will Baptist Pentecostals joined—loosely—with similar groups in North Carolina. But the two state groups ended up incorporating separately, with the North Carolina group being known as the Pentecostal Free-Will Baptist Church.

151. International Church of the Foursquare Gospel (ICFG)

The ICFG was incorporated in 1927, though it actually dates from evangelist Aimee Semple McPherson's founding of her Angelus Temple in Los Angeles (see 474 and 52). The denomination's name comes from an inspiration that Sister Aimee had while preaching on Ezekiel's vision of the four-faced cherubim. She took the four faces to symbolize the "foursquare gospel": Christ as Savior, Baptizer (in the Holy Spirit), Healer, and Coming King. (These were not new ideas, since evangelist A. B. Simpson had used almost the same titles for Christ in his book *The Four-fold Gospel*.)

The denomination arose because students graduating from the Angelus Temple's L.I.F.E. Bible College had gone out to establish branch churches, the Fourfold Gospel Lighthouses. Sister Aimee served as its president until her death in 1944, and the Angelus Temple served, and still serves, as the "mother church." Under her leadership, the denomination was active not only in evangelism and healing but also in social assistance, particularly during the depression.

Rolf McPherson succeeded his mother as president of the denomination, and it grew considerably around the world. Rolf worked to bring the ICFG into relation with other Pentecostal and evangelical churches. The ICFG is quite healthy, operating several Bible schools in the U.S. and Canada. Aid for the poor and people who have been stricken by disasters continues. Jack Hayford's vibrant Church on the Way in California is probably the best-known ICFG church today (see 48 [Church on the Way]).

Membership in the ICFG is about 227,000 in the U.S., 2.2 million worldwide.

152. Holy Spirit Teaching Mission (HSTM)

The Holy Spirit Teaching Mission grew out of a charismatic Bible study meeting weekly in Fort Lauderdale, Florida. The interdenominational group incorporated in 1966 and expanded its scope with teaching conferences, later sponsoring conferences in other states. It further expanded with teaching tours and cruises. In 1969 it launched a magazine, *New Wine*. In 1972 it changed its name to Christian Growth Ministries. (See 153 [Integrity Communications].)

153. Integrity Communications

It began in Fort Lauderdale, Florida, as the Holy Spirit Teaching Mission (see 152) and changed its name in 1972 to Christian Growth Ministries. In 1982 it became Integrity Communications, and its base is Mobile, Alabama. Founded by five pastors—Don Basham, Derek Prince, Charles Simpson, Ern Baxter, and Bob Mumford—the group claims that the true church, the body of Christ, is independent of denominational structures, and that this true church is a pyramid of spiritual authority. Many churches have used this model, though many charismatics who have remained within their denominations have objected to the controversial concept of shepherding (see 201). Baxter and Prince left the group in 1984, Mumford left in 1986, and Basham died in 1989. *New Wine* magazine ceased publication in 1986, and Simpson launched a new magazine, *Christian Conquest.*

154. messianic Jews

Jews who believe that Jesus (*Yeshua*) is the Messiah are known as messianic Jews. Technically, they are Christians, since they believe in Christ as Lord and Savior, but they also adhere to their Jewish identity (a fact that causes more conflicts with other Jews than with Christians). They refer to themselves as "completed Jews." While they are only a small part of the Jewish community in the world, they are active in evangelism, and quite a few are charismatic in orientation, emphasizing the gifts of the Spirit in evangelism and in the daily walk. Messianic Jews operate the Messiah Yeshiva in Maryland, a Bible and graduate school for training messianic workers.

155. Order of St. Luke (OSL)

Devoted to healing, the OSL was founded by Episcopalians John Gayner Banks and his wife, Ethel, in 1947. The aim was to restore the practice of healing that had been demonstrated by Christ and His apostles. Participants in the OSL sought the gift of healing and, in so doing, often experienced other gifts of the Spirit, such as speaking in tongues. In 1963, however, the OSL announced that it opposed glossolalia practiced under its auspices.

156. Community of Jesus

This interdenominational group began as the Rock Harbor Fellowship. Located on Cape Cod in Massachusetts, it was founded by Cay Andersen and Judy Sorensen, who had a joint healing ministry. Both were baptized in the Holy Spirit, and in 1970 they renamed their group the Community of Jesus, which has about three hundred full-time residents, several clergy in residence, and a nonresident membership of about six hundred. (See 91 [community fellowship].)

157. Word of God community (WG)

Founded in 1967, this charismatic community in Ann Arbor, Michigan, began as a Catholic group but has become interdenominational. The WG became a center of worldwide Catholic renewal and a role model for other charismatic communities around the world. It has played a major role in training leaders in the Catholic charismatic renewal. The WG publishes *Pastoral Renewal* and has its own publishing house, Servant Publications. (See 91 [community fellowships].)

158. Reba Place Fellowship

Located in Evanston, Illinois, just north of Chicago, this charismatic community is known for its inner-city ministry. It is one of many community fellowships (see 91) that emphasize not only a rich fellowship among Christians living together but also an outreach to the surrounding community.

159. Pentecostal Church of God (PCG)

Historically, Baptists do not believe in requiring any fixed creed for church members. When the newly formed Assemblies of God (AG) adopted a creed (statement of faith), some Pentecostals influenced by the Baptist mind-set objected and formed their own denomination, the Pentecostal Assemblies of the U.S.A., later changed to the Pentecostal Church of God. Its leader was John Sinclair, formerly executive presbyter of the AG. Oddly enough, by 1933 the PCG found it necessary to create its own statement of faith—similar to the one of the AG.

Headquartered in Joplin, Missouri, the PCG grew during the 1940s and was noted for its work among Native Americans. By the 1980s the church had more than a thousand churches in the U.S., with roughly 120,000 members. The PCG publishes the magazine *Pentecostal Messenger* and operates three Christian colleges.

160. Assemblea Cristiana

Say "Italian" and people think *Catholic*. Not always. The Assemblea Cristiana is Pentecostal, organized in Chicago in 1907 by a group of Italian immigrants on the north side. It grew out of the group that had been converted in the evangelistic meetings of William H. Durham. Members traveled to other Italian communities in the U.S. and South America and planted hundreds of Italian Pentecostal churches.

161. Pentecostal Fellowship of North America (PFNA)

The group grew out of Pentecostal leaders hobnobbing at gatherings of the National Association of Evangelicals, to which many Pentecostal churches did and do belong. The formation of the Pentecostal World Fellowship in 1947 gave further stimulus to form an American association. The PFNA organized in 1948 at Des Moines, Iowa, with a view toward "endeavoring to keep the unity of the Spirit until we all come to the unity of the faith" (from the PFNA statement of objectives). The PFNA adopted a statement of faith that included belief in the Trinity. This had the effect of excluding Oneness Pentecostals (see 216).

162. Pentecostal Free-Will Baptist Church

The Free Will Baptist Church has not been particularly open to the charismatic renewal. As far back as 1855 some Free Will Baptists, accepting and emphasizing baptism in the Spirit, formed their own organization, becoming a denomination in 1959. Beginning in the South, the denomination is still concentrated there but has sent missionaries to Mexico, South America, India, and the Philippines. It is one of countless examples of a new denomination forming because the parent denomination was not open to the exercise of spiritual gifts. Membership is about twelve thousand.

163. United Pentecostal Church (UPC)

The UPC traces its roots back to Charles F. Parham (see 476), but then, so do most Pentecostal groups. More particularly, the UPC stems from the growth of Oneness Pentecostalism (see 216), which insisted that baptism should take place in the name of Jesus only, not in the name of Father, Son, and Holy Spirit. Many Pentecostals, following Oneness teaching, were rebaptized. Oneness ministers and their followers began to organize, and in 1945 a merger of two large Oneness groups resulted in the UPC. The churches practice footwashing and hold to traditional Holiness standards in terms of worldliness (no makeup or jewelry, women do not cut their hair, etc.). The UPC is the largest of the Oneness denominations and has grown steadily since its founding, with about 500,000 U.S. members. Headquarters are in Hazlewood, Missouri.

164. Kansas City Fellowship

Are there still Christian prophets? Kansas City Fellowship (KCF), an independent charismatic church, had within its leadership some men who, beyond any doubt, could prophesy. Paul Cain, one of the church's pastors, visited the Vineyard Christian Fellowship headquarters in 1988. He predicted earthquakes would occur the day he arrived and the day he left. They did—one in Pasadena, the other in Armenia. Vineyard head John Wimber (see 572) was deeply moved, saying he was led to take prophecy seriously for the first time in his life. He took Cain and other prophets from KCF on a world tour.

165. Mülheim Association (MA)

German Pentecostals? Yes, there are many. The MA was formed in 1913, taking its name from the town of Mülheim, which had been the gathering place for Pentecostal conferences for several years. It was interdenominational in scope, including members from the state Lutheran churches and from independent congregations. The MA emphasizes the spiritual gifts, though it does not insist on glossolalia as evidence of being baptized in the Spirit.

166. Old Catholics

In 1870 the Roman Catholic Church's Vatican Council proclaimed that the pope was infallible when speaking *ex cathedra*—that is, when speaking from his official position as head of the church. Many Catholics in Germany, Austria, and Switzerland split from Rome and formed the Old Catholic Church. The new group rejected several Catholic teachings that had developed over the centuries and, of course, refused to recognize the pope's authority. The Old Catholics were open to signs and wonders, healing, prophesyings, and other spiritual gifts. There are still some in North America.

167. Ethiopian Overcoming Holy Church

Contemporary readers may not even be aware that the word *Ethiopian* used to refer to black Americans. A black Oneness Pentecostal pastor, William T. Phillips, founded the Ethiopian Overcoming Holy Church of God in 1917, later changing the name "Ethiopian" to "Apostolic," which it still uses. With its headquarters in Birmingham, Alabama, it has about thirteen thousand members.

168. Assemblies of God of Great Britain and Ireland (AGGBI)

Despite the obvious similarity of names, the AGGBI was not a spin-off of the U.S. Assemblies of God. The British group was founded in 1922 by several Pentecostal leaders who wished to unite churches to preserve the true gospel and keep congregations faithful to it. The founding leaders established several Fundamental Truths, which are common to most Pentecostals: baptism in the Spirit (as evidenced by speaking in tongues), premillennial return of Christ, and several others. There are about six hundred congregations today, with about forty thousand members.

169. Salvation Army

Certainly one of the most visible Christian groups in the U.S., the Army was founded by William Booth in England in the 1800s. Booth wanted to bring the gospel to the urban poor and others who were not being reached by the mainline churches. The Army spread to the U.S., where it is still active in social service and in preaching. Though it is not usually considered part of the renewal movement, Army officials have stated that, yes, the Army has always been empowered by the Spirit and that it still considers itself a charismatic movement.

170. Universal Catholic Church

Germany's state-supported churches (both Lutheran and Catholic) had become quite boring in the 1800s. Around 1863 a German charismatic group calling itself the Universal Catholic Church (later the New Apostolic Church) sprang into being, with exercise of such spiritual gifts as healing, prophecy, tongues, and interpretation of tongues.

171. Assemblies of the Lord Jesus Christ

With its headquarters in Memphis, Tennessee, this racially integrated denomination is a Oneness Pentecostal body, founded in 1952. As with many Pentecostal groups, it practices footwashing and insists that women not cut their hair. It does not insist on grape juice in Communion but allows the use of wine.

172. Pentecostal World Conference (PWC)

Founded in 1947, the PWC is the Pentecostals' alternative to the World Council of Churches (with so much controversy about the WCC's theological liberalism and social gospel). The interdenominational PWC meets every three years to promote spiritual fellowship among Pentecostals and to show the world the unity of Spirit-baptized believers. This is a good thing, since so many Pentecostal denominations (and the many independent congregations) have begun as splinter groups, often splitting from their parent bodies over trivial matters. One problem: the PWC does not have any ties to the charismatic renewal, most of which has taken place in the mainline denominations. However, the Spirit moves where He will, and fellowship (often at the grassroots level) among Pentecostals and charismatics does take place, even without a world council to encourage it.

173. Aglow International

Begun in 1967 in Seattle as the Women's Aglow Fellowship, this was originally a local luncheon group with prayer and fellowship. It has grown to more than a thousand chapters worldwide. Its World Literature Trusts distributes Bible study guides abroad. It also publishes the magazine *Aglow*. In many ways it is a female counterpart to the Full Gospel Business Men's Fellowship.

174. Wesleyan charismatics

The many splinter denominations from the Methodist church have typically been Holiness churches, but not very open to Spirit filling. The Wesleyan Holiness Charismatic Fellowship was formed to provide fellowship for those who have left these denominations (Church of the Nazarenes and Free Methodists, for example) or who are in the denominations and feeling isolated. In some cases the members have not left the denominations freely but have been disfellowshipped, mainly because of speaking in tongues.

175. Mount Sinai Holy Church

"Bishop" Ida Robinson wanted a church where both men and women served as leaders, so she organized the Mount Sinai Holy Church of America, which allowed women to be pastors and bishops. She claimed that in 1924 she had fasted and prayed and received from God a vision telling her to "loose the women."

176. Seventh-day Pentecostal Church of the Living God

As its name indicates, this group worships on Saturday instead of Sunday. It is a Oneness body (see 216) and thus baptizes only in the name of Jesus, not the Trinity. Founded in the 1940s, and now with about a thousand members, the group is mostly in Washington, D.C., and the adjoining states.

177. Church of God in Christ

The COGIC (or, sometimes, CGIC) is America's largest black Pentecostal body. In fact, it is one of the largest denominations in the U.S., though many people have never heard of it. Its chief figure for many years was Charles H. Mason, who in 1893 claimed to be entirely sanctified. He left the Baptist church and organized a new congregation meeting in a shed in Lexington, Mississippi. The new group, following Mason, emphasized sanctification and the outpouring of the Spirit. Mason and other leaders went to California to investigate the Azusa Street revival. Mason experienced the baptism of the Spirit and speaking in tongues. His church split on his return, with the non-Pentecostal party forming the Churches of Christ (Holiness). Mason and his followers became the Church of God in Christ. When Mason died in 1961, the church's membership was about 400,000. Today it has about 5.4 million members, an amazing rate of growth.

178. United House of Prayer for All People

This denomination of about twenty-five thousand members is mostly urban and definitely unrestrained in its worship style (being noted for speaking in tongues, dancing, trances, etc.). The original House of Prayer was founded by "Sweet Daddy" Grace in 1919, who reached out to the poor in such metropolitan areas as New York, Atlanta, and Washington, D.C. Grace was succeeded in 1961 by "Sweet Daddy" Walter McCullough.

179. Congregational Holiness Church (CHC)

This group split from the Pentecostal Holiness Church (PHC) in 1920, primarily because some PHC leaders taught that Christians should never rely on medicine or doctors to treat illness. Some other members had criticized the church's bishops and wanted a congregational form of government. Watson Sorrow, one of the critics, was expelled in 1920, and he led his followers to form the CHC. The church's charter emphasized the importance of congregational government. The CHC has about eight thousand members in the U.S., mostly in Georgia.

180. Church of God (Huntsville, Alabama)

A church with a membership of *thirty million?* That was what this denomination once reported. It appears that its founder, Homer Tomlinson (see 223), was estimating how many members the church had "in the spiritual domain." Actual membership appears to be in the hundreds. The group is a splinter group from the Church of God of Prophecy (see 189). Tomlinson died in 1968, and his successor moved the headquarters to Huntsville, Alabama, while still adhering to the doctrines of Homer Tomlinson, including "the kingdom of God on earth," which reflected his desire to influence politics.

181. Church of the Living God, Christian Workers for Fellowship

This predominantly black denomination is Pentecostal, but with a few differences. It allows tongues speaking, but only in recognizable languages. It has three ordinances: baptism, Communion (with *water* instead of grape juice), and footwashing. The Lord's Prayer is the only prayer "prayed by all Christians." It approves of the Masons (unusual in churches, but in this case its founder was a Mason). It believes that some of the saints in the Bible were black. The group has about 275 churches (always called temples) and about 45,000 members, with headquarters in Cincinnati.

182. Pentecostal Assemblies of the World (PAW)

Growing out of the Azusa Street revival in Los Angeles, the PAW incorporated in 1919. It is a Oneness Pentecostal group (see 216), baptizing in the name of Jesus only. The PAW is mostly black and has about 500,000 members worldwide. Like many Pentecostal bodies, it practices foot-washing but, unlike many others, uses wine in Communion.

183. United Holy Church of America

Several black Holiness churches in the southeastern U.S. joined in 1916 to form this denomination. The church claims "no earthly founder" and says that Christ and the power of the Holy Spirit have established the church. The denomination emphasizes baptism in the Spirit and encourages (but does not insist upon) speaking in tongues as evidence of the baptism. There are about thirty thousand members.

184. credential agencies

To whom are independent pastors accountable? To God, obviously. But a recurring problem among independents is that there is no authority overseeing candidates for ministry. To fill this need, various credential-granting organizations have developed—providing a form of quality control to ensure that a congregation is getting a minister who holds to certain basic beliefs and practices. There are many of these among Pentecostals and charismatics, just one example being the Full Gospel Fellowship of Churches and Ministers International.

185. Church of the Lord Jesus Christ of the Apostolic Faith

This predominantly black denomination began in the 1930s with the radio ministry of Sherrod C. Johnson. He taught the Oneness doctrine (baptism in the name of Jesus only, not in the name of the Trinity), footwashing, wine in Communion, no military service, and no celebration of Easter or Christmas. The head of the denomination is apostle and general overseer of about seven thousand members.

186. Charisma in Missions

Geared toward evangelizing the world's Spanish-speaking peoples, Charisma in Missions was organized in 1972 by Marilyn Kramar and has gained the approval of Catholic authorities. Dedicated to training lay evangelists, it sponsors the Latin Encounter for Youth, an annual International Latin Encounter for Renewal and Evangelization, and other ministries.

187. Christ for the Nations Institute (CFNI)

Healing evangelists Gordon and Freda Lindsay (see 638) founded this school in Dallas to train pastors and evangelists. It grew out of teaching seminars at the Lindsays' church, Dallas Christian Center. The CFNI opened in 1970, and its alumni have established similar institutes in

Germany, Jamaica, Argentina, Mexico, Thailand, and other nations.

188. Bethany Fellowship

Bethany is best known today as an evangelical publishing house (noted for its prairie romances), but it began in 1945 as a community for supporting and training missionaries. Members merged their resources to buy a large tract of land near Minneapolis. Graduates of its mission training program have gone out to Brazil, Mexico, the Caribbean, the Philippines, Japan, and elsewhere. Students train for missions not only in the Bible and evangelism but also in practical matters such as construction, maintenance, or printing. While it positions itself as evangelical, it teaches that gifts of the Spirit are still at work in the church.

189. Church of God of Prophecy

A major split occurred in the Church of God (Cleveland, Tennessee) (see 146), generally around the issue of overseer A. J. Tomlinson's leadership. The pro-Tomlinson group evolved into the group that, since 1952, has been the Church of God of Prophecy. Its headquarters are, like the group it split from, in Cleveland, Tennessee. In many ways similar to the Church of God, the Church of God of Prophecy has emphasized the importance of group worship, with meetings on several nights per week, often several hours long. Worship features the altar, a bench for those seeking spiritual renewal (a legacy from the anxious bench of revivals in the 1800s). At the altar one can seek God, ask for salvation or healing, or receive guidance (calls) from God. Services are usually flexible, open to interruption by any person seeking guidance or extended prayer. Membership worldwide is about 170,000, with about 72,000 in the U.S.

190. Apostolic Faith Mission (Portland, Oregon)

Founded by Florence Crawford (see 482), the AFM grew out of the Apostolic Faith movement in Los Angeles. She left Los Angeles for Oregon and launched her mission there on Christmas Day, 1906. She began a paper, *The Apostolic Faith,* and became very critical of worldliness among some Pentecostals. Those in the AFM had to adhere to a strict moral code—no dancing, cards, theater, smoking, or drinking; no makeup, bobbed hair, shorts, or slacks for women. Ministers were prohibited from either soliciting funds or taking regular offerings. The source of funding was an offering box.

191. Church of God of the Mountain Assembly (CGMA)

As its name suggests, the CGMA is a mountain denomination, reaching out to the people in the mountainous regions of eastern Kentucky and Tennessee. Its headquarters are in Jellico, Tennessee, and it grew out of a movement of Baptist ministers preaching a "closer communion with God." Learning that the name Church of God had already been taken by the Cleveland, Tennessee, group, they added the Mountain Assembly to their name. As a distinctively

Pentecostal group, it endured some persecution in its region but grew anyway. Small as the denomination is (about seven thousand members), it sponsors missions in Africa, India, and the Caribbean.

192. Christian and Missionary Alliance (CMA)

The CMA is (as its name implies) a missionary denomination, with more than two million members in fifty-one countries. It grew out of the Holiness movement of the 1800s, and it emphasizes sanctification. Its key founder was A. B. Simpson (see 478), a strong influence on Charles Parham. In the early 1900s the growing Pentecostal movement caused a split in the CMA. Some members, having experienced the baptism of the Spirit, chose to remain in the CMA, while others left. Simpson was fairly open toward Pentecostal signs, but after his death, the CMA distanced itself from the movement. A 1908 denominational statement noted that speaking in tongues was "capable of abuse and wild excesses," and that it was not God's plan that all believers should speak in tongues. The CMA's governing board used the phrase "seek not, forbid not," indicating openness to tongues but no particular urge to seek the gift. Later the denomination stated that tongues should be prohibited in "certain services of the church."

193. Elim Pentecostal Church

Welsh evangelist George Jeffreys (see 512) established the Elim Evangelistic Band in northern Ireland in 1915. The movement spread and consisted of 15 assemblies by 1920.

By 1926 Elim had converted a former Catholic convent into Elim Bible College. By 1928 there were 70 congregations, and by 1987 a total of 380 in Britain. The group emphasizes Christ as Savior, Healer, Baptizer, and Coming King.

194. Open Bible Standard Churches (OBSC)

This Pentecostal denomination began, as have so many, with a break from another—in this case, *two* others. Fred Hornshuh, a pastor with the Apostolic Faith (AF), broke from the AF in 1919 over such issues as the AF's aloofness toward other Pentecostals. Hornshuh began publishing the *Bible Standard* magazine, which lent its name to the new breakaway group. This was the "first wave" of the OBSC. The other began with a splinter group from the International Church of the Foursquare Gospel (ICFG). Several ICFG pastors in Iowa formed the Open Bible Evangelistic Association. The Bible Standard Churches and the Open Bible Evangelistic Association merged in 1935. The OBSC has about forty-six thousand members.

195. Pentecostal Fire-Baptized Holiness Church (PFBHC)

Just how worldly can Christians be? In the past Pentecostals, particularly the women, were easily recognized by their simplicity. But now that charismatics and (to a slightly lesser degree) Pentecostals dress pretty much the same as everyone else, some believers advocate a stricter, more traditional standard. The PFBHC was founded in

1918 mainly to maintain strict standards, which include no neckties for men; mid-calf–length dresses for women; no jewelry for women or cutting of their hair; no attendance at swimming pools or theaters. In other respects the denomination, which is very small, is traditionally Pentecostal, stressing sanctification and speaking in tongues. Headquarters are in Toccoa Falls, Georgia.

196. Mount Sinai Holy Church of America

This denomination, primarily black, is traditionally Pentecostal in belief and practice with an emphasis on strict moral standards (e.g., no alcohol, tobacco, or "artificial adornings"), but one thing that sets it apart from many denominations is that women may serve as bishops and elders. The Pentecostal and Holiness churches have historically been open to women in preaching and teaching, but this denomination (founded by a woman, Ida Robinson, in 1924) also allows for women in the top offices.

197. Maranatha Campus Ministries International (MCMI)

American college campuses may lean toward political correctness, but Christian ministries are still part of the college scene. Bob and Rose Weiner launched the MCMI at Murray State University in Kentucky in 1972, hoping to reach students with the gospel and to disciple them through Maranatha Christian churches, which provide education and fellowship. (Technically, the MCMI was a denomination as well as a campus ministry.) It was active on about two hundred college campuses and had about five hundred full-time staffers worldwide. Maranatha was dissolved in 1989.

5

Controversies, Scandals, and Such

198. Jim and Tammy Faye Bakker

The Holy Spirit does not work through perfect people, since there are none. The Bakkers—heads of the PTL Club and its related ministries, based in Charlotte, North Carolina—have become a byword for shady financial dealings and sexual misconduct, and they have given skeptics cause to laugh at Christians. But there is no doubt that PTL, as most media ministries, gave comfort and spiritual sustenance to many. James Orsen Bakker (b. 1940) and Tammy Faye Bakker (b. 1942), now divorced, were a popular husband-wife talk show team during their PTL days in the 1970s and 1980s. In 1987 Jim resigned and gave up his Assemblies of God ministerial credentials. He spent several years in prison for the club's misuse of contributions. In

1997, he published a forthright book, *I Was Wrong*, and began an apparently sincere attempt at a spiritual comeback. He claimed he had repented of preaching a prosperity gospel. (See 790 [PTL].)

199. snake handling

This practice provokes a lot of snickers from non-Christians and even from many Christians. Mark 16:18 records the risen Jesus' words to His followers, telling them what they will be capable of: "They will take up serpents; and if they drink anything deadly, it will by no means hurt them." Did Jesus mean the words about snakes *literally?* Hard to say. Acts 28 relates that Paul, shipwrecked on Malta, was bitten by a viper, but he shook the snake off into the fire and suffered no ill effects. The people expected him to fall dead, but after waiting a long time and seeing nothing unusual happen to him, they believed he was a god.

Snake handling today is associated with a "backwoodsy" religion. George Went Hensley, following his Spirit baptism in a Church of God (Cleveland, Tennessee) congregation, took an interest in Mark 16:18. He prayed to God to let him find a serpent, and he found a rattlesnake, which he handled with no harm to himself. He repeated the act at his church, but eventually, the Church of God stated that it did not approve of such acts. Such behavior continues, though most Pentecostal denominations have condemned the practice, particularly since people have been injured or killed.

200. Jimmy Swaggart (b. 1935)

A cousin of rock 'n' roll legend Jerry Lee Lewis, Swaggart was (like Lewis) born in Ferriday, Louisiana, and was and is a talented musician. He was baptized in the Spirit at age eight and began preaching at age seventeen. He became an evangelist at twenty-two, but Swaggart and his "golden gospel piano" were not appreciated by the Assemblies of God, which for a year denied him ordination. He was not particularly effective as a local church pastor, but his style of preaching and music did well on radio, a ministry that he began in 1969. His gospel albums sold well and gave exposure to his preaching ministry, and Swaggart was a rival to Billy Graham in national fame.

In 1981 he gave up his radio broadcasts in favor of a more effective medium, television, which had broadcast his programs since 1973. Swaggart reached out not only with the message of the gospel but also with an emphasis on social and political issues (some of the same emphases as Jerry Falwell, but with a more dramatic preaching style). Many people concerned for moral decline in the U.S. gave him their support, widening his influence far beyond Pentecostals. He established his Family Worship Center, the Jimmy Swaggart Bible College, and a monthly magazine.

Then, the scandal: the Assemblies of God (AG) defrocked him in 1988 because of allegations of his involvement with a prostitute. Swaggart confessed and repented but refused to accept the AG's discipline, which resulted in his ouster. His ministry suffered when giving declined dramatically. In the great tradition of American churches—and

·perhaps in the tradition of Christians always getting another chance—he did not disappear from the scene altogether.

201. shepherding / discipleship

The shepherding movement (also known as the discipleship movement) arose because of the phenomenal growth of the charismatic movement in the 1960s and 1970s. Many new believers found a spiritual home in denominations such as the Assemblies of God, while others remained within their own denominations. But some did not feel comfortable with any particular denomination. Some concerned people—notably the six men who founded the Holy Spirit Teaching Mission (HSTM) in Florida (see 152)—propagated the idea (a valid one) that doing one's own thing was not an option for Christians, since true believers need to be spiritually accountable to someone. Bob Mumford of HSTM authored the book *The Problem of Doing Your Own Thing* (1973), which outlined the pyramid scheme of spiritual authority. The HSTM changed its name to Christian Growth Ministries (CGM) and continued teaching that being a Christian required spiritual submission to some man (*man* in the male sense—there were no women shepherds), the shepherd.

Some Christian leaders, notably Pat Robertson, claimed that this kind of submission seemed to be cultish instead of Christian. Along with several other charismatic notables, he refused any fellowship with the CGM leaders. At the center of the controversy was the fear that the "sheep" were asked to make their "shepherd" the ultimate authority in their lives, not God or the Bible.

The CGM leaders admitted there had been abuses of shepherding. One of the leaders, Derek Prince, published *Discipleship, Shepherding, Commitment,* which set out guidelines for the movement, emphasizing the Bible as the final authority. There arose a truce, more or less, between the CGM leaders and other charismatics. The CGM no longer exists, but its successor organization, Integrity Communications (see 153), continues, having moved from Fort Lauderdale to Mobile, Alabama. At its peak in the mid-1970s the movement probably involved 150,000 people.

202. David Berg and the Children of God

Can a good man turn bad? Indeed. By 1971, Arizona pastor David Berg had about four thousand young followers living in forty colonies, emphasizing Scripture memorization, witnessing in pairs, and a communal and Spirit-centered life. Many young people found peace and community among the Children of God, but Berg aroused controversy over his attempt to get followers to sever all ties with their families and to put their lives under strict control of his "elders." In time Berg communicated to his flock only via his "MO" letters. Berg and the group created scandal by their alleged sexual indiscretions, many of them revealed in his daughter's autobiography. Berg died in 1994. The group is now known as The Family.

203. "open and gross sin"

B. H. Irwin founded the Fire-Baptized Holiness Church in 1895 and was its head until 1900, when he confessed to "open and gross sin." Irwin sort of disappeared from history after that, and people have puzzled over the nature of the unspecified sin.

204. Hobart E. Freeman (1920–84)

What happens when people of faith let their own children die? National scandal, of course. This happened in 1978 when David and Kathleen Bergmann, members of Hobart Freeman's Faith Assembly, let their child die without receiving medical aid. The parents received ten-year prison sentences. Freeman himself was, at the time of his death, under indictment for his role in the death of a fifteen-year-old girl whose parents were indicted and later convicted.

Freeman, born in Kentucky, had been healed of polio as a child and became pastor of the large Faith Assembly in Wilmot, Indiana. It was a "closed" church, with services open only to members, and Freeman prohibited members from having any religious teaching outside the church. On the subject of healing he took a firm stand: medical doctors and drugs are rooted in witchcraft and demonic power, and any true healing must come from God alone. Indeed, many miraculous healings were reported at the church. Regrettably, several people who had medically treatable ailments also died. The story of the Bergmanns' child was a national scandal, though Freeman's attitude toward healing is not typical of most people who believe in divine healing.

205. Oneida Community

John Humphrey Noyes (1811–86) was a minister and a
"perfectionist" who believed true Christians were free from
all sin. Declaring himself sinless, he found some other (supposedly) sinless people and formed a commune at Oneida,
New York. Noyes read Acts 2:44—"all who believed were
together, and had all things in common"—and applied it to
his "perfect" community. The people had all things in common, including spouses. The commune prospered materially, but because of the group's questionable morals, Noyes
had to flee the U.S. He died in Canada.

The community believed in faith-healing, and Noyes
claimed that Christians should expect release from disease
and evil spirits just as the first Christians had.

206. Unification Church

What do the Moonies have to do with the Spirit? The
Unification Church, founded by Sun Myung Moon, is officially called the Holy Spirit Association for the Unification
of World Christianity. Moon, a Korean, claimed that Jesus
appeared to him on Easter 1936 and told him to establish
the kingdom of God on earth.

207. Leroy Jenkins (b. 1935)

The late comic Flip Wilson sometimes portrayed a hip pastor who preached at the Church of What's Happening
Now. But there was a real church of that name, pastored by
the often-controversial Leroy Jenkins. Jenkins's arm was

healed in a tent meeting in 1960. Following that, he began preaching and healing, and throughout the 1960s, he toured with his ten-thousand-seat revival tent. The Pentecostal pastor had quite a following but created scandals after divorcing his wife and being arrested on drug charges.

208. seed faith

In Mark 10:29–30, Jesus assured His disciples that those who followed Him would "receive a hundredfold now in this time . . . and in the age to come, eternal life." This assurance has become a part of the message of many prosperity gospel evangelists (see 784), some of whom tell listeners that giving one dollar for the gospel's sake gives back one hundred, ten dollars gives back one thousand, and so on. It is called seed faith, though it might more appropriately be called seed giving. It has its critics both inside and outside the Christian fellowship.

209. Charles Hamilton Pridgeon (1863–1932)

Is hell eternal, or just a limited time of purification? In his later years, Pridgeon came to believe that there would be a "restitution" of all things. This universalism came to be called Pridgeonism and the Pridgeon doctrine, and the Assemblies of God condemned it as a heresy. Pridgeon had been orthodox in his earlier days. He had founded a missionary society that sent missionaries to China, India, and Africa. He encouraged a remarkable outpouring of the Spirit among students at the Pittsburgh Bible Institute, which he had founded. In 1918 he began airing his controversial beliefs about hell.

210. the antiordinance movement

Before the Pentecostal movement, the Holiness movement (see 449) was already emphasizing guidance by the Spirit. In the 1880s some Holiness preachers began what became the antiordinance movement. Teaching that reliance on the Spirit alone is the key element in the Christian life, some preachers advocated doing away with baptism and the Lord's Supper (the ordinances). The belief spread in Texas and surrounding states and was taken to extremes as some people began to reject all authority, including the Bible, the church, even the law. Several couples broke up their marriages (or cohabited without marriage), saying that the Spirit had led them to do so. The movement quickly ran out of steam, but had the unfortunate result of making Spirit-led Christians appear silly or even dangerous.

211. *Prime Time Live,* November 1991

With an audience of fifteen million viewers, Diane Sawyer dealt a body blow to televangelists in a program that profiled Larry Lea, Robert Tilton, and others. The program was designed to show how some televangelists bilk their contributors out of funds. Lea, the only one of the evangelists profiled who would actually grant an interview to Sawyer, took his program off the air soon afterward. The program's producers insisted that the show was *not* anti-Christian.

212. Robert G. Tilton (b. 1946)

Tilton's TV ministry was dealt a severe media blow, the 1991 *Prime Time Live* program (see 211) with its allegations of financial abuses. Membership at his Word of Faith Outreach Center in Dallas dropped from ten thousand to less than one thousand, and his TV show, *Success-N-Life*, went off the air for a time, but later returned. Televangelists have proved to be a resilient lot.

213. The Way

Can speaking in tongues be *taught?* According to Victor Paul Wierwille (1916–85), yes. Wierwille started out in the mainstream, ministering through a radio Bible study called *Vesper Chimes*. In 1951 he spoke in tongues, influenced by an evangelist who claimed to know a technique for bringing it about. Wierwille developed a twelve-session Power for Abundant Living course that, at its end, taught the "method" for speaking in tongues. In 1957 he opened the headquarters for The Way on a farm in Ohio. The group, divided into local fellowships called twigs, has been accused of being more of a cult than a Christian community. At the time of Wierwille's death the group numbered about 30,000 in about 2,500 twigs.

214. William Marrion Branham (1909–65)

A noted healing evangelist, Branham was born in a log cabin in Kentucky and reported heavenly visitations at ages three and seven. Feeling the call to preach, he conducted a tent revival in Jeffersonville, Indiana, and later built Branham Tabernacle there.

According to Branham, an angel appeared to him in a secret cave in 1946 and guided him throughout his life. He had the amazing power to read people's thoughts and understand their illnesses. Many of his healings were well attested medically, and he astounded people with his understanding of their ailments. People were drawn to him, and he packed stadiums.

Some of his beliefs and practices aroused controversies. He believed that Eve had had sexual relations with the serpent and that some people are descended from the "serpent's seed" and destined for hell, which is not eternal. The seed of God are those who respond to Branham's teaching, and though people might be saved in the mainline denominations, they would have to endure the Tribulation. Branham claimed he was the angel of Revelation 3:14 and 10:7. When he died in 1965, some followers believed he would be resurrected.

215. Jack Coe (1918–56)

This noted healing evangelist did not have a promising beginning. His parents abandoned him to an orphanage, and he became an alcoholic early in life. But in World War II while in the army he experienced a divine healing and became a minister, ordained by the Assemblies of God (AG). In the late 1940s and early 1950s his magazine *Herald of Healing* was widely read, and he established the Dallas Revival Center in 1952. However, the AG questioned some of his methods and expelled the flamboyant evangelist in 1953. Even so, his church grew. Scandal erupted in 1956: Coe, leading a healing crusade in Miami, was arrested for practicing medicine without a license. The judge dismissed the case, but Coe died in December of that year.

216. Oneness Pentecostalism

Most Pentecostals and charismatics hold to the traditional belief in the Trinity: God is Father, Son, and Holy Spirit—three-in-one and one-in-three. But around 1914 evangelist Frank J. Ewart and others began teaching that the God of the Old Testament was, with Jesus and the Spirit, one person—not three-in-one. The difference sounds trivial to many people, but the Oneness evangelists irked some people by baptizing not in the usual way ("in the name of the Father, Son, and Holy Spirit") but only "in the name of Jesus." Ewart ruffled feathers by insisting on *rebaptizing* Christians who had been baptized with the old formula. Quite a few Pentecostals opted for rebaptism. The Assemblies of God did not accept this innovation, and Ewart left to form a Oneness church. There are now several Oneness denominations, the largest being the United Pentecostal Church.

217. Finis Dake (1902–87)

Dake's refers to the popular *Dake's Annotated Reference Bible*, which became *the* study Bible for many Pentecostals. Published in 1963, it contains Dake's marginal notes with their distinctive Pentecostal brand of dispensationalism.

Pentecostal preachers loved it (and still do). It is still published by Dake Bible Sales under the leadership of his son, Finis Jr. Alas, Dake was the center of a scandal in his younger days. He was pastor of an Assemblies of God church in Zion, Illinois, and in 1937 he received a six-month jail sentence for transporting a sixteen-year-old from Wisconsin to St. Louis, with several hotel stops along the way. He pleaded guilty to violating the Mann Act (transporting a minor across state lines for immoral purposes). His wife and church members supported him, but the Assemblies of God booted him out. He later became an independent Pentecostal.

218. "finished work"

Is sanctification an instantaneous experience given to believers sometime after their conversion, or is it a gradual, over-the-whole-lifetime thing? Methodist founder John Wesley seems to have taught that it could be instantaneous, and many Holiness churches in America (since so many began as breakaway groups from the Methodist) have followed this teaching. Making the question even more complicated was the fact that Pentecostals began to emphasize the baptism in the Spirit. Was this, some asked, the same as instantaneous sanctification? How were they related?

Most early Pentecostal leaders believed that sanctification and Spirit baptism were separate, and that Spirit baptism was always accompanied by tongues. Thus, three stages: conversion (justification), entire sanctification, then baptism of the Spirit. But noted preacher William Durham (see 499) questioned this neat scheme and stated that sanctification was a *process,* not an instantaneous experience. He believed that traditional teaching undercut the Christian's need to grow steadily in grace. He found many who accepted this teaching, but more traditional Pentecostals resisted. It became the most divisive issue among Pentecostals for years after his death in 1912.

219. historically correct?

Stanley H. Frodsham wrote *With Signs Following: The Story of the Pentecostal Revival in the Twentieth Century.* Although it is still regarded as a good history of the early Pentecostal movement, it has a notable omission: the key leader Charles F. Parham is never mentioned, even though the book devotes several pages to the Kansas revival that took place under Parham's influence. Why the omission? Parham's arrest in 1907 on a sodomy charge. Though the charges were dropped, the scandal wrecked his reputation. Frodsham apparently chose to write him—and the scandal—out of history.

220. Levi Lupton (1860–1929)

"The apostle Levi" was the name Levi Lupton took as director of the Apostolic Evangelization Company, which he founded in 1907. At a large camp meeting in that year the noted Pentecostal evangelist urged the participants to do something new: undertake foreign missions. He was probably the most noted spokesman for foreign missions among Pentecostals, and he was a key player in founding the Pentecostal Missionary Union. Regrettably, the dynamic man confessed to adultery in 1910 and became persona non grata among his former Pentecostal brethren.

221. MC510

This was the number for a course at Fuller Theological Seminary, The Miraculous and Church Growth, taught by adjunct professor John Wimber (see 572). Launched in 1982 in a church basement, the course enrolled more than one hundred students from various backgrounds. Wimber's course involved two hours of theological discussion followed by an hour of lab in which students were to practice what they had learned about how God can cast out demons, heal the sick, and even raise the dead.

Some healing occurred in the class, including that of Peter Wagner (see 574), who sat on a stool in front of the class while Wimber prayed over him. Wagner had been on blood pressure medication for years. A few days later his doctor found that it had fallen. Medication was reduced and finally discontinued. Wagner himself began to lay hands on the sick and minister to them. The course, not surprisingly, became extremely popular, though the seminary discontinued it in 1986 because of the controversy it had generated. The following spring Wagner began teaching MC550, The Ministry of Healing in World Evangelization.

222. Shiloh manslaughter trials

Frank Sandford (1862–1948), a Maine boy, burned with the desire to establish God's kingdom on earth. Beginning as a pastor, he found his true calling as head of the Holy

Ghost and Us Bible School. (He referred to the Spirit as "my Companion.") He moved the school to a hilltop in Maine, and the site, named Shiloh, became a Christian community of six hundred residents. Believing God spoke to him directly, Sandford claimed that he was Elijah, Melchizedek, and David—prophet, priest, and king. Somehow money came in to keep the community afloat (he attributed this to faith and prayer), but there were lean times. During one fast that he mandated, one member died, and Sandford was tried for manslaughter but served no time. Even so, the hostile press had a field day. (Like some other healers, he prohibited any use of medical science in healing.)

Later he purchased two yachts to be used in missions. In 1911 one was wrecked off the coast of Africa, and the people on it boarded the other yacht. When it reached the coast of Maine, six of the people had died from lack of food and water. The situation caused a scandal, with people accusing Sandford of autocratic rule. He was convicted of manslaughter and served a seven-year prison sentence, while Shiloh continued, awaiting his release. After prison, Sandford lived in seclusion.

223. "King of the World"

Homer Tomlinson (1892–1968) had an advertising career before he was a church administrator, and his background showed in his colorful self-promotion. Tomlinson called himself "King of the World" and staged "coronations" in the capitals of 101 countries. The press (eager to publicize what they considered a Christian buffoon) showed up when he arrived, dressed in a scarlet robe, holding an inflatable globe, crowning himself, and making promises of peace and prosperity. He claimed to have ended revolutions in Haiti, Costa Rica, and Guatemala, as well as a war between Israel and the Arabs. He claimed the Vietnam War continued because he could not be crowned in Vietnam. Four times he ran as Theocratic Party candidate for president (claiming he would have cabinet posts such as secretary of the Bible and secretary of righteousness). His book *Shout of the King* seems more like fantasy than autobiography.

His father was the respected A. J. Tomlinson (see 530). Homer expected to succeed A. J. as head of the Church of God of Prophecy, but when that did not happen, he resolved *not* to be a minister. A small band of his followers endures as the Church of God (Huntsville, Alabama). (See 180.)

224. Latter Rain movement

The movement began in Saskatchewan, Canada. In February 1948, at the Sharon Orphanage and Schools, some students came under the power of God, with a prophecy given about a great work of God about to take place. Within two days several miraculous healings occurred. Brothers George and Ern Hawtin, both employees at Sharon, led revival meetings in Vancouver, British Columbia, and people from across the U.S. and Canada attended. Those attending took the news of the revival back home, spreading the flame just as had occurred with the Azusa Street revival forty years earlier.

The Latter Rain movement emphasized the "blaze of prophetic light" that had come upon the church, with God working through "prophets and apostles of His own choosing." Many pastors who identified with the movement were ousted from their churches, as occurs in all renewals. Note: the early Pentecostal revival had been called the Latter Rain by some people. For an explanation of the name, see 256 (Joel's "latter rain").

225. opening the books

Alas, some crooked evangelists give all evangelists a bad name. In recent years the IRS and an anti-Christian attitude of the public (and the media in particular) have made it essential that Christian ministries have an "open air" policy regarding their finances. (The problems of the Bakkers in the 1980s come to mind.) Curiously, one evangelist of the past who was not crooked but who disdained auditing was healer Finis Yoakum of California (see 491). He drew multitudes to Los Angeles in the early 1900s, and Yoakum's policy toward contributions was this: *if you don't trust, don't give; if you do give, trust*. A sound policy—*if* all workers for the Lord were as honest as he was.

226. black or white origins?

In the 1970s, James Tinney, editor of a magazine for black Pentecostals, caused—or tried to cause—a controversy. He claimed that Pentecostals traced their beginnings to the 1901 Topeka revival led by white pastor Charles F. Parham. In fact, the movement really began with the Azusa Street revival led by black pastor William J. Seymour. Happily, Christians in the renewal movement shrugged this off as a nonissue. Both Parham and Seymour made valuable contributions to the movement, but renewal is ultimately due to the Spirit.

227. strychnine, anyone?

There are snake-handling Christians and poison-drinking Christians. Both base their acts on Mark 16:18, in which the risen Jesus prophesied that His followers "will take up serpents; and if they drink anything deadly, it will by no means hurt them." Some persecuted Christians who were forced to drink poisons suffered no ill effects. But some Christians on the fringe have drunk poison—strychnine seems to be the one preferred—deliberately to show that Jesus' words were true. Some of them have lived—and some have died.

228. passions good and bad

Christians are human, and even the most spiritual sometimes fail, often in the area of sex. The Swaggart scandal in the 1980s was one of many reminders that the flesh is weak. Some keen observers of the renewal movement have noticed some connections: emotional experience is important to Pentecostals and charismatics, and both religion and sex provide (in different ways) intense experiences. No one has ever proved that sexual misconduct is any more common among Spirit-led Christians than among any others.

229. exotic practices

The amazing growth of the Toronto Airport Christian Fellowship was typical of many churches in the Vineyard Fellowship. But in 1995, Vineyard head John Wimber booted the Toronto congregation out of the Fellowship, citing "exotic practices" of roaring, barking, and making other animal noises. The Toronto church did not cease to grow, however.

230. James G. Watt (b. 1938)

He was the "Pentecostal in the cabinet," Ronald Reagan's controversial secretary of the interior. He drew criticism and snickers when he stated that he didn't want the Beach Boys performing at a Fourth of July celebration, but he really drew fire for his remark that a political commission included "a black, two Jews, and a cripple." He eventually was compelled to resign from the cabinet. The politically incorrect Watts was in many ways a good administrator and, unknown to the general public, a member of the Assemblies of God.

231. A. A. Allen (1911–70)

People of faith often come from deplorable family situations. Asa Alonso Allen, who had been an alcoholic in his younger days, had an alcoholic father and a wayward mother but was converted to Christ in 1934. He was licensed to preach by the Assemblies of God and by 1953 was broadcasting *The Allen Revival Hour* on radio. His

Miracle Magazine was launched in 1954 and widely read. He became one of the best-known healers of the 1950s and 1960s, reaching out in particular to the poor and to minorities. Alas, he was arrested for drunk driving in 1955. He gave up his Assemblies credentials but started his own Miracle Revival Fellowship. His divorce from his wife in 1967 caused some murmuring.

232. Church of God, Jerusalem Acres

Grady Kent, a black preacher from Georgia, was beaten by Ku Klux Klan members in 1939. The episode brought him to the attention of A. J. Tomlinson of the Church of God (Cleveland, Tennessee), who placed Kent in a CG church as pastor. Kent was semiliterate and had a speech impediment but was apparently a spellbinding speaker. However, he became "full of himself" and identified himself as one of the "two witnesses" of Revelation 11 and "John the Revelator" (and called St. John II). (Like many misguided prophets, Kent was obsessed with the book of Revelation.) Tomlinson asked Kent to either resign or retract such statements, and Kent resigned in 1957. He formed his own group, the Church of God of All Nations, with him as chief bishop. He bought land in Cleveland, Tennessee, which he planned to call Jerusalem Acres. Kent died in 1974, and some followers believed he would rise from the dead. The denomination barely exists, with a very small membership.

233. annihilationism

Hard as it is to believe, many people in the renewal movement had quarreled over what might seem an unimportant matter: Is hell forever, or does God simply snuff out the wicked? Charles F. Parham, one of the founding fathers of the Pentecostal revival in this century, claimed that annihilationism was "the most important doctrine in the world today." Later Pentecostals took pains to emphasize that, yes, hell really was permanent. Parham's statement indicates that in the early days of Pentecostalism, not everyone saw speaking in tongues as the key feature of the movement. Annihilationism is also called *conditional immortality*.

6

The Spirit in the Book: Old Testament

234. the hovering Spirit

The first mention of the Spirit in the Bible is at the very act of creation. According to Genesis 1:2, "the Spirit of God was hovering over the face of the waters." The Hebrew word that we translate as "Spirit" was *ruach*, which could mean "spirit," "wind," or "breath."

235. "strive" or "abide" or what?

One of the most puzzling verses in the Bible is Genesis 6:3: "The LORD said, 'My Spirit shall not strive with man forever, for he is indeed flesh; yet his days shall be one hundred and twenty years.'" The word we translate "strive" could also be translated "abide in" or "contend with" or "remain in," as various contemporary translations have it. But no one agrees on just what the verse means. However, since the verse occurs in a story of how God sees how wicked mankind has become, we can assume that the withdrawal of the Spirit—as indicated by the shortening of man's life span—is a sign of God's righteous reaction to sin.

236. Old Testament Trinity

Genesis 18 relates that the Lord appeared to Abraham as he was sitting in his tent doorway. But "the Lord" appeared as three men. Abraham entertained them hospitably, and "He" (the Lord—but which of the three men was speaking?) spoke a prophecy to Abraham. The passage refers to "the Lord" and "He" but also insists that *three* men, not one, visited Abraham. Was one of the three men God-in-the-flesh while the other two were angels? Some readers have suggested that this was the Trinity—what the New Testament refers to as God the Father, Son, and Spirit. So perhaps Abraham's visitors were an Old Testament Trinity.

237. inspired artist

We talk of some creative people as being inspired. In the book of Exodus, this was literally true, for the craftsman Bezalel was, as God told Moses, "filled . . . with the Spirit of God, in wisdom, in understanding, in knowledge, and in all manner of workmanship, to design artistic works" (Ex. 31:3–4). Bezalel had the important task of constructing the tabernacle, the center of Israel's worship. The Spirit-filled Bezalel is the first person mentioned in the Bible as having the Spirit. In this case the Spirit in him was used to accomplish a particular task.

238. Israel's seventy elders

Moses was a great leader of Israel, but he often found it burdensome to direct the griping, quarrelsome Israelites. God directed him to select seventy elders to aid in administration. God told Moses, "I will take of the Spirit that is upon you and will put the same upon them; and they shall bear the burden of the people with you, that you may not bear it yourself alone" (Num. 11:17). Later this did indeed occur, with God coming down in a cloud and placing the Spirit upon the seventy. Afterward, Moses exclaimed, "Oh, that all the LORD's people were prophets and that the LORD would put His Spirit upon them!" (11:29).

239. a false prophet with the Spirit

Numbers 22–24 tells the curious tale of the Moabite prophet Balaam, who was sent by the king, Balak, to place curses on the Israelites as they were passing through the area. Thanks to an angelic visitor and his own donkey (which spoke!), Balaam put aside this task and, instead of cursing Israel, pronounced blessing upon it. He did so under the influence of the Spirit: "Balaam raised his eyes, and saw Israel encamped according to their tribes; and the Spirit of God came upon him" (24:2).

240. Joshua, successor to Moses

Moses' faithful assistant, Joshua, succeeded him as Israel's leader. Numbers 27:18 records the first instance of a laying on of hands (Moses upon Joshua) as an act of bestowing the Spirit upon another person. Deuteronomy 34:9 claims that Joshua was given the spirit (or Spirit, depending on the translation) of wisdom, so the children of the Lord followed him and obeyed.

241. military men and the Spirit

The book of Judges tells the often violent stories of the Israelites and their struggles in their new homeland of Canaan. In the days before Israel had a king, God raised up judges (more like military leaders than judges in our modern sense) to lead the people against their enemies. Several of the more notable judges—Othniel, Gideon, and Jephthah—are described as coming under the power of the Spirit. (See 242.)

242. Spirited muscleman

The Hebrew strongman Samson (a violent character and hardly a role model in sexual matters) does not impress us as a "spiritual person," but he definitely was empowered by the Holy Spirit. More than once "the Spirit of the LORD came mightily upon him" (Judg. 14:6; 15:14). He tore a lion apart with his bare hands and slew his enemies, the Philistines.

243. poor King Saul

Israel's first king, the tall, handsome Saul, was an admirable but, finally, pitiful man. For reasons that the Bible does not make clear to us, Saul was under the good influence of the Spirit, but later, the Spirit was withdrawn from him and "a distressing spirit from the LORD troubled him" (1 Sam. 16:14). Saul could be rash and impulsive at times, and God told the prophet Samuel, who had first anointed Saul, to anoint the young David as Israel's king. David, not Saul, then had the Spirit (16:13). Oddly, though, at a later time Saul was again under the Spirit's influence, and he "prophesied" (1 Sam. 19:23–24).

244. the Spirit as architect

Exodus records that the talented Bezalel, who constructed Israel's tabernacle, was filled with the Spirit for his task. First Chronicles 28:11–13 records that the plans given by King David to his son Solomon for the Lord's temple and other buildings were "had by the Spirit." It is the second instance in the Bible of creative artistry being attributed not to human ingenuity but to the Spirit.

245. dis-Spirited David

Psalm 51, attributed to Israel's King David, is the prayer of a guilt-stricken man to be forgiven and cleansed by God. Verse 11 has the pitiful man crying to God, "Do not cast me away from Your presence, and do not take Your Holy Spirit from me." This is one of only two places in the Old

Testament that refer to the Spirit as the Holy Spirit (the other place is Isa. 63:10–11). David's predecessor as king was the ill-fated Saul, who had the Spirit but, later, had Him withdrawn. The guilt-stricken David no doubt remembered the sorry state of a man without God's Spirit.

246. Psalm 103:2–3

Psalm 103, attributed to David, proclaims, "Bless the LORD, O my soul, and forget not all His benefits: who forgives all your iniquities, who heals all your diseases." In the late 1880s, the faith-healing movement often referred to these verses, which combine forgiveness of sin with healing from sickness. One of the driving forces behind the healing movement was this belief that Christ came to heal both body and soul.

247. the omnipresent Spirit

Psalm 139 could have the title "He's Everywhere, He's Everywhere!" In the psalm, David stated his awareness of God being with him everywhere and at all times, even aware of his every thought. In verse 7 he asked, "Where can I go from Your Spirit? Or where can I flee from Your presence?" The answer, of course, is "nowhere." But the awareness of the Spirit's presence everywhere is a source of comfort.

248. "the voice of the turtle"

Do turtles sing? According to the Song of Solomon (in the King James Version), "the time of the singing of birds is come, and the voice of the turtle is heard in our land" (2:12). The "turtle" is the turtledove, not a singing reptile. The New King James Version has "turtledove." The Song of Solomon, a book of love songs, does not mention God, the Spirit, or anything even remotely spiritual. Many clever people have interpreted the book allegorically. When read this way, the passage about the turtledove becomes a prophecy of the Spirit. The dove is the Spirit, and the "voice" is the sound of speaking in tongues. Far-fetched? Bernard of Clairvaux, one of the most noted preachers and saints of the Middle Ages, interpreted the passage in just that way.

249. Isaiah and the Spirit

Isaiah referred to the Spirit more than any other Old Testament book did. The prophet mentioned the Spirit in connection with the promised Messiah (also known as the Servant), upon whom the Spirit would rest (11:2; 42:1; 61:1). These prophecies were fulfilled in the life of Christ. Isaiah looked forward to a time when more than a few select individuals would have God's Spirit (32:15; 34:16; 59:21). Consider 44:3: "I will pour water on him who is thirsty, and floods on the dry ground; I will pour My Spirit on your descendants, and My blessing on your offspring." (See 251 [Suffering Servant].)

250. Jesse's descendant with the Spirit

Jesse's sole claim to fame in the Bible is that he was King David's father and thus an ancestor of Jesus. But Isaiah 11 contains an interesting prophecy: "There shall come forth a Rod from the stem of Jesse, and a Branch shall grow out of his roots. The Spirit of the LORD shall rest upon him" (vv. 1–2). Christians believed this rod or shoot (descendant, that is) was Jesus. Artists liked to depict a Jesse tree, showing the sleeping Jesse with a tree coming up from his loins—a literal family tree with the kings of Israel and, of course, Jesus. It was a favorite subject for stained-glass windows, and many an old church has a Jesse window.

251. the Suffering Servant

Several passages in Isaiah speak of a "servant of the Lord," a meek and innocent person who endures suffering but is God's chosen One, the Messiah. The passages (42:1–4; 49:1–6; 50:4–9; 52:13–53:12) are often called the Servant Songs, and the person they refer to is known as the Suffering Servant. In 42:1, God announced, "Behold! My Servant whom I uphold, My Elect One in whom My soul delights! I have put My Spirit upon Him." The early Christians believed these passages applied to Jesus, Israel's Messiah, the innocent man suffering for the guilty.

252. Jeremiah

Jeremiah's book is one of the longest in the Bible, yet it never mentions the Spirit by name. As a prophet of God, Jeremiah undoubtedly spoke by the Spirit, so we marvel that the saintly and sensitive man never actually spoke of the Spirit who touched his life so deeply. Yet the message of renewal of the heart by God is certainly present in the book.

253. Ezekiel's "lift"

The prophet Ezekiel is best known for his dramatic visions, notably the valley of the dry bones in chapter 37 (see 254). But Ezekiel is also noted for the times he mentioned the Spirit as a presence that physically lifted him up and moved him! Several times the prophet described being "set on his feet" or "lifted up" or otherwise moved by the Spirit. The prophet also foresaw a time when the Spirit would be poured out not on a few select individuals but on all of Israel (39:29).

254. the Spirit and the valley of the dry bones

The prophet Ezekiel had several unusual visions, none more striking than that of a valley filled with dry bones. God asked him, "Can these bones live?" Ezekiel replied, "O Lord GOD, You know," and God commanded him to preach to them, saying, "O dry bones, hear the word of the LORD!" Ezekiel did so, and the bones reattached to one another and came to life. God told Ezekiel that the bones represented Israel, which thought itself spiritually dead. Yet God could and would put His Spirit in the people and return them to their homeland. The story, found in Ezekiel 37, is the basis of the old spiritual, "Dem Bones, Dem Bones, Dem Dry Bones."

255. Joel and Pentecost

The prophet Joel's brief book is quoted often by Christians in the renewal movement because Joel, in 2:28–32, predicted the Holy Spirit being poured out on mankind: "I will pour out My Spirit on all flesh; your sons and your daughters shall prophesy, your old men shall dream dreams, your young men shall see visions. And also on My menservants and on My maidservants I will pour out My Spirit in those days . . . And it shall come to pass that whoever calls on the name of the LORD shall be saved." Peter, in the book of Acts, quoted this prophecy in his stirring sermon on the day of Pentecost (see 284). The significance of Joel's prophecy is that in the Old Testament the Spirit empowered only a select few people—prophets, military deliverers, and kings. The early Christians saw the Spirit empowering all who put their faith in Christ, fulfilling Joel's prophecy.

256. Joel's "latter rain"

Many Pentecostals and charismatics today would agree that the gift of speaking in tongues largely (but never totally) disappeared from Christian history, down to the present day. They would also say that the outpouring of this and other spiritual gifts today is the "latter rain" (Joel 2:23) prophesied in Acts 2:16–21. (See 224 [Latter Rain movement].)

257. Micah

The faithful prophet Micah observed the difference between true prophets and false ones, noting that "truly I am full of power by the Spirit of the LORD, and of justice and might" (3:8). False prophets were moved by their own wickedness and greed, not by the Spirit.

258. Haggai

The brief book of the prophet Haggai is probably one of the least-read parts of the Old Testament, mostly because its purpose (encouraging the rebuilding of the Jerusalem temple) strikes most people as dead history. However, the tiny book contains a word of eternal significance: God, speaking to Israel, reminded the people that "I covenanted with you when you came out of Egypt, so My Spirit remains among you; do not fear!" (2:5).

259. Zechariah

The book of the prophet Zechariah contains an often-quoted verse regarding the Spirit: "'Not by might nor by power, but by My Spirit,' says the LORD of hosts" (4:6). It is a reminder that reliance on human power is bound to lead to frustration, for the power of the Spirit of God is infinitely greater.

7

The Spirit in the Book: New Testament

260. *pneuma*

We find the Greek word *pneuma* in our words *pneumonia* and *pneumatic*. (And the French word for automobile tire is *pneu*.) The word *pneuma* meant, like the Hebrew word *ruach* in the Old Testament, "wind" or "breath" or "spirit"—in other words, very real things that are invisible but also powerful and alive. In the New Testament, *pneuma* referred to the Spirit of God—also invisible, powerful, and alive. In John 3, Jesus referred to the unpredictable wind that blows wherever it will—powerful and untamable, as the Spirit is. The same word *pneuma* is used for both "wind" and "Spirit" in these verses. The idea harks back to Genesis 1, with its image of the Spirit "hovering over the face of the waters."

261. John the Baptist

This colorful and engaging New Testament character had close connections with the Spirit, even before his birth. John's birth to the aged Zacharias and Elizabeth was foretold by the angel Gabriel, who told the startled father-to-be that the child would be "filled with the Holy Spirit, even from his mother's womb" (Luke 1:15). Gabriel later announced an even more miraculous conception: the Virgin Mary would bear a son. When the expectant Mary went to visit her kinswoman Elizabeth, the unborn John "leaped in her womb; and Elizabeth was filled with the Holy Spirit" (Luke 1:41). After John's birth, his delighted father "was filled with the Holy Spirit, and prophesied," uttering a song of praise to God (Luke 1:67–79).

All four Gospels report John's ministry of baptizing repentant people in the Jordan River. John told his listeners that he baptized with water, "but One mightier than I is coming . . . He will baptize you with the Holy Spirit and fire" (Luke 3:16). He was referring to Jesus, who came to John for baptism, at which time the Spirit descended upon Jesus in the form of a dove.

262. Christmas and the Spirit

The gospels of Matthew and Luke are the only books of the Bible that mention Jesus' miraculous conception by the Virgin Mary. The books give no details of how the conception took place except that "that which is conceived in her is of the Holy Spirit" (Matt. 1:20). The angel Gabriel had prophesied this to the puzzled Mary, telling her, "The Holy

Spirit will come upon you, and the power of the Highest will overshadow you" (Luke 1:35).

263. Simeon

Luke's gospel is often called the "gospel of the Spirit" because of the many times he referred to the Holy Spirit. Alone of the gospel writers, he told the story of the devout Simeon, who had been awaiting the Messiah and had been told by the Spirit that he would not die until he had indeed seen the Christ. In the temple he encountered the infant Jesus with Mary and Joseph. Knowing that Jesus would be the Messiah, Simeon took the child in his arms and praised God.

264. anointing

Christ and *Messiah* both mean "the Anointed One." Using the thumb or a finger, a person daubs an oil (usually olive oil) to mark a person or object as being special in some way. A sacred anointing meant the person or thing was being dedicated to God. The Old Testament records many things being anointed—the tabernacle, prophets, priests, and kings. In time the marking with oil came to symbolize the Holy Spirit. It meant that the person was set apart and empowered for a particular work in God's service. Samuel anointed Saul (and, later, David) as king. David several times used the phrase "the LORD's anointed" to refer respectfully to Saul. In the New Testament the "anointing with the Spirit" is a spiritual reality, not a matter of daubing oil. Jesus was said to be anointed with the Spirit, a fact the

Gospels mention at His baptism. Jesus' disciples are also said to be anointed with the Spirit (2 Cor. 1:21; 1 John 2:20).

265. Jesus' baptism

This act, performed by Jesus' kinsman John the Baptist, marked the beginning of Jesus' public life. All four Gospels report it. When Jesus came out of the water, the Spirit descended on Him "like a dove," and a voice from heaven said, "This is My beloved Son, in whom I am well pleased." Jesus received a divine and public approval of the ministry He was beginning. Paintings of Jesus' baptism always show a dove (the Spirit) over His head. The baptism is the chief reason that the Holy Spirit is always symbolized by a dove.

266. the Spirit and the temptation

According to the Gospels, immediately after Jesus' baptism, the Holy Spirit descended upon Him. And what was the first evidence of the Spirit in Jesus' life? "Jesus was led up by the Spirit into the wilderness to be tempted by the devil" (Matt. 4:1). Mark's gospel phrased it more bluntly: "The Spirit drove Him into the wilderness. And He was there in the wilderness forty days, tempted by Satan" (Mark 1:12–13). It is often forgotten that before Jesus began teaching and healing, the Spirit first led Him into a meeting with Satan, whose aim was to divert Jesus from His true calling.

267. returning in power

The gospels of Matthew, Mark, and Luke record that the Spirit came upon Jesus at His baptism and afterward led Him to the wilderness to face temptation by Satan. Luke's gospel also records that "Jesus returned in the power of the Spirit to Galilee, and news of Him went out through all the surrounding region" (Luke 4:14). Luke connected the Spirit with *power*, which Jesus soon revealed in His healings, exorcisms, and other miracles.

268. Jesus' rejection at Nazareth

The Gospels tell the sad story of Jesus being rejected in His hometown. In the synagogue at Nazareth He stood up to read from the scroll of the prophet Isaiah, and He read these words: "The Spirit of the LORD is upon Me, because He has anointed Me to preach the gospel to the poor; He has sent Me to heal the brokenhearted, to proclaim liberty to the captives and recovery of sight to the blind, to set at liberty those who are oppressed; to proclaim the acceptable year of the LORD." He concluded the reading by saying, "Today this Scripture is fulfilled in your hearing." The people He had known for years were "filled with wrath, and rose up and thrust Him out of the city" (Luke 4:17–29). They were blind to the fact that His words were true, and that at His baptism the Spirit had descended upon Him.

269. blasphemy against the Spirit

This deadly serious sin is mentioned in the gospels of Matthew, Mark, and Luke. In Mark's gospel, Jesus stated, "I say to you, all sins will be forgiven the sons of men, and whatever blasphemies they may utter; but he who blasphemes against the Holy Spirit never has forgiveness, but is subject to eternal condemnation" (3:28–29). Millions of sensitive souls have agonized over this, wondering, Have I committed the unpardonable sin? Most people have no clear idea of what blasphemy against the Spirit is. But the Gospels make it clear: Jesus' words in Mark followed an accusation by His enemies that His power to cast out demons came from Satan. In other words, they attributed the holy power to the power of darkness—calling Jesus a servant of Satan. They called good evil, something the Bible heartily condemns (Isa. 5:20). This does not seem to be a sin that a person could accidentally commit, so people who agonize over the unpardonable sin can feel certain that they have not committed it.

270. Jesus and the Sadducees

The Sadducees were the establishment class of the Jewish religion in Jesus' day. While He had some harsh words for the Pharisees, condemning their hypocrisy, Jesus also came down hard on the Sadducees. Many of them were priests, meaning they were officially the religious cream of the crop. Yet they seemed content to go through the rituals and sacrifices without giving much thought to God. On one occasion Jesus accused them of "not knowing the Scriptures nor the power of God" (Matt. 22:29). His words could well serve as a condemnation of the church through the centuries, not knowing the Bible or the power of God. The renewal movement has worked to remedy this situation.

271. the Seventy

Jesus chose twelve men as His close group of disciples, but Luke's gospel also mentioned a larger group, "the seventy": "The Lord appointed seventy others also, and sent them two by two before His face into every city and place where He Himself was about to go." He told them to "heal the sick there, and say to them, 'The kingdom of God has come near to you.'" Apparently, they had some success: "The seventy returned with joy, saying, 'Lord, even the demons are subject to us in Your name'" (Luke 10:1–17). Worth noting: Jesus gave power of healing and casting out demons to those who were not part of His "inner circle," the twelve disciples. Spirit-led believers see this as a foreshadowing of the spiritual gifts of healing and exorcism described in Acts.

272. trial and the Spirit

The gospels of Matthew and Mark record Jesus' assuring words about His disciples facing the hour of trial. When persecution came, as it inevitably would, the disciples should not be afraid about what they would say at their trials, "for it is not you who speak, but the Spirit of your Father who speaks in you" (Matt. 10:20). Persecuted Christians have taken great comfort in these words.

273. Jesus' warning

The New Testament gives witness to the power of the Spirit seen in many wonders—prophesying, casting out demons, and other miracles. Jesus promised such things. Yet He also gave a stern warning to those who would pursue miracles for their own sake: "Not everyone who says to Me, 'Lord, Lord,' shall enter the kingdom of heaven, but he who does the will of My Father in heaven. Many will say to Me in that day, 'Lord, Lord, have we not prophesied in Your name, cast out demons in Your name, and done many wonders in Your name?' And then I will declare to them, 'I never knew you; depart from Me, you who practice lawlessness!'" (Matt. 7:21–23). Signs and wonders are good, but the heart must be right with God.

274. open warfare

Jesus stated, "If I cast out demons by the Spirit of God, surely the kingdom of God has come upon you" (Matt. 12:28). Jesus was saying that the exorcisms He (and later His disciples) performed were signs that the kingdom of God and the kingdom of Satan were in obvious and open conflict. With its emphasis on deliverance from demons, the renewal movement has brought this important teaching into the open once again.

275. the Spirit as water

The Spirit is often compared to fire, but the New Testament in one passage compares Him to water. Jesus told His disciples, "'If anyone thirsts, let him come to Me and drink. He who believes in Me . . . out of his heart will flow rivers of living water.' But this He spoke concerning the Spirit, whom those believing in Him would receive" (John 7:37–39). The Old Testament had often pictured water as a refreshment from God. In a region noted for lack of water, living water must have sounded wonderful.

276. Helper and Comforter

The Greek word *paraklete* refers to a "counselor," "supporter," or "comforter." John's gospel uses *paraklete* to refer to the Spirit, and the various English versions translate *paraklete* as "Helper," "Comforter," "Counselor," and "Advocate" (John 14:16; 15:26; 16:7). All convey the idea of one who consoles and supports and (like an advocate— that is, an attorney) is more than just a fair-weather friend. John's verses on the Spirit are some of the most quoted and most memorable passages on the role of the Spirit in the believer's life. Jesus reminded His disciples—then and now—that though He is no longer physically present, the Helper is always present.

277. reproof

In our age, tolerance is considered the supreme virtue. But the Bible makes it clear that reproof—reminding people of their sins and failings—is a noble work. It is also one of the key works of the Spirit. Jesus told His disciples that the Spirit (called Helper or Comforter or Counselor, depending on the translation) will "convict the world of sin, and of righteousness, and of judgment" (John 16:8). The key idea is that the Spirit causes people to see the truth. When Jesus was physically present on earth, His sinless life as well as His teachings served the purpose of reproof. After His ascent to heaven, the invisible Spirit acts on people for the same purpose.

278. giving up His spirit

In John's gospel, the crucified Jesus said, "'It is finished!' And bowing His head, He gave up His spirit" (John 19:30). In the Greek New Testament there is no difference between "Spirit" (meaning the Holy Spirit) and "spirit"—the word *pneuma* serves for both.

279. the breath of life

John's gospel records that on the first Easter, the risen Jesus breathed on His disciples and told them, "Receive the Holy Spirit" (20:22). Many readers have observed the connection between this and the creation of Adam in Genesis 2:7, where God "breathed into his nostrils the breath of life; and man became a living being." In a sense the giving of the Spirit to the disciples is a new creation. In both Greek and Hebrew, the words we translate "breath" and "Spirit" are the same. And the Greek words of John are more accurately translated "breathed into" the disciples, not "breathed on" them.

280. one Pentecost, or two?

The descent of the Spirit upon Jesus' apostles at Pentecost is reported in Acts 2, a favorite passage for people in the charismatic movement. But what do we make of John 20:22, where the risen Jesus, on the day of His resurrection—before His ascension and before Pentecost—"breathed on them, and said to them, 'Receive the Holy Spirit'"? We must assume that John was reporting the truth: the disciples received the Spirit on Easter Sunday. Then what occurred at Pentecost? We can only assume that the Pentecost outpouring of the Spirit was a *fuller* experience, as evidenced by the apostles proclaiming the word in foreign tongues.

281. Mark's longer ending

Depending on which Bible translation you use, the gospel of Mark may end at 16:8. Bible scholars enjoy debating whether this is the true ending of the gospel or whether verses 9–20 are the real ending. At any rate, 16:17 reports the risen Jesus telling His disciples that "these signs will follow those who believe: In My name they will cast out demons; they will speak with new tongues." This is the only place in the Gospels where speaking in tongues is mentioned. Was Jesus referring to *glossolalia*, speaking in one's unknown praise language to God, or to *xenolalia*, addressing someone in a real language that one has never learned—or both? The book of Acts shows that both occurred among the early Christians, fulfilling Jesus' prophecy.

282. Jesus' ascension

The descent of the Spirit on Jesus' apostles dates from the Pentecost, described in Acts 2. Jesus had made it clear to them that the Spirit would come after He departed. (Note John 7:39: "The Holy Spirit was not yet given, because Jesus was not yet glorified.") In Peter's dynamic sermon at Pentecost he stated that Jesus had been raised from the dead and ascended to heaven, where He was "exalted to the right hand of God, and having received from the Father the promise of the Holy Spirit, He poured out this which you now see and hear" (Acts 2:33).

283. Acts

The book of Acts, written by Luke, is a kind of sequel to Luke's gospel. Acts is Luke's "book of snapshots" of the early church, showing how it believed and practiced. Time and time again throughout Christian history, sensitive Christians have read Acts and noticed the contrast between the early church's vitality and the colorless, boring church that emerged later. The Pentecostal and charismatic movements today are in many ways attempts to "get back to Acts," back to the guidance of the Spirit in the church's life.

284. Pentecost

This is celebrated by both Jews and Christians, but in different ways. Israel's Feast of Pentecost (also called Feast of Weeks) was (and still is) celebrated fifty days after Passover (*Pentecost* means "fiftieth"). It marks the completion of the wheat harvest, and part of the ritual involved offering the Lord the firstfruits of their produce (Lev. 23:15–21).

Christians celebrate Pentecost as the day the Holy Spirit came upon the believers gathered in Jerusalem to celebrate the Jewish Pentecost. Acts 2 dramatically describes the incident in which the apostles were filled with the Holy Spirit and began to speak in other tongues. Many Jews from various nations gathered for the Pentecost celebration. The apostle Peter preached them a stirring sermon, and three thousand became Christians. This fulfilled Jesus' words to them in Acts 1:8, predicting they would receive power when the Spirit came on them and would be His witnesses across the earth. Christians often refer to Pentecost as "the birthday of the church."

285. the Tower of Babel, in reverse

The miraculous ability to speak in a foreign language one has not learned is reported in Acts 2, where the apostles at Pentecost were able to preach the word so that various foreigners understood them. This is known as *xenolalia* (see 31) and has occurred many times. Many Christians have observed that this miraculous occurrence at Pentecost is a kind of reversal of the Tower of Babel story found in Genesis 11:1–9. There people, who originally spoke just one language, were so filled with pride that they attempted to build a tower reaching into heaven. God came down and struck them with a diversity of languages. Thus, man's separateness is a kind of curse for human pride. But the Spirit undoes this, enabling the preacher of the gospel to communicate with the foreigner.

286. baptism in the Holy Spirit

John the Baptist baptized people in water to symbolize repentance and turning to God. He predicted Someone greater who would "baptize you with the Holy Spirit" (Matt. 3:11). The prophecy of Spirit baptism was fulfilled in a dramatic way in Acts 2, when the twelve apostles "were all filled with the Holy Spirit and began to speak with other tongues, as the Spirit gave them utterance" (v. 4). One of the apostles, Peter, then preached a stirring sermon, ending it with these words: "Repent, and let every one of you be baptized in the name of Jesus Christ . . . and you shall receive the gift of the Holy Spirit" (Acts 2:38). Acts and Paul's letters mentioned baptism of the Spirit several times (Acts 1:5; 8:16; 10:47; 11:16; 1 Cor. 12:13). Baptism in the Spirit refers to the person experiencing—sometimes dramatically—the active presence of God in his life. Many Christians believe that water baptism is only an outward sign, while the Spirit baptism is more significant. This belief has led to the growth of Pentecostal and charismatic churches (see 731 [Pentecostals] and 732 [charismatics]). Baptism of the Spirit is mentioned many, many times in this book.

287. Peter and the priests

Peter was, as the Gospels show, a bold (even impulsive) speaker. Acts 4 records that the Jewish authorities had some of the apostles arrested and, the following day, confronted them, asking, "By what power or by what name have you done this?" In spite of the intimidating gathering of the

Jewish establishment, Peter spoke out boldly, for he was "filled with the Holy Spirit" (Acts 4:1–8). Peter, the Galilean fisherman, was empowered by the Spirit and felt no fear in confronting the hostile group.

288. lying to the Spirit

The book of Acts tells the sad story of Ananias and Sapphira, a couple who sold some property and donated some (but not all) of the proceeds to the Christians in Jerusalem. Peter, speaking for the apostles, asked the husband, "Ananias, why has Satan filled your heart to lie to the Holy Spirit and keep back part of the price of the land for yourself? . . . You have not lied to men but to God." Ananias then immediately fell down dead, and shortly afterward the wife (not knowing of her husband's fate) also lied to Peter about the proceeds. Peter told her that she and her husband had "agreed together to test the Spirit of the Lord." Like her husband, she fell down dead (Acts 5:1–11). Many sensitive readers consider this an extremely cold-hearted story. Why kill two people just for lying? We don't know. The story only drives home the point that lying is not merely a sin against man but a sin against the God of truth.

289. Peter's shadow

Acts shows how the Spirit empowered the first Christians to do mighty works, including healing and other miracles. Acts 5:15 relates that some believers brought the sick into the streets so that "at least the shadow of Peter passing by might fall on some of them." Did the shadow actually bring healing, or did the believers just think it did? Acts does not say. But it is a testimony to the people's faith in the Spirit's power.

290. the disappearance of Philip

Philip was one of the seven men (usually called the deacons) appointed by the apostles to serve the church in Jerusalem. All are described as "full of the Holy Spirit and wisdom" (Acts 6:3). The Spirit told Philip to preach the faith to an official of the queen of Ethiopia. Philip explained to the man that the words of Isaiah that he was reading were fulfilled in the life of Jesus. Philip baptized the man in water, then "the Spirit of the Lord caught Philip away," and the man saw him no more (Acts 8:26–39).

291. Stephen

The first Christian to die for his faith was one of the seven men (usually known as the deacons) whom the apostles appointed (with the Spirit's guidance) to meet the needs of the Christians in Jerusalem. All seven are described as "full of the Holy Spirit and wisdom," but Acts mentions Stephen in particular as being a man full of faith and the Holy Spirit, who "did great wonders and signs among the people." Some hostile Jews accused him of blasphemy against their religion, and he was called to defend himself by the high priest. His eloquent speech recounted Israel's history in brief, and Stephen ended it by telling the Jews, "You always resist the Holy Spirit." The speech inflamed them, and even more so when Stephen looked toward heaven and said that he saw Christ standing at the right hand of God. They dragged him out of the city and stoned him to death, proving that what he said was true: they resisted the Spirit and persecuted God's prophets (Acts 6–7).

292. simony

Sorcery and occult practices were common in Bible days. Acts 8 tells of Simon the sorcerer, who attracted quite a following. He was baptized as a Christian and was impressed that the apostles could, by laying hands on people, give them the Holy Spirit. He offered the apostles money for the same ability. Peter was outraged, and he told Simon to repent of such wickedness.

Centuries later, when the church became wealthy and church officials were well paid, the word *simony* was used to describe the practice of buying a church position. But Simon's real sin was that he thought that the power of the Spirit could be bought and sold.

293. the apostles and the Samaritans

As Jesus' parable of the good Samaritan makes clear, the Jews looked down on the Samaritans. Yet Acts records that the faith spread to them under the evangelist Philip (Acts 8:12). The apostles in Jerusalem sent Peter and John to investigate. They arrived in Samaria and prayed that the believers would receive the Spirit, who had not yet come upon them. The two apostles laid hands on them, and they received the Spirit (8:15–17). This is quite dramatic, for it is the Bible's first mention of non-Jews receiving the

Spirit. Clearly, the Spirit saw no barriers in terms of race or location.

294. the Acts of the Spirit

In the original Greek, the New Testament book of Acts is simply called that—Acts. But Christians have traditionally called it Acts of the Apostles, since some of its main characters (such as Paul and Peter) were indeed apostles. But some attentive Bible readers have noted that the book could just as well be called Acts of the Holy Spirit, since the Spirit is mentioned in Acts more than fifty times.

295. Ananias and the blind Saul

Saul's dramatic conversion on the road to Damascus is related in Acts 9. Saul, blinded when confronted by the risen Christ, was staying in Damascus. The Lord called upon Ananias, a Christian, and told him to go to Saul to restore his sight. Ananias did as he was told, saying to Saul, "Brother Saul, the Lord Jesus, who appeared to you on the road as you came, has sent me that you may receive your sight and be filled with the Holy Spirit" (9:17). Saul's sight was restored, and he was baptized. His filling with the Spirit followed the Lord's words to Ananias that Saul (later Paul) was his "chosen vessel" to bear the gospel to many people. The "filling" was not for Saul's delight but for the building up of the church.

296. Peter and Cornelius

The author of the book of Acts, Luke, was probably a Gentile, so it is no wonder that he delighted to tell of Christianity's spread to the Gentiles. Acts 10 tells the story of Peter's witness to the kindhearted Roman centurion, Cornelius, a meeting that had been divinely arranged. After Peter preached to Cornelius's household, "the Holy Spirit fell upon all those who heard the word." Peter and his fellow Jews were astonished "because the gift of the Holy Spirit had been poured out on the Gentiles also" (vv. 44–45). They spoke with tongues and praised God, so Peter knew that Gentiles could receive the Spirit just as Jewish believers had.

297. the prophet Agabus

Prophecy is one of the gifts of the Spirit, and the book of Acts relates the stories of a few Christian prophets, one of them named Agabus: "In these days prophets came from Jerusalem to Antioch. Then one of them, named Agabus, stood up and showed by the Spirit that there was going to be a great famine throughout all the world, which also happened in the days of Claudius Caesar" (Acts 11:27–28). History records that Agabus's Spirit-given prophecy proved correct. Agabus appeared later in Acts, again led by the Spirit to prophesy, predicting that Paul would be bound and delivered over to the Gentiles, which was fulfilled when Paul was arrested and taken to Rome.

298. "to the Holy Spirit, and to us"

Acts 15 speaks of the meeting of the apostles in Jerusalem, after which they sent a letter to the Christians at Antioch. The letter contained these words: "For it seemed good to the Holy Spirit, and to us . . ." (Acts 15:28). It is an interesting example of the early church's belief that its leaders' decisions were guided by the Spirit—that the Spirit was serving (as Jesus had prophesied) as the Counselor.

299. "forbidden by the Holy Spirit"

Acts 16 relates that Paul and his fellow missionary, Silas, had gone through the districts of Phrygia and Galatia, but "they were forbidden by the Holy Spirit to preach the word in Asia. After they had come to Mysia, they tried to go into Bithynia, but the Spirit did not permit them" (16:6–7). It is one of many cases in Acts where the Spirit played the role of Counselor—the Divine Adviser—that Jesus had prophesied.

300. Paul's Macedonian vision

Paul and the other apostles had spread the gospel through much of the Near East. Acts 16:6–10 tells how they came to take the faith into Europe. In the town of Troas, Paul had a vision of a man of Macedonia standing and begging, "Come over to Macedonia and help us." Christian missionaries through the centuries have loved repeating this story, picturing people around the world saying, "Come over and help us." More than a few Spirit-led missionaries have taken the gospel to the far corners of the earth because they recalled Paul's vision.

301. the Paul-Barnabas split

A basic fact: Christians will disagree at times. Acts 15:36–39 records that missionary partners Paul and Barnabas came to a parting of the ways—over a personal matter, not over a matter vital to faith and belief. Acts relates this very matter-of-factly: Barnabas continued as a missionary without Paul, and Paul continued without Barnabas. The Spirit continued to work, even when two old friends had parted company. Christians are sometimes dismayed at the number of denominations that exist because of squabbles (sometimes over trivial matters). Yet the faith goes on. Who is to say that one denomination would be better than one hundred?

302. puzzled Ephesians

Acts 19 relates a curious story in the life of the young church. In the town of Ephesus, Paul encountered some believers and asked them, "Did you receive the Holy Spirit when you believed?" They replied, "We have not so much as heard whether there is a Holy Spirit" (v. 2). Paul, under the power of the Spirit, baptized the believers, then laid hands on them, and they received the Spirit, speaking in tongues and prophesying.

303. regeneration

Titus 3:5 is the one place in Scripture that refers to regeneration and the Spirit: "He saved us, through the washing of regeneration and renewing of the Holy Spirit." Of course, the idea of being renewed and born again is present in many other places in the Bible. The idea is that a new life has begun. Jesus made clear that this was the work of the Holy Spirit (John 3:5).

304. indwelling

The Old Testament refers several times to the Spirit being "in" a person selected for an important task. We don't take this literally, of course, since an invisible Spirit doesn't need to be "inside" or "on" a person's physical body. The idea is that God's presence is "with" the person. The Spirit is "in" all believers, as Paul made clear in 1 Corinthians 6:19: "Do you not know that your body is the temple of the Holy Spirit who is in you, whom you have from God, and you are not your own?"

305. sealing

In times past, people often had signet rings or other devices to "seal" or "brand" an object as being their own—somewhat like a monogram today. The Bible states that Christians are "sealed" by the Spirit: "Having believed, you were sealed with the Holy Spirit of promise" (Eph. 1:13); and "Do not grieve the Holy Spirit of God, by whom you were sealed for the day of redemption" (Eph. 4:30). The seal is a mark of God's ownership of Christians, but also a promise of better things to come—somewhat like an engagement ring, a spiritual down payment.

306. illumination

Most of us desire to be illumined, enlightened. According to the New Testament, this is one of the tasks of the Spirit: "When He, the Spirit of truth, has come, He will guide you into all truth" (John 16:13); and "We have received, not the spirit of the world, but the Spirit who is from God, that we might know the things that have been freely given to us by God" (1 Cor. 2:12). The knowledge here is not abstract knowledge, but knowledge of the workings of God and His purposes for us and the world.

307. inspired prophets

The Bible says little about itself, but one of the few passages that does is this: "No prophecy of Scripture is of any private interpretation, for prophecy never came by the will of man, but holy men of God spoke as they were moved by the Holy Spirit" (2 Peter 1:20–21). The "Scripture" referred to here is the Old Testament, which the early Christians accepted as divinely inspired. (Since the New Testament was still being written, "Scripture" didn't yet include it.) Peter echoed the early Christians' belief that the Spirit inspired the prophets and other authors of the Bible. So the Bible is inspired not in the usual sense of imagination or cleverness, but in the sense of being guided by the Spirit Himself.

308. "God-breathed"

In 2 Timothy 3:16–17, Paul told Timothy, "All Scripture is given by inspiration of God, and is profitable for doctrine, for reproof, for correction, for instruction in righteousness, that the man of God may be complete, thoroughly equipped for every good work." Though the Spirit is not actually mentioned here, the idea is present. The Greek word that we translate as "by inspiration of God" is *theopneustos*—literally, "God-breathed." The word *pneustos*—"breathed"—is related to the word *pneuma*, "Spirit."

309. you are God's temple

The early Christians set high standards for sexual morality—a striking contrast to the morals of unbelievers. In 1 Corinthians, Paul stressed that a Christian's body is not his own possession but is "the temple of God," in which dwells the Holy Spirit. Paul advised the Corinthian Christians (living in a city infamous for sexual immorality) to "flee sexual immorality. Every sin that a man does is outside the body, but he who commits sexual immorality sins against his own body. Or do you not know that your body is the temple of the Holy Spirit? . . . Therefore glorify God in your body" (1 Cor. 6:18–20).

310. the whole armor of God

In Ephesians 6:10–18, Paul spoke of the spiritual armor that Christians wear to face the powers of evil. The "whole armor of God" includes the belt of truth, breastplate of righteousness, shoes of the gospel of peace, shield of faith, helmet of salvation, and sword of the Spirit. Christian art often pictures the apostle Paul with a sword, which is based on the sword of the Spirit mentioned in this passage.

311. "Jesus is Lord"

Probably the oldest statement of Christian belief is "Jesus is Lord," mentioned by Paul in 1 Corinthians 12:3. The three words are rich with meaning, for by calling Jesus "Lord," the person is saying, "Jesus is ruler over my life." Paul made it clear that no one could make this dramatic statement unless moved by the Holy Spirit. Put another way, a person may admire Jesus as a great teacher, but until moved by the Spirit, the person cannot really accept Jesus as master of his life.

312. the priesthood of all believers

Israel had priests, but the New Testament (particularly the epistle to the Hebrews) teaches that Christ is the great High Priest, the one mediator needed between God and man. But 1 Peter goes a step farther: all Christians are, in a sense, priests—that is, people with direct access to God. Peter told his readers, "You are a chosen generation, a royal priesthood, a holy nation, His own special people" (2:9). When the Reformation began in the 1500s, its leaders reacted against the Catholic priesthood (which was often corrupt) and emphasized the priesthood of all believers. The renewal movement has done much to restore the importance of laymen in worship and church life.

313. adoption

God has no children, genetically speaking. People *become* sons and daughters of God, so every child of God is an adopted child. Other religions had crude stories of gods literally producing children, but for Israel, God has only spiritual children—those who obey Him as a Father. Paul referred to Christians as being "adopted" by God: "You received the Spirit of adoption by whom we cry out, 'Abba, Father'" (Rom. 8:15). Although Christians are already children of God, the "full" adoption occurs after death: believers "groan within ourselves, eagerly waiting for the adoption, the redemption of our body" (Rom. 8:23).

314. *arrabon*

The apostle Paul used this Greek word to refer to the Spirit. It basically meant "down payment," and Paul was referring to the Spirit as God's down payment in the believer's life, an assurance of more to come. Ephesians 1:13–14 speaks of "the Holy Spirit of promise, who is the guarantee [*arrabon*] of our inheritance."

315. too deep for words

Speaking of the Spirit's role in believers' prayers, Paul stated that "we do not know what we should pray for as we ought, but the Spirit Himself makes intercession for us with groanings which cannot be uttered" (Rom. 8:26). Some readers believe Paul might be referring to speaking in tongues, or he might be stating that the Spirit has a better grasp of our real needs than we do.

316. quench not the Spirit

This command occurs near the end of Paul's first letter to the Thessalonians. Paul commanded, "Do not quench the Spirit. Do not despise prophecies. Test all things; hold fast what is good" (5:19–21). The early Christians saw frequent use of spiritual gifts; however, it is clear from Paul's warning here that some Christians were trying to "quench the Spirit." The modern renewal movement has been a valiant attempt to cease such quenching.

317. firstfruits

Literally, firstfruits were the first fruits to ripen for harvest. Paul explained to the Christians that we are already God's children—already but, in a way, not yet fully, since we are still living in a sinful world. Romans 8:23 reminds believers of "the firstfruits of the Spirit," meaning that while we endure life in this world, waiting on the better life in heaven, the Spirit serves as a kind of preview or appetizer of the glorious life to come.

318. "through a glass, darkly"

Paul addressed the issue of spiritual gifts in great detail in 1 Corinthians 12–14. He insisted that the gifts are wonderful but that finally, in eternity, they will not be needed: "For now we see in a mirror, dimly, but then face to face"

(13:12). (The King James Version has, rather poetically, "through a glass, darkly.") He was saying that our spiritual life now is the equivalent of seeing things in an imperfect mirror, while in the future we will see "face to face." Christians in the past took his words to mean that the spiritual gifts have *already* passed from the scene, something that applied only to the first Christians. The renewal movement today has sounded a resounding "No!" to this misinterpretation.

319. "the natural man"

The word *natural* is considered a positive thing today, but not in the writings of Paul, who contrasted *natural* with *spiritual*. For Paul, "the natural man" was man in his usual state, a sinner, needing to be reconciled to God: "The natural man does not receive the things of the Spirit of God, for they are foolishness to him" (1 Cor. 2:14). Paul divided mankind into two categories: the natural, who had not yet experienced conversion, and the spiritual, who had.

320. "Spirit of Christ"

This phrase occurs only twice in the Bible (Rom. 8:9; 1 Peter 1:11), but it affirms that the early Christians truly believed Christ was God. Romans 8:9 mentions the "Spirit of Christ" and the "Spirit of God" in the same verse.

321. *teleios*

Paul asked the Galatian Christians, "Having begun in the Spirit, are you now being made perfect by the flesh?" (Gal. 3:3). The Greek word *teleios* is usually translated "perfection" in the Bible, and the idea of Christian perfection has been around for centuries. It is regrettable that the word *perfect* now means "flawless," because that isn't what the Greek word suggests at all. Rather, it means "complete" or "full grown" or "morally mature." That was how Paul used it several times. He was telling the early Christians that with life in the Spirit, believers could become complete—that is, all that God intended them to be. In Galatians 3:3 he was reminding them that this completeness would come through the working of the Spirit.

322. out-of-the-body experiences

Paul described an anonymous Christian (perhaps himself) who had been caught up in the "third heaven . . . whether in the body or out of the body I do not know" (2 Cor. 12:2–3). Paul seemed to be describing a vision of heaven, but some Christians today have claimed to have out-of-the-body experiences similar to Paul's. Some would call such people the lunatic fringe, though others might say that if Paul had such an experience, couldn't Christians today?

323. the Spirit as writer

Paul told the Christians at Corinth that they were epistles of Christ, "written not with ink but by the Spirit of the living

God" (2 Cor. 3:3). So Christians are living epistles, witnesses to the world of the Spirit's power.

324. drinking the Spirit

Paul told the Corinthians that "we were all baptized by one Spirit into one body . . . and we were all given the one Spirit to drink" (1 Cor. 12:13 NIV). He seemed to be saying that the Spirit fills Christians just as liquid fills a glass and that the Spirit refreshes Christians inwardly.

325. wine or Spirit?

Paul told the Ephesians, "Do not be drunk with wine, in which is dissipation; but be filled with the Spirit" (5:18). Paul wasn't arguing here for total abstinence (since elsewhere he told Timothy to take a "little wine for the stomach"), but he was saying that drunkenness is not proper for the Christian, particularly since the joy of being Spirit-filled far surpasses the fleeting pleasure of alcohol.

326. John "in the Spirit"

The last book of the Bible, Revelation, is a series of visions given by the Spirit to John, in exile on the island of Patmos. The visions, showing the persecution of believers and the ultimate triumph of God over evil, were revealed to him "in the Spirit," a phrase he used several times (1:10; 4:2; 17:3; 21:10).

327. the sevenfold Spirit of Revelation

The book of Revelation mentions the Spirit several times, including a description as the "sevenfold Spirit" or, in some translations, "the seven Spirits" (1:4; 3:1; 4:5; 5:6). The Greek here can be translated either way, although "sevenfold Spirit" is probably accurate, with the number seven (a "good" number in the Bible) suggesting fullness and power. John, the author of Revelation, was writing to seven Christian communities in the province of Asia, so it is appropriate that the Spirit was described as "sevenfold."

328. the Spirit's invitation

The book of Revelation ends with a vision of the heavenly city, the New Jerusalem, pure and spotless. Following this dazzling vision, John recorded these words: "The Spirit and the bride [the heavenly city] say, 'Come!' . . . And let him who thirsts come. Whoever desires, let him take the water of life freely" (22:17). This is the Bible's last mention of the Spirit, a fitting conclusion to the whole, since the Spirit is inviting everyone to take the water of eternal life.

8

The Spirit's Working, Pre-1800

FOLLOWING THE APOSTLES

329. "Spirit-bearers"

In the early church, after the period of the New Testament, the apostles and other authors of sacred writings were sometimes referred to as *pneumatophoroi*—"Spirit-bearers." The idea was that the Christians, like the prophets of the Old Testament, were inspired by the Holy Spirit.

330. *A History of Christianity*

Considered *the* history of the faith for many years, this 1953 classic by Professor Kenneth Scott Latourette is still widely read. In his chapter on the birth of Christianity and how it

impressed nonbelievers, Latourette wrote, "Through the
Holy Spirit promised by Jesus came the moral transforma-
tions which were so marked in the Christian fellowship."
(On the other hand, Latourette's book does not even mention the Pentecostal movement of the early 1900s—a
notable omission!)

331. the Didache

The ancient book called the *Didache* (also called the
Teaching of the Twelve Apostles) was written sometime
around A.D. 100. The brief book sheds light on how the
early Christians viewed the gifts of the Spirit, particularly
people claiming to have the gift of prophesying. The
Didache gives detailed instructions on distinguishing false
prophets from true ones. A key element is that true
prophets are not to ask for money or linger more than a
few days in one area (which would suggest they were free-
loading).

332. Ignatius of Antioch (d. ca. 107)

Tradition has it that he knew the apostle John personally
and was appointed bishop of Antioch by Peter. He was
arrested during the persecutions of Emperor Trajan and
sent to Rome, where he was killed by lions in the arena.
While on the way to his martyrdom, Ignatius dictated letters to seven churches. In one of the letters he referred to
himself as having the gift of prophecy, claiming that the
Spirit spoke to him, and through him, while preaching,

making him aware of a problem of disunity in one of his congregations.

333. *The Shepherd of Hermas*

This popular devotional work was written sometime in the second century. It included guidelines for a problem that vexed the early Christians, how to distinguish between true and false prophets. The work affirmed that the gift of prophecy was still to be found, but that false prophets seeking fame and money or both were to be avoided. It reiterated Jesus' teaching that true prophets would be known by their fruits.

334. the Gnostics

The Greek word *gnosis* means "knowledge," and in the early days of Christianity the people known as Gnostics were serious rivals in the marketplace of beliefs. The Gnostics were a diverse group but had several beliefs in common, a key one being that salvation comes through knowledge, not through faith. Most Gnostics believed that matter was evil and that only spirit was good. Gnostics who considered themselves Christians said they believed in Christ as a teacher but not as a Savior. If Gnostics spoke of the Holy Spirit at all, it was as an agent of a "higher knowledge" that would save the person. Certain individual Gnostics could receive special revelations from the Spirit, but the Spirit was not for all believers, for most believers were not ready for true *gnosis*. One unfortunate result of Gnosticism was that it led true Christians to be suspicious of anyone claiming to have a word of knowledge, even though that gift is (according to the Bible) given to some believers.

335. Marcion (second century)

Before the Christian church had decided finally on the twenty-seven books that we now call the New Testament, Marcion, a wealthy businessman, had come up with his own "canon." Regrettably, Marcion's beliefs were out of line with genuine Christian teaching. Marcion completely discarded the Old Testament and much of what became the New. He had no place for a belief in the Holy Spirit. Christian authors who wrote to defend right belief attacked Marcion on many points, including his rejection of the Holy Spirit.

336. *The Martyrdom of Polycarp*

Written about 160, this document describes the holy death of the saintly Polycarp, bishop of Smyrna. The story of his martyrdom in the arena mentions that the Spirit gave fortitude to those who died for the faith.

337. Theophilus (second century)

This is not the same Theophilus to whom Luke addressed his gospel and Acts. This one was bishop of Antioch and author of the *Apology,* a defense of Christianity addressed to a pagan friend. Theophilus sometimes spoke of the Trinity as Father-Son-Wisdom, and sometimes equated the Spirit with the divine Wisdom described in Proverbs 1:20–33. This is not surprising, since in Proverbs 1:23, Wisdom says, "Surely I will pour out my spirit on you."

338. Justin Martyr (d. 165)

"Martyr" was not his last name but a title: he died as a Christian martyr during one of the Roman persecutions. Justin, a former pagan, wrote to defend his new faith against pagan critics. In his two *Apologies* he compared Christianity to pagan religions and found it far superior in truth and morals. One curious fact about his writings: he seemed to suggest that the Logos (the Word, a title for Christ found in John's gospel) and the Spirit were similar, perhaps even the same.

339. the Montanists

Around A.D. 170, a Christian named Montanus began to prophesy in north Africa, along with two followers, Prisca and Maxilla. The three claimed to speak on behalf of the Paraclete (the Holy Spirit), and they encouraged Christians not to fear the martyrdom they faced during the Roman Empire's persecutions. The followers of these three became known as Montanists, and they were noted for being "puritans"—allowing no sexual relations of any kind, fasting often, and eating only very simple food. Like many "puritans," they repelled many people but attracted others.

Paul mentioned prophesying as one of the gifts of the Spirit (1 Cor. 12:10), and the Montanists particularly emphasized this gift. However, many bishops feared that the

Montanists were becoming unorthodox, so Montanus and his followers were excommunicated—officially thrown out of the church. Even so, the pure life of the Montanists and their willingness to die for their faith were admirable. More notable, they emphasized the leading of the Spirit at a time when Christianity was turning into an institutional faith.

340. Tertullian (ca. 200)

A former lawyer, Tertullian defended the faith against its pagan critics. He also coined the term *Trinitas* (which we use as *Trinity*) to refer to Father, Son, and Holy Spirit.

In Tertullian's lifetime, the writings that we now call the New Testament were still fairly new—so much so that Christians did not always agree on just which writings were holy and inspired by God. Tertullian was a Montanist (see 339), and though he read and honored the writings of Paul and other Christians, he also emphasized the leading of the Spirit, not just the reading of sacred writings. When a Christian council voted on which writings were truly inspired, Tertullian was appalled. He responded by saying, "They have shut the Holy Spirit up in a book." He feared that Christians would substitute the Bible for the daily guidance of the Spirit.

341. Athenagoras (second century)

As his name suggests, Athenagoras was from Athens in Greece, and in that city famous for its philosophers, he set out to compare Christianity with pagan philosophies. In his well-written *Apology* (which in those days meant "defense") he spoke of the various pagan philosophers, including the great ones such as Plato and Aristotle. He claimed that their teachings were based solely on their own conjectures, while the teachings of Christianity were divine (and true) because the prophets of God had the inspiration of the Spirit.

342. Clement of Alexandria (ca. 155–ca. 220)

This noted theologian taught at the Christian academy in Alexandria, Egypt, the Roman Empire's intellectual capital. Clement reflected the common belief of Christians in that era, teaching that all knowledge comes from the Spirit, as do all spiritual gifts. Clement claimed that the Jews, spiritual predecessors of Christians, are "silver," while Christians, because they have the Holy Spirit, are "gold."

343. Hippolytus (d. ca. 236)

Living in Rome, Hippolytus wrote *The Apostolic Tradition,* which gives a vivid picture of Christian belief and practice in that period. He had much to say about the exercise of spiritual gifts and, in contrast to some later writers, was sure that laity, not just clergy, could exercise gifts of the Spirit. Although the church was beginning to neglect the gift of healing, Hippolytus made it clear that the gift was still in evidence.

344. Origen (ca. 185–ca. 254)

The Egyptian-born theologian named Origenes Adamantius was one of the great Christian thinkers in the ancient world. Origen wrote massive Bible commentaries and books of theology. He also took literally Jesus' words about becoming eunuchs for the kingdom of God (Matt. 19:12) and had himself castrated. Origen gave an interesting interpretation to the Trinity (God as Father, Son, and Spirit). He taught that Christians derive their existence from the Father, their rational nature from the Son (Christ), and their holiness (sanctification) from the Spirit.

345. Novatian (d. ca. 258)

A split occurred in Christianity because some Christians had renounced their faith under the persecutions of Roman emperor Decius (ca. 250). Some Christians said, fine, let's receive them back into the church, but other Christians said, no, since they denied the faith and must be excommunicated. Novatian was one of this strict party. He was a theologian, author of the first long discussion of the Trinity—Father, Son, and Spirit. The *Treatise Concerning the Trinity* speaks of the Spirit as bestowing the various gifts that make the church holy and righteous. Novatian died as a martyr under Emperor Valerian.

346. Cyprian (ca. 200–ca. 258)

The early Christians were dependent on the leading of the Spirit, as the book of Acts shows. But eventually, Christianity came to be institutionalized, with rituals and the clergy replacing the dynamic work of the Spirit. The change did not happen overnight. A major figure in the development of what became the Catholic system of bishops was Cyprian. Raised as a wealthy pagan in north Africa, Cyprian became a Christian. Regarding his conversion, he wrote, "A second birth created me a new man by means of the Spirit breathed from heaven." He became bishop of the great city of Carthage in north Africa. In time, Bishop Cyprian came to believe that the institutional church (with its priests and bishops in charge) was the true channel of the Spirit. This seems a long way from the church of the New Testament, with every believer working under the power of the Spirit.

347. Gregory the Wonder-Worker (ca. 213–ca. 270)

He was called by the Greek name *thaumaturgus*, meaning "wonder-worker." Gregory was a pagan but converted to Christianity under the teaching of Origen (see 344). He became a bishop and made many converts. He was known as *thaumaturgus* because of the many miraculous healings that occurred through his ministry.

348. Eusebius of Caesarea (ca. 265–ca. 339)

The "father of church history" made the first systematic attempt to write the chronicles of Christianity, set down in his book *The History of the Church*. It begins with the New Testament period, moves on to the spread of the faith throughout the Roman Empire, and includes the harsh persecutions under the Roman emperors. Eusebius was a close friend of Emperor Constantine, who accepted Christianity and ended the persecutions. Eusebius reflected the common belief of early Christians that the Holy Spirit led men to the writing of the Bible. In more than one place in his *History* he used the phrase "the Holy Spirit Himself says . . . ," followed by a Bible passage.

349. Emperor Constantine (d. 337)

Constantine was the first Roman emperor to be a Christian. He ended the brutal persecutions of the church and in 313 recognized Christianity as a legitimate religion. Historians, especially Christian ones, agree that this was both good and bad. Good, because Christians were no longer being harassed and executed. Bad, because when the faith became "legit," it in time lost its fire.

After Constantine, some of his successors began to favor Christianity over other religions, and soon it became the official religion of the empire. The result? Nominal Christians, joining the church because "everyone did it," especially if they wanted government jobs. The church became "establishment" and well organized, but the spiritual gifts were harder to find.

350. Nicene Creed

Most early creeds focused on Christ and said little about the Spirit. The famous Apostles' Creed acknowledges the Spirit, but only with the bare words "I believe in the Holy Spirit" (and a mention that Jesus was "conceived by the Holy Spirit"). The longer Nicene Creed says more. Dating from the fourth century, the creed (originally written in Greek) states belief in "the Holy Spirit, the Lord, the giver of life, who proceeds from the Father and the Son, who with the Father and Son together is worshiped and glorified, who spoke by the prophets."

351. Hilary (ca. 315–68)

He was bishop of Poitiers in Gaul (what we now call France) and wrote *De Trinitate*, a book about the Trinity. In it he spoke of the Spirit and of spiritual gifts, noting that Paul's words on gifts in 1 Corinthians 12 still applied—that is, the gifts were still operating, even though the church had become the "establishment" religion of the Roman Empire and the spiritual gifts were less and less in evidence.

352. Sarapion (ca. 350)

The bishop of Thmuis in Egypt composed a collection of prayers for his flock, interesting for the light they shed on belief in the Spirit. In one prayer he asked God, "Give us the Holy Spirit, that we may be able to speak and expound your unspeakable mysteries. May the Lord Jesus Christ speak in us, and the Holy Spirit, and hymn you through us."

353. Ephraem of Syria (ca. 306–ca. 373)

He wrote in the ancient language known as Syriac. While living in a cave he wrote hymns, devotional poetry, and theological works. He wrote so much about the Spirit that tradition calls him "the Harp of the Holy Spirit." He often spoke of the Spirit as fire, imparting warmth to the soul, burning away sin, and melting away the icy bonds of sin and Satan.

354. Basil of Caesarea (d. 379)

He was bishop of Caesarea in Palestine and such a famed theologian that he was known as Basil the Great. He showed his social concern by building on the outskirts of Caesarea a hospital and hostels for the poor, a complex called the Basilead. Miraculous healings were reported at Basil's hospital. Basil wrote so much about the work of the Spirit that he was known as Doctor of the Holy Spirit. Basil wrote that to be a *pneumatophor*—a "Spirit-bearer"—involves self-denial and full obedience to God.

355. Gregory of Nyssa (d. 395)

The younger brother of Basil (see 354), Gregory became a bishop of the church and a noted theologian, famous for his *Sermo Catecheticus,* a handbook of theology. Gregory also wrote *The Making of Man,* in which he developed a theology of healing, based on the healing miracles of Christ. Though the spiritual gifts were beginning to wane at this period of history, Gregory testified to having witnessed healings. Gregory often spoke of the Spirit as the "Breath of God."

356. Gregory of Nazianzus (330–89)

A friend and associate of Basil (see 354), Gregory was a bishop and a noted theologian. One of his five great *Theological Addresses* was *On the Holy Spirit.* He compared people who denied the reality of the Spirit to the New Testament Sadducees whom Jesus criticized. In his *Oration on Pentecost* he recounted the role the Spirit played in the lives of the men of the Bible and observed that He is still active in the church in healing (including Gregory's parents), in prophecy, and in other gifts.

357. the Pneumatomachi

Their name means "fighters against the Spirit." Around the year 375 they were a party in Palestine that denied the Spirit is truly God. In that period, Christians argued constantly over the doctrine of the Trinity, the ongoing question being, "Just how are the Father, Son, and Spirit three-in-one and one-in-three?" Some of the Pneumatomachi claimed that the Spirit was merely an angel that visited God's people from time to time.

358. Cyril of Jerusalem (ca. 310–86)

Cyril was bishop of Jerusalem and author of twenty-four *Catecheses,* lectures on Christian beliefs for people preparing to join the church. In them he summarized major Christian beliefs, including the doctrines of the Holy Spirit. Cyril based his teachings strictly on the Bible, being aware that heretical groups such as the Gnostics had gone astray with their wild, unbiblical ideas about Christ and the Spirit.

359. Didymus the Blind (d. 398)

Blind from the age of four, Didymus was a respected teacher at the Christian academy in Alexandria, Egypt. Jerome, famous for translating the Bible into Latin, was one of Didymus's pupils, and he translated his teacher's *On the Holy Spirit* into Latin. Didymus claimed that the anointing of the Spirit strengthens the soul to share in the life of God.

360. John Chrysostom (344–407)

His last name means "golden mouth" and refers to his reputation as a great preacher. John was head of the church in the important city of Constantinople, and one of the most respected theologians in Christian history. Regrettably, John taught that the spiritual gifts listed in the New Testament no longer operated. They were, he said, part of the age of the apostles—important in spreading the Christian faith, but no longer needed, since Christians now had the Bible and the clergy to guide them. As the church became more powerful, church authorities made that view official (for obvious reasons). The view is one reason that church authorities often persecuted people claiming to exercise the spiritual gift of prophecy.

361. Ambrose (339–97)

Ambrose was bishop of Milan in Italy, noted for his kindness to poor people and for his theological writings. He had amazing influence in politics, particularly in forcing Roman Emperor Theodosius to make amends for killing thousands of people involved in a revolution. Ambrose wrote *De Spiritu Sancto*, a major theological work on the Holy Spirit. He was a friend of and a tremendous influence on Augustine (see 362).

362. Augustine (354–430)

Augustine's *Confessions* is probably one of the most-read Christian books of all time, a thoughtful man's account of his long road to finding peace with God. Augustine became bishop of the city of Hippo in north Africa, where he wrote some of the world's greatest theological works. Regrettably, this influential man shared a common belief among Christian leaders: the age of the spiritual gifts listed in the New Testament is past. Augustine believed that the gifts of the Spirit were at work in the early church but once the faith was established (and set down forever in the Bible), they were no longer needed. He frowned on speaking in tongues, which he connected with frantic pagans who spoke in tongues, prophesied, and claimed to do miracles.

363. Athanasian Creed

Many of the ancient creeds, such as the Apostles' Creed and the Nicene Creed, state Christians' belief in God the Father,

Son, and Holy Spirit. But most of them do not define too clearly the whole matter of the Trinity (see 736). In other words, in what way are the three persons also one God? The church came closer to defining this mystery (if defining a mystery is possible) with the statement known as the Athanasian Creed, named for the theologian Athanasius. Written in the fifth century, this creed states that "the Father is God, the Son is God, and the Holy Spirit is God, and yet they are not three Gods, but one God." It was the first Christian creed to state explicitly that the three persons are equal in their divinity.

THE MIDDLE AGES

364. the Middle Ages

In terms of how people viewed the work of the Holy Spirit, the Middle Ages were the Dark Ages. The official church authorities had little interest in how Christians could exercise the gifts of the Spirit, since official teaching was that these gifts were confined to the New Testament period. (See 360 [John Chrysostom].) In the Middle Ages the clergy took a dim view of any layman who claimed to exercise any spiritual gift, particularly the gift of prophecy. The Inquisition and other agencies helped ensure that the official church was the only channel for the work of the Spirit. Since most laymen could not read the Bible (which was only in Latin, not in the people's languages), they were kept ignorant of the Bible's teaching on the Spirit.

365. the Lateran Council

The officials of the medieval Catholic church did not approve of individuals exercising spiritual gifts. Yet some individuals did so, often in the area of healing. But in 1123 the churchwide Lateran Council prohibited clergymen from attending people who were sick except to give them spiritual direction (meaning, in practice, preparing them for the afterlife). The idea was to discourage maverick clergymen from trying to perform healings.

366. infant exorcism

In the Middle Ages almost everyone in Europe was baptized as an infant. The baptismal ritual included the *exsufflatio*—breathing three times on the infant's face and saying, "Depart from him, unclean spirit, and give place to the Holy Spirit."

367. the Waldensians

Peter Waldo was a twelfth-century Frenchman who was appalled at the immorality and worldliness of the official church. He gathered around him followers, known as the Poor in Spirit and later called (after Waldo) the Waldensians. Facing persecution from Catholic authorities, they nonetheless established their own communities and attempted to lead lives based on the New Testament. Their worship, in contrast to most worship of the Middle Ages, allowed for the gifts of the Spirit, particularly prophesying. Despite persecution, they survived for years in remote mountain locales. When the Reformation came in the 1500s, they happily joined it.

368. Hildegard (1098–1179)

She was an abbess (the head of a convent) in Germany and a noted devotional writer. She claimed to receive divine visions, which in her day could lead to charges of heresy by the church authorities. But the authorities believed she was sincere and made no attempt to silence her. She wrote the book *Lingua Ignota,* which means "unknown tongue." In Hildegard's day, speaking in tongues was highly suspect. But in *Lingua Ignota* she attempted to write down her prayer language, consisting of nine hundred words and an alphabet especially devised for the purpose. One witness spoke of her singing in unknown tongues as her "concerts."

369. Richard of St. Victor (d. 1173)

He was head of the monastery of St. Victor in Paris, well versed in the Bible and theology. His famous book *On the Trinity* taught that the Spirit is the means by which divine love is given to the believer and takes root in him.

370. *Rituale Romanorum*

This Catholic document, written sometime in the eleventh century, states that speaking in unknown tongues and/or interpreting them were signs of demon possession. That was an odd position for the Catholic church to take, considering that the practice was reported in the Bible and in the lives of some of the Catholic saints. The document reflected the Catholic church's growing suspicion of any spiritual gifts.

371. Joachim of Fiore (ca. 1130–1202)

He was a mystic philosopher who claimed his visions opened the Scriptures to him. Joachim divided history into three ages—Father, Son, and Spirit. Studying the Bible, particularly Revelation, he concluded that the third age, the age of the Spirit, would begin in 1260 and result in the conversion of the world. Joachim, a monk, predicted that the third age would be the age of monks—resulting in the entire world, under the influence of the Spirit, leading a simple (and celibate) life like that of monks.

372. Francis of Assisi (ca. 1181–1226)

The wealthy Italian boy who gave up his riches (and even his clothing) to live a life of Christian poverty has always been an appealing figure. Disinherited by his father (who believed him insane), Francis became a beggar-preacher, finding joy in nature and closeness to God. People were attracted to the gentle, Christlike Francis, and his followers formed an order known as the Franciscans. Healings were attributed to Francis, and Francis admitted to being "drunk in the Spirit," caught up in a divine ecstasy, losing all awareness of time and place. The Spirit assured him that all his sins had been forgiven, then bathed him in a wondrous light. The Franciscans spread throughout Europe, but every year gathered at Assisi on the day of Pentecost.

373. Bonaventure (1221–74)

Born Giovanni di Fidanza in Italy, he was healed of a sickness through the prayers of the beloved Francis of Assisi (see 372). He joined the Franciscan order and was eventually elected minister general of the group. He wrote a popular biography of Francis, presenting him as a man filled with joy through the Spirit. Bonaventure, a devout man as well as a noted theologian, claimed that he wrestled with the Spirit and felt the joy of being inflamed by the Spirit's fire. He spoke of the sevenfold grace of the Spirit, harking back to Revelation's mention of the "sevenfold Spirit" (1:4; 3:1; 4:5).

374. "singing in jubilation"

The Catholic church in the Middle Ages was not keen on laymen exercising spiritual gifts, but the Spirit manifested Himself anyway. In Easter celebrations, congregations might sing at the end of a hymn's "Alleluia" without any set words or melody. That is, in the fullness of Easter joy, they could cut loose and sing out whatever leaped into their hearts. Some referred to this as "singing in jubilation," and it is possible (even likely) that some of the people were singing in tongues.

375. Clare of Montefalco (ca. 1268–1308)

She was an abbess, head of a convent, and was credited with performing healings and other miracles. Friends claimed that she experienced ecstatic trancelike states while in the

Spirit, speaking in tongues, which listeners referred to as "heavenly words."

376. Catherine of Siena (1347–80)

This medieval saint has been a favorite of Catholics for many years. People sought her out as a spiritual adviser in her native Italy, and she was said to have worked miracles of healing and even a word of knowledge (she knew of a secret vow the pope had made, one he had revealed to no one).

377. Geoffrey Chaucer (1342–1400)

His *Canterbury Tales* are still read and loved. Chaucer was a keen observer of the world around him, and like most men of his time, he was appalled at the corruption and immorality of many of the Catholic clergy. In his *Tales* he portrayed one saintly clergyman, the Parson, who (appropriately enough) delivers a very serious sermon in which he speaks of the horror of "sinning in the Holy Ghost . . . above all other sins, this sin is most displeasing to Christ, and most hateful."

378. Vincent Ferrer (1350–1419)

Vincent, born in Spain, belonged to the religious order known as the Dominicans, widely known for their preaching. He became famous as a preacher all over Europe and, though he spoke only Spanish in his sermons, was said to possess the gift of tongues, for Germans, Greeks, and Hungarians were said to understand his preaching.

THE 1500s

379. Martin Luther (1483–1546)

Luther was the key figure in the Protestant Reformation of the 1500s and one of the great Christian leaders of all time. In his many writings he touched on all aspects of Christian belief, including the Holy Spirit. Like all the Protestant leaders, Luther emphasized getting back to the Bible—that is, God's Word is more important than church rituals. But Luther also emphasized the role of the Spirit in leading believers to understand the Bible: "Where the Spirit does not open Scripture, it is not understood." But there was a flip side to this teaching: just as there is no understanding of the Bible without the Spirit, so there is no understanding of the Spirit without the Bible: "Do not seek the Spirit only through solitude or prayer, but read Scripture."

380. John Calvin (1509–64)

Predestination is probably the most famous teaching of Calvin, one of the noted theologians of the early Protestant movement. But Calvin's famous theological work *Institutes of the Christian Religion* also has a lot to say about the work of the Spirit. Basing his beliefs on the Bible, Calvin said that the Spirit moves a person to place his faith in Christ. The Spirit leads the person to repentance and to love toward God and his neighbor, resulting in a life of sanctity and purity. However, Calvin said little about such spiritual gifts as tongues, healing, or prophesying; he seemed to believe that these gifts were only for the first generation of Christians. The Presbyterian and Reformed churches that are Calvin's spiritual descendants have generally followed suit. Calvin wrote that "Scripture is the school of the Holy Spirit."

381. Robert Bellarmine (1542–1621)

A cardinal in the Catholic church, he was also a theologian who lived at a time when Catholics were still defending their beliefs and practices against the Protestant Reformation. Bellarmine observed that Reformation leaders such as Luther and Calvin claimed that the spiritual gifts in the New Testament are no longer available. Bellarmine, trying to smear the Protestants, speculated that their disdain for spiritual gifts proved that they were not truly Christian. If they taught the truth, he asked, where were the miracles?

382. Anabaptists

In the 1500s the Protestant Reformation was a welcome housecleaning of Christianity, sweeping aside a lot of dead ritual and getting back to the Bible. The Anabaptists were part of the effort, but they differed from Protestant leaders such as Martin Luther and John Calvin in their emphasis on such spiritual gifts as healing, miracles, and speaking in tongues. So the Anabaptists were considered radicals, and both Catholics and Protestants persecuted them throughout Europe. Although the Protestants accepted the Anabaptists' attachment to the Bible, they could not accept the use of spiritual gifts. Many of the Anabaptists died for their faith. The Mennonites were one noted branch of the Anabaptists.

383. Ambrosians

They were a sect of the Anabaptists (see 382) in the 1500s, led by a man named Ambrose, who taught that ministers were unnecessary, since believers had the Bible and the Spirit to lead them spiritually. Ambrose caused some controversy when he claimed that he had received direct revelations from the Spirit, revelations that were of higher authority than the Bible.

384. Hans Denck (1500–1527)

Denck became an Anabaptist (see 382) only two years before his death by plague in his native Switzerland. In that brief period he wrote several works putting forth Anabaptist beliefs. Like most Anabaptists, he emphasized the role of the Spirit in all Christians' lives. Although he adhered to the truth of the Bible, Denck stressed that the Bible without the Spirit is worthless: "Whoever thinks that he can observe the law by means of the Book ascribes to the dead letter what belongs to the living Spirit."

385. Pilgram Marpeck (ca. 1556)

Marpeck was a noted Anabaptist author and one of the few Anabaptist leaders to die a natural death (many of them were martyred by both Protestants and Catholics). Marpeck said a great deal about the work of the Spirit in the church and agreed with other Anabaptists that the external aspects of church life—teaching, preaching, social service, etc.—were important, but they were meaningless without a genuine internal rightness that only the Spirit could bring about. He wrote, "The gifts of the Spirit are weighty. He moves us, when and where he wills, giving them to whomever he desires."

386. Menno Simons (1496–1561)

His name continues in the denomination known as Mennonites. He was a beloved leader among the Anabaptists (see 382) in Germany and the Netherlands. In his writings he emphasized, as did all Anabaptists, the continuing work of the Spirit in the Christian life, particularly the role of sanctifying the believer, "restraining the old man with his lusts and destroying the sins in their flesh."

387. Martin Bucer (1491–1551)

Bucer, a German, was a key figure in the Protestant Reformation. Like most of the Reformers, he emphasized getting back to the Bible. Bucer believed that though the Bible was critical to the Christian life, it was a "dead letter" unless the person reading it was guided by the Spirit.

388. the *Book of Common Prayer*

After the Church of England split from the Catholic church, it compiled its own worship book, which (after many revisions) is still in use today. The book has a reading for the day of Pentecost (Whitsunday, as the English call it), which speaks of the Holy Spirit as "lighting upon the apostles, to teach them, and to lead them to all truth, giving them both the gift of diverse languages, and also boldness with fervent zeal constantly to preach the gospel unto all nations."

389. Ignatius of Loyola (1491–1556)

Born in Spain, Ignatius had a conversion experience while recuperating from a war wound (a cannonball wound, to be specific). He founded the zealous order of men known as the Society of Jesus, or Jesuits, still a major force in the Catholic church. Ignatius was said to have practiced *loquela*, singing in tongues.

390. Francis Xavier (1506–52)

The Spanish-born Francis was one of the most remarkable missionaries of all time, working in the Far East. He was a friend of the famed Ignatius of Loyola, who established the Catholic order known as the Society of Jesus, or Jesuits (see 389 [Ignatius of Loyola]). In 1539 the king of Portugal sent Francis to evangelize India, where he baptized thousands. He arrived in Japan in 1549, studied the Japanese language, and made many converts until Buddhist monks began persecuting the young Christian community. More than 700,000 conversions were attributed to his work, and the Catholic church officially named him Patron of Foreign Missions. Like a number of missionaries, Francis was credited with the ability to speak in tongues. Apparently, he spoke in an unknown prayer language (some said he spoke the "language of angels"), but he also could communicate with listeners whose languages he did not know.

391. Louis Bertrand (1526–81)

Bertrand was a missionary among Native Americans in the New World, and the Catholic church recognized him as being miraculously endowed with the gift of tongues—not speaking in unknown tongues, but, as with the apostles at Pentecost, the ability to communicate in a language that had not been learned. In the history of missions this phenomenon of the Spirit has occurred more often than most people know. (See 31 [xenolalia].)

1600–1800

392. Huguenots

This name applied to the French who converted to a form of Protestantism based on the teachings of John Calvin. Some of the French kings, wanting to keep France Catholic, persecuted the Huguenots. In 1572 occurred the horror known as the St. Bartholomew's Day Massacre, in which thousands of Huguenots were brutally murdered. They were not exterminated, though in 1685 King Louis XIV ordered them all to convert or else. Many Huguenots, particularly in the south of France, practiced speaking in tongues, a rarity among Protestants in those days.

393. Johann Arndt (1555–1621)

A German Lutheran pastor, Arndt is remembered for his book *True Christianity*, in which he emphasized that belief in the correct doctrines is not enough, for the Christian life must include moral living and growth in grace. His writings helped pave the way for the Lutheran renewal movement known as Pietism.

394. Lewis Bayly (1565–1631)

A Welsh bishop, Bayly penned an extremely popular devotional book, *The Practice of Piety*, which went through dozens of editions and was much loved by Puritans in Britain and America. Bayly, who was also a chaplain in the household of King Charles I, emphasized the role of the Holy Spirit in the Christian's daily walk.

395. Galileo (1564–1642)

Are religion and science in conflict? The renowned Italian scientist Galileo, who discovered that the earth and the other planets revolve around the sun, did not think so. He saw that science could discover truths about the universe but could not save the soul. He wrote, "The intention of the Scripture was to persuade men of the truths necessary to salvation. Science could not do this, but only the Holy Spirit."

396. Westminster Confession

The Westminster Assembly of 1643 was a gathering in which English Puritans formulated their basic beliefs. The essentials became the Westminster Confession of Faith, still used in some Protestant churches. One of the greatest legacies of the confession is its teaching on the inspiration of the Bible. It stated that the Bible was the sole authority for Christian belief. The Bible in its original languages was "inspired by God . . . and kept pure in all ages." However, the full assurance of divine authority is "from the inward work of the Holy Spirit."

397. Sealers

These were a group among the English Puritans in the 1600s. They focused on the Spirit's sealing work, which occurs following conversion and enables the person to commune with God, resting in the assurance of belonging to Him (Rom. 8:16). One Sealer, Thomas Goodwin, wrote that the Spirit's sealing is experienced as "a light that overpowereth a man's soul and assureth him that God is his and he is God's."

398. John Milton (1608–74)

England's famed Puritan poet, Milton knew the Bible by heart (in the original Hebrew and Greek, to boot). His most memorable work was *Paradise Lost*, the story of Adam and Eve's temptation by Satan and their expulsion from the Garden of Eden, with the promise that God would send a

Savior. Since *Paradise Lost* was an epic, Milton followed the old tradition of invoking the Muse—that is, beginning his epic with a prayer to the Muse (guiding spirit) of poetry, asking for inspiration. But since the poem is Christian, Milton prayed to the Spirit as the Muse. In only a few lines Milton showed how well he knew the Bible's images of the Spirit: "thou from the first / Wast present, and with mighty wings outspread, / Dovelike sat'st brooding on the vast abyss." He was referring to the Spirit being present at creation (Gen. 1:2) and being in the form of a dove (Matt. 3:16). In *Paradise Regained*, Milton told the story of Christ's temptation by Satan. Again he asked the Spirit to inspire him, referring to the Spirit as the One who drove Christ into the wilderness to meet Satan, as the Gospels say (Matt. 4:1, Mark 1:12).

399. Jansenists

A French bishop named Cornelius Jansen (1585–1638) published the controversial book *Augustinus,* which emphasized the Bible's concept of salvation by grace, not by works. Catholic authorities frowned on the notion, but Jansen had many followers, known as the Jansenists. Though they never broke from the Catholic church, they opposed the way that the pope and the bishops dictated Christian belief. The Jansenists, or some of them, spoke in tongues, which provoked a negative reaction from the Catholic authorities.

400. Quakers

The movement begun by George Fox (see 401) called itself the Society of Friends, but they are better known as Quakers. They took their name from John 15:15, where Jesus told His disciples, "No longer do I call you servants . . . but I have called you friends." They believed Christian worship was overly ritualized, while the true Christian life consists of living according to the Bible and also by the "Inner Light," the guidance of the Spirit. The idea of the Spirit as daily guide is a sound one (Matt. 10:20; John 14:15–26; 16:5–15), but the Friends suffered incredible persecution, as have most Christians who pursued a simple lifestyle and attempted to take Jesus' teaching literally. Robert Barclay, an early Quaker theologian, stated that all Christians, not just ministers, should be "free to speak or prophesy by the Spirit."

401. George Fox (1624–91)

He was founder of the Friends, better known as the Quakers (see 400). Fox had a crisis conversion in 1646 and began teaching that rituals and regular church services meant nothing, for God spoke directly to each believer. Fox was sometimes jailed for interrupting church services and appealing to the authority of the Bible and the Holy Spirit. He frequently prayed for the sick and laid hands on them. After his death, followers found that he had kept a "Book of Miracles" in which he recounted more than 150 healings that had occurred under his ministry.

402. James Naylor (ca. 1617–60)

Naylor was a noted preacher among the early Quakers in England. Like many of them, he was pilloried, whipped, and jailed as he traveled about the country preaching. Like Quaker founder George Fox, he was never officially ordained but, like all Quaker preachers, believed the Spirit's empowerment was more important than any title of Reverend.

403. Valentine Greatrakes (1629–83)

The man with this unlikely name was a noted healer in a time when the official churches in Britain were settling into a kind of dead orthodoxy, with little room for exercising spiritual gifts. Between 1662 and 1666 he traveled in England and Ireland, laying hands on many people and healing them.

404. Camisards

Louis XIV, France's Sun King, decided he could no longer tolerate Protestants in his country, so in 1685 he revoked the old edict of toleration. Many Protestants fled to England or elsewhere, but some resisted, notably the group called the Camisards. Reacting to Louis's execution of some twelve thousand Protestants, the Camisards offered armed resistance. Some of the "prophets" among the Camisards spoke in tongues. Observers said that some semiliterate Camisards uttered "discourses in good and intelligent

French such as they never used in their conscious hours."
(See 392 [Huguenots].)

405. Isaac Newton (1642–1727)

The familiar image of Isaac Newton is the man discovering
the law of gravity when an apple dropped on his head.
Newton was one of the greatest scientists of all time. In
modern times, many scientists are unbelievers, not men of
faith. That wasn't true of Newton, however. He claimed
that each of his discoveries was communicated to him by
the Holy Spirit. He was fascinated by the Bible and wanted
to reconcile science with religion.

406. Philipp Jakob Spener (1635–1705)

Spener was a German Lutheran pastor and author of *Pia
Desideria,* a small but influential book about the need for a
life of prayer, Bible study, and leading by the Spirit. Spener's
book influenced the movement known as Pietism, a spiritual awakening in Germany. Spener stated that all laypeople
are to share in the ministry of the gospel: "Not only ministers but all Christians are made priests by their Savior, are
anointed by the Holy Spirit, and are dedicated to perform
spiritual-priestly acts." He was asking that the Lutheran
church put into practice what Martin Luther taught: the
priesthood of all believers. (See 407 [Pietism].)

407. Pietism

Originally, the Protestant Reformation, which began in Germany in the 1500s, was a spiritually rich movement. But in time Protestant theology became more important than living a Spirit-led life. Even so, various movements in Germany kept alive the vision of the Spirit moving in individuals' lives. The seventeenth-century grassroots movement known as Pietism emphasized groups meeting in homes to pray, study the Bible, and engage in a deeper fellowship than was possible in Sunday worship. Emphasis was on the laymen's need to study the Bible and apply its truths to life, not just to listen passively to the Sunday sermons. Lutheran officials took a dim view of Pietism (mostly because laymen meeting without a minister present suggested too much independence from authority). In many ways the renewal movement today resembles the Pietists of yesterday. (See 406 [Spener].)

408. Gottfried Arnold (1666–1714)

A German Lutheran pastor and devotional writer, Arnold was saddened at the deadness of church life in his day. Looking back on the church as described in the book of Acts led him to write *The First Love of the Fellowship of Christ*, in which he praised the warmth and spontaneity of the first generation of Spirit-led Christians. In contrast with the Lutherans who emphasized the importance of correct doctrine, Arnold stressed that though doctrine was important, the true church was present when believers were born again and led by the Spirit.

409. August Hermann Francke (1663–1727)

Francke was a shining example of a scholar who was also a man of the people, for he not only taught theology but also established an orphanage and school for poor children. At the University of Halle in Germany, Francke worked to make the school a center of Bible study and missionary training. Francke was part of the Lutheran movement called Pietism (see 407), a renewal movement in Lutheranism in the 1600s and later. It emphasized the new birth and the daily walk in the Spirit.

410. Brugglers

Misguided people have sometimes claimed to operate under the influence of the Spirit. In the 1740s in Brugglen, Switzerland, brothers Christian and Hieronymus Kohler formed their own Christian sect. The two claimed to constitute the Holy Trinity, along with a female convert, Elizabeth Kissling, as the Spirit. They predicted the end of the world would be Christmas 1748. The local government branded them heretics and sent them into exile. One of the brothers was executed as a heretic. Their followers survived for a time in remote mountain areas.

411. Count Zinzendorf (1700–1760)

Nicholas von Zinzendorf was a deeply religious German nobleman whose travels took him to an art gallery where he saw a picture of Christ wearing the crown of thorns. The painting had the inscription "What have you done for me, since I have done this for you?" Seeing that was a spiritual turning point for the count, who turned his estate into a refuge for persecuted Christians. The estate, Herrnhut (Lord's Watch), became the center of a new denomination, the Moravians, noted for their deep spirituality. Gifts of the Spirit were exercised at Herrnhut, and Zinzendorf referred to them as "apostolic powers." Zinzendorf was a friend of and influence on John Wesley (see 415).

412. William Law (1686–1761)

An English minister, Law wrote an extremely popular devotional book, *A Serious Call to a Devout and Holy Life* (1728). In it he called for renouncing the world and dedicating oneself absolutely to God, taking up the cross of Christ. All of life is to be offered as a sacrifice to God, and the goal is Christlikeness. The book influenced a whole generation of believers, including John Wesley, evangelist George Whitefield, and many others. The flaw in Law's teaching is that he made duty the cornerstone of life (not a bad idea in itself) and neglected the joy of being filled with the Spirit.

413. Great Awakening

Before "separation of church and state" became a watchword of American life, several of the colonies were designed by their founders to be Bible commonwealths, guided by Christian principles. But after their settlement in the 1600s, spirituality declined. Beginning in the 1720s, various revivals broke out in New Jersey, New England, and other colonies.

Jonathan Edwards (see 414) was a key revivalist, as was the renowned English evangelist George Whitefield. The Awakening preachers called for a living, Spirit-filled faith, not just a respectable cultural Christianity that involved churchgoing but little investment of one's emotions. The Awakening was the first colonywide movement in the Americas, in some ways a preparation for the colonies' break from England in the 1770s.

414. Jonathan Edwards (1703–58)

One of the significant Americans of the colonial period was both intellectual and revivalist. The brilliant Edwards was a key figure in the colonial revival movement known as the Great Awakening. In his home church at Northampton, Massachusetts, Edwards saw that "the Spirit of God began extraordinarily to set in." Individuals clamored to be sure of their salvation, and the church was packed with eager listeners. "The town," Edwards wrote later, "seemed to be full of the presence of God. It never was so full of love, nor so full of joy, and yet as full of distress, as it was then." Strife, backbiting, and gossip disappeared. Practically everyone in town became a regular attender.

Years later Edwards wrote about the Awakening, aware that it led to some emotional excesses, yet certain that, all in all, it was evidence of the Spirit of God moving in human hearts. He looked upon the revival period from 1720 to 1740 as fruitful years for the church. (See 413 [Great Awakening].)

415. John Wesley and the Methodists

Many Holiness denominations had their roots in the Methodist church founded by John Wesley in the 1700s. Wesley (1703–91), a minister in the spiritually dry Church of England, emphasized the "warm heart" transformed by God—Christianity as a life-changing, life-enhancing reality, not just a matter of correct belief and "proper" worship. Wesley's followers (dubbed Methodists by their critics) engaged in Bible study, small group fellowship, and heart-felt hymn singing that changed lives in England and America. In time, as the Methodist churches became settled, many Methodists harked back to Wesley's original ideals—not only the *feeling* part of Christian life, but also Wesley's emphasis on perfection—that is, excluding willful sin from one's life. The 1800s was the golden age of Methodist splinter groups forming new churches that wanted to restore the original aims (and feel) of Wesley. The Wesleyan Church and the Church of the Nazarene are only two of them. See 991 (Wesley's Aldersgate experience).

416. David Brainerd (1718–47)

Born in Connecticut, he went to Yale to study for the ministry but was booted out because of his "intemperate, indiscreet zeal." He went to the Native Americans in Pennsylvania as a missionary, riding thousands of miles on horseback. He died young, leaving his intriguing *Journal*, in which he frequently spoke of "the assistance of God's Spirit" in preaching the gospel on the rugged frontier.

417. Dunkers

Officially known as Church of the Brethren, the Dunkers (so called because they baptized by immersion) were begun in Germany by Alexander Mack. Persecuted there, many of these devout people settled in Pennsylvania in the 1700s. The Dunkers believed strongly in anointing the sick with oil and praying for (and expecting) healing, and many healings were reported among the group.

418. Shakers

The group is probably best known today for simple, well-made furniture. The movement began as a spin-off of the Quakers (notice the similarity in names). "Mother" Ann Lee of England led several followers to settle in New York State in 1774. The group's actual name was the United Society for Believers in Christ's Second Appearing. Members got the name Shakers from their ecstatic dance in worship. The Shakers encouraged speaking in tongues and divine healing, though they also were known as practitioners of herbal medicine.

419. Thomas Walsh (1700s)

One of the foremost preachers among John Wesley's Methodists, Walsh wrote in his diary on March 8, 1750, "This morning the Lord gave me language that I knew not of, raising my soul to Him in a wonderful manner."

420. John Fletcher (1729–85)

Fletcher was John Wesley's designated successor as head of the Methodists, though he declined. He had been converted under Methodist influence and was, like Wesley himself, a pastor in the Church of England, ministering to coal miners and achieving a reputation for saintliness. Fletcher was for many years the most widely read theologian of Methodism, and he might have been the one who actually coined the phrase "baptism of the Holy Spirit." He might not have been referring to a one-time event but to the ongoing process of sanctification.

421. John Barclay and the Bereans

Barclay (1734–98) was a pastor in the Church of Scotland, but he left it to form his own denomination, the Bereans (named for the noble-minded Christians mentioned in Acts 17:11). The Bereans differed from the Church of Scotland in ways we would consider minor. Based on Barclay's teachings, they taught that the revealed truth of the Bible can be received only through the illumination of the Holy Spirit. They also believed that the "sin against the Holy Spirit" is unbelief.

422. Isaac Backus (1724–1806)

Churches in the American colonies faced a curious split. Some Christians wanted the church to be a believer's church, made up of members who had had a personal experience of conversion, who knew Christ in their own hearts.

They became known as the New Light Christians. The Old Light establishment opposed this idea and was willing to open membership to any person who would profess basic Christian beliefs. Backus was a New Light pastor, who believed the Spirit had called him to preach. He pastored a Baptist church in Connecticut but traveled widely to encourage Baptist churches throughout the colonies. His three-volume *History of New England* contains many references to the work of the Spirit in colonial church growth.

423. Francis Asbury (1745–1816)

In a 1771 Methodist gathering in England, leader John Wesley asked, "Our brethren in America call aloud for help. Who are willing to go over and help them?" Asbury went, and for forty-five years he traveled thousands of miles on horseback. He saw Methodism in America grow from zero to two hundred thousand. Like most frontier preachers, Asbury was "on fire for the Lord." One observer noted that "under the rush of his utterance, people sprang to their feet as if summoned to the judgment bar of God." Asbury encouraged weeping, falling down, and other manifestations of people being convicted of sin, yet had little to say about the gifts of the Spirit.

9

Renewal in the 1800s

424. 1801 Cane Ridge meeting

The golden age of camp meeting revivals was the early 1800s. In August 1801, thousands poured into Cane Ridge, Kentucky, about twenty miles west of Lexington. Called a *Communion* (no one had coined *camp meeting* yet), it began on Friday, August 6, and several preachers from different denominations whipped the thousands of people into a spiritual frenzy (including Kentucky's governor). People shouted, cried, fell on the floor, fell into comas, or became hysterical. When the fallen ones finally spoke, people hung on their every word. Laymen became "spontaneous exhorters," prophesying in warnings or words of wisdom. Preaching continued day and night. Loud hymn singing continued into the night. The numbers: probably 20,000 in attendance, perhaps 3,000 conversions, and probably 3,000 "slain in the Spirit."

425. circuit riders

Without circuit-riding preachers, Americans on the frontier would have had little contact with religion. The riders, most of them Methodists, were radically different from the more restrained clergy in the East. One preacher admitted, "People love the preacher who makes them feel," and one Methodist superintendent told his preachers to "feel for the power, brothers." One circuit rider, who had been converted at a camp meeting, stated that he would preach a few minutes, "and the fire would break out among the people, and the slain of the Lord everywhere were many."

426. Barton W. Stone (1772–1844)

This American frontier preacher was a popular revivalist, and his *Autobiography* records the physical manifestations accompanying his preaching. Stone never referred to "baptism in the Spirit," yet he vividly described listeners falling to the floor as if dead, jerking all over, dancing, grunting (or "barking," as some called it), an indescribable laughing, and singing that "silenced everything . . . most heavenly."

427. Lorenzo Dow (1777–1834)

Some called him Crazy Dow. He was tall, gaunt, and scraggly, but a dynamic revival preacher. Dow had an on-again, off-again connection with the Methodists, but was basically an independent, crisscrossing the frontier and preaching up to twenty sermons per week. Like many frontier preachers, he encouraged people's bodily reactions to his preaching.

During one of his sermons, a woman started screaming in religious ecstasy. Instead of calling her deranged (which would have happened in the "proper" churches on the East Coast), Dow yelled out, "God is here—He is with that woman!" Dow's revivals could appear out of control, but conversions resulted. The frontier had its own Spirit-made rules.

428. James B. Finley (1781–1856)

A Methodist circuit rider in western Ohio, Finley ministered to the Wyandot tribe. Some became Christians, and he was impressed with the Wyandots' ability to focus intently on a preacher, screening out all distractions. He observed, as did most missionaries to the Native Americans, that they referred to God as the Great Spirit. At an 1828 camp meeting they behaved with intensity that Finley described: "While they were praying the Spirit came down upon them, and the power of God was manifested . . . the whole encampment was in a flame of religious excitement. . . . All that the preachers and people had to do was to follow the leadings of the Spirit."

429. Sing Sing

Before it was the site of an infamous New York State prison, Sing Sing was a popular site for camp meeting revivals. A preacher who had worked revivals throughout New York State claimed that at an 1838 camp meeting he had seen more than a hundred people "slain by the Spirit of the Lord" in one night.

430. the early Mormons and tongues

Revivals on America's frontier were accompanied by all kinds of physical phenomena, but speaking in tongues was definitely *not* common and was frowned on. Many preachers associated it with a new group known as the Mormons. Methodist evangelist Peter Cartwright (1785–1872) described a camp meeting where a Mormon couple drew attention: the woman shouted, then swooned in her husband's arms, after which he told the people that she would soon speak in an unknown tongue, which he would interpret. Cartwright believed the whole thing was faked. He grabbed the woman's arm as she spoke and ordered her to hush her "gibberish," which he called "presumptuous and blasphemous nonsense."

431. Bennet Tyler (1783–1858)

Born in Connecticut and educated at Yale, Tyler was a Congregationalist pastor who watched and encouraged the revival movements that historians call the Second Great Awakening (roughly 1790–1825). He wrote that "God, in a remarkable manner, was pouring out his Spirit on the churches of New England. Within the period of five or six years, not less than one hundred and fifty churches in New England were visited with times of refreshing from the presence of the Lord."

432. Asahel Nettleton (1783–1844)

Born in Connecticut, he attended Yale and was pleased at the Yale revival of 1807. He became an evangelist and was noted for the "inquiry meetings" he held after his sermons, giving seekers an opportunity to ask questions about the faith before making a commitment. He preached throughout the U.S. and Britain and is credited with more than twenty-five thousand converts. Nettleton used an unemotional approach in his preaching, believing that the doctrines of sin and redemption, when preached rightly, would be used by the Spirit to convict the listener of sin.

433. the burned-over district

The western part of New York State became the burned-over district because so many revival fires had burned there in the early 1800s. As time passed, many of the residents were burned out, having heard so many preachers and having been convicted of sin so many times that they no longer responded to further preaching. This phenomenon occurs again and again in the history of Christianity. It is discouraging, yet always the Spirit manifests Himself somewhere.

434. the Bible Christians

This is one of many denominations that split off from the Methodist church. William O'Bryan, an itinerant Methodist preacher in England, led the split (1815), and the Bible Christians spread widely in parts of England. They came to be called unofficially Quaker Methodists because their simple worship style reminded people of the early Quakers. Like the Quakers, they emphasized the direct illumination of the Holy Spirit. The movement produced many notable preachers.

435. Hans Nielsen Hauge (1771–1824)

The chilly country of Norway may not seem an ideal place to be an evangelist on foot, but that was what the dedicated Hauge was. In 1796 he felt God calling him to preach, so he traveled about Norway, calling people to repentance. He was a lay preacher, never ordained. The Lutheran church of Norway prohibited itinerant preaching, and Hauge was arrested and imprisoned several times. He was widely loved by the people, however. He wrote several books emphasizing the new birth and the importance of laymen in the Christian fellowship.

436. Irvingites

Edward Irving (1792–1834) was a renowned Church of Scotland preacher who drew enormous crowds at his church in London. He became friend to such notables as historian Thomas Carlyle and poet Samuel Taylor Coleridge. Irving aroused some controversy, however, when he encouraged speaking in tongues during his worship services. Irving was booted out of the Church of Scotland. His followers formed the Catholic Apostolic Church, sometimes known as the Irvingites. The group is important in history for being pre-Pentecostal Pentecostals, seventy years before the movement began in America.

437. Thomas Arnold (1795–1842)

Back when schools were *supposed* to teach Christianity and morals, Arnold was headmaster of England's prestigious Rugby School. He believed that Christianity was more a matter of pure living than a matter of ritual and lifeless beliefs. Arnold emphasized the priesthood of all believers in a day when the ministers were emphasizing their own importance. Arnold was quoted as saying, "He who does not know God the Holy Spirit does not know God at all."

438. Plymouth Brethren

This small denomination began in Britain around 1831. Similar to the original Quakers in some ways, the Brethren rejected having any distinct clergy in the church. In their meetings, any member who was illumined by the Spirit could give an address or officiate at the Lord's Supper. (See 439 [John Nelson Darby].)

439. John Nelson Darby (1800–1882)

Darby was one of many sensitive, deeply religious souls who never felt quite at home in the state-supported Church of England, in which he was a minister. The church in that age was "correct" in its doctrine, but Darby desired the kind of vibrant church life he read about in the book of Acts. Declaring the Church of England to be "in ruins," Darby departed the denomination in 1828 and helped form the Plymouth Brethren movement (see 438). The Brethren believed that a true Christian community had a sense of genuine fellowship and a ministry guided by the Holy Spirit. The meetings of the Brethren were a notable contrast to spiritual deadness in most Church of England parishes.

440. MacDonald twins

Born in 1800 in a village on the west coast of Scotland, James and George MacDonald received the filling of the Spirit in the same year, 1830. Their sister, who lay dying, prayed that James might receive the Spirit, and it occurred immediately. He told his sister to get out of bed, and she did so, being healed instantly. Not long afterward George began suddenly to speak in tongues and prophesy, as did James.

441. Peculiar People

The Quakers (see 400) sometimes went by this name, but it is usually applied to an evangelical faith-healing group in England. Leader of the group was William Bridges, and the group began around 1838, concentrated in southeastern England. Known as simple and devout people, the Plumstead Peculiars, as they were also called, prayed for and sometimes received divine healing in a time when it was largely forgotten in the Church of England. The name of the group comes from Titus 2:14, where Paul referred to Christians as a "peculiar people" (KJV)—*peculiar* meaning not "weird" but a sense of "special" or "separated."

442. Robert Murray M'Cheyne (1813–43)

The state-supported Church of Scotland experienced its dramatic "disruption" in 1843, when evangelicals led almost half the church to form the Free Church of Scotland. M'Cheyne was one of the evangelicals. The saintly M'Cheyne served a large church in Dundee, where he was known for his excellent sermons, deep compassion, and tireless visitation of sick and troubled people. One of his biographers wrote that he began every day by reading the Bible and praying that he might bring healing of body and soul through the power of the Spirit.

443. Amana Society

The company now famous for its appliances started out as a Christian group, the Community of True Inspiration. The group arose in 1714 in Germany among Christians who believed that prophecy and direct inspiration from God could still be had. To escape persecution in Germany, the group came to America, eventually settling in Amana, Iowa, in 1855. They used a simple form of worship, with readings from the Bible and exhortations by elders, who were believed to be inspired by the Spirit.

444. Gilded Age

This was the name given to the 1870s and 1880s, a time of tremendous economic growth in the U.S. Churches grew, but the "frontier" feel of Christianity (allowing for the emotions of the camp meeting) was on the wane, replaced by a more "respectable" Christianity. Newer and larger churches were built, places in which poor people could hardly feel comfortable. "Respectable" churches and educated clergy largely forgot the destitute. In some ways the Gilded Age was a preparation for the Pentecostal renewal at the beginning of the 1900s, for the lower classes were looking for a vital, emotion-charged faith that was mostly missing from the "respectable" churches. "Has God not chosen the poor of this world to be rich in faith and heirs of the kingdom?" (James 2:5).

445. *The Baptism of the Holy Ghost*

There had been plenty of revivals in America in the 1800s but not much real focus on the Spirit. (The Spirit's work, of course, does not always depend on people's awareness of it.) Asa Mahan, a Presbyterian minister and president of Oberlin College in Ohio, published *The Baptism of the Holy Ghost* in 1870, lending his theological respectability to such terms as *holiness, Christian perfection, entire sanctification,* and *baptism of the Holy Spirit.* These terms weren't new, but Mahan's clout popularized the ideas. Mahan was an associate of the great evangelist Charles G. Finney (see 446).

446. Charles Grandison Finney (1792–1875)

One of America's greatest evangelists was a former lawyer and a man of keen intellect. But Finney knew that rationality alone would not convert people to Christianity. He stated, "Mankind will not act until they are excited." The revivalist and the Holy Spirit, working together, would get the Word to the people. But emotionalism for its own sake is wrong. The excitement and heightened emotion should turn people's minds to higher things—God's claim on their lives and the loathsomeness of their own sin. Finney's lectures on how to conduct revivals were extremely influential in American Christianity. He stated that "the baptism of the Holy Ghost is a thing universally promised to Christians . . . and that blessing is to be sought and received after conversion."

447. Horace Bushnell (1802–76)

As a theologian, Bushnell is a favorite of liberals, since his book *Christian Nurture* emphasized "growing into faith" rather than having a dramatic conversion experience. This was a serious shift in American thought, but in time it became what everybody believed. It is one reason that many "respectable" people were slow to respond to the renewal movement (which emphasized dramatic conversions and baptism in the Spirit). But Bushnell also made a curious prediction, which happened to come true: he foresaw a new wave of miracles and other supernatural happenings in the church.

448. James Caughey (1810–97)

Born in northern Ireland, Caughey came to the U.S. in his youth and became a Christian at age twenty-seven. Ordained as a Methodist, he began to read about the need of the power of the Spirit in preaching, and in 1839 he had the experience that he believed empowered him to preach boldly. He preached widely in England and was well received, but the English Methodists disliked his emotionalism and what they called his "new measures" in preaching. Nonetheless, he made more than twenty thousand converts in Britain.

449. Holiness movement

There have always been Christians who sought a deeper spirituality, something more demanding than just attending church and appearing nice. In America in the mid-1800s, several groups spun off from the Methodists, whose founder, John Wesley, wrote *A Plain Account of Christian Perfection*. Wesley's book claims that the Bible holds up a standard of perfection so that a Christian can live without deliberate sin. A National Holiness Association was formed, and there is now some overlap of Holiness groups and Pentecostals (see 731). Both groups emphasize the power of the Holy Spirit (see 743) and the importance of sanctification in the person's life (see 739 [sanctification]). (Many entries elsewhere in this book refer to the Holiness movement and its ties to charismatics and Pentecostals.)

450. Walter Palmer (1804–90) and Phoebe Palmer (1807–74)

A prosperous physician, Walter and his wife, Phoebe, were noted speakers at churches and camp meetings. Phoebe claimed that twenty-five thousand people got "pardon" (accepted Christ) at their meetings. Phoebe and her sister Sarah hosted interdenominational women's meetings to promote holiness. These were held weekly beginning in 1835, and Phoebe claimed to experience "purity," or entire sanctification, on July 26, 1837. In 1839 men were admitted to the meetings. The Palmers claimed that the old nature was killed by a second work of grace. Phoebe helped establish the National Association for the Promotion of Holiness in 1867.

451. Gift People

R. W. Swan, a pastor in Providence, Rhode Island, was part of an outpouring of the Spirit in 1875 when he, his wife, and six church members spoke in what he called "the unknown tongue." One of the women in the church held her mouth shut when she felt the impulse to speak, but eventually, she yielded to the Spirit and broke forth in tongues. Healings occurred, including invalids and disabled people, and word about the events spread. Local people mocked the group, calling them the "Gift People."

452. Holiness Baptists

An Arkansas man, Jethro Walthall, was filled with the Spirit in 1879, speaking in tongues and sometimes falling prostrate under God's power. This occurred *before* he knew anything about the Bible's teaching on tongues or the baptism in the Spirit. He became a Baptist pastor but knew that the Baptists would disapprove of his experiences. They charged him with heresy, citing his beliefs in baptism in the Spirit and divine healing. He joined the movement known as Holiness Baptists and later joined the Assemblies of God.

453. Hannah Whitall Smith (1832–1911)

She may be one of the most-read Christian authors in the past hundred years, for her classic *The Christian's Secret of a Happy Life*, published in 1875, has been loved by millions. Hannah and her husband, Robert Pearsall Smith, were both popular speakers at interdenominational Higher Christian Life conferences in America and Britain, and the two were key shapers of the Keswick movement (see 454). Prior to writing her classic, Hannah had struggled with depression and spiritual emptiness, but she came to experience a life of spiritual victory and contentment. She and her husband were eager to lead others into the life of victorious living through Christ. She pointed to Romans 6:6, with its promise of victory over sin, as the keystone of her experience.

454. Keswick Higher Life movement

Keswick is in England's lovely Lake District, and for years it has been a meeting place for Christians seeking an enriched spiritual life. In the 1870s, Robert Pearsall Smith, his wife, Hannah Whitall Smith, and W. E. Boardman were noted authors of devotional books about the Spirit-filled life. The three, along with other Christian leaders, spoke at an 1874 conference, which was widely publicized throughout Europe. From that conference and later ones, Robert Smith launched a magazine, *The Life of Faith*, the organ of Keswick. The conference that gave the Keswick movement its name actually met at the town of Keswick in 1875, generally considered the movement's birthday.

Since the Smiths and Boardman were American, the Keswick movement is, in a sense, a development of the American Holiness tradition on English soil. Following this, the Keswick conventions emphasized sanctification and a fullness of the Spirit that give power for living the Christian life. Particular "fillings" of the Spirit are there for times of special need.

455. *In the Power of the Spirit*

Devotional writer William E. Boardman had a huge success with *The Higher Christian Life*, which helped spread the Holiness movement worldwide. In another successful book, *In the Power of the Spirit* (1875), he proposed an idea that all renewal Christians now take for granted: the Spirit's power is not for a select few but for all true Christians. Boardman's book in some ways prepared the ground for the Pentecostal movement at the turn of the century.

456. *Sickness and the Gospel*

Otto Stockmayer of Switzerland published this book on faith-healing, and it helped to spread the message globally. Stockmayer had been healed on Easter 1867 when Samuel Zeller laid hands on him and prayed for his healing. Stockmayer opened a faith home and lectured widely on the subject of divine healing. His book emphasized that healing was a vital aspect of proclaiming the whole work of salvation. Christ, he said, intended not just to save from sin but to destroy all the works of the devil, including sickness. He was sometimes called "the theologian of healing by faith."

457. The Lord That Healeth Thee

William Boardman was a widely read devotional author and a key figure in the Holiness movement of the 1800s. His book on sanctification, *The Higher Christian Life,* was published in 1859 and became a favorite among Holiness and other Christians. In 1881 he published *The Lord That Healeth Thee,* a look at the importance of divine healing. Boardman lent his prestige as a Christian author to the healing movement.

458. Richard C. Trench (1807–86)

A saintly man and archbishop of Dublin, Trench is remembered as defending the reality of the miracles in the Bible and also providing for some new understanding of the miracles of healing. Critics of miracles have often said that they can't be real because they interrupt the laws of nature. Trench explained that miracles of healing were not against nature, since (as the New Testament makes clear) sickness itself is against nature.

459. The Atonement of Sin and Sickness

The 1880s was a great decade for faith-healing, and for books that popularized it. R. Kelso Carter published *The Atonement of Sin and Sickness: A Full Salvation for Body and Soul* (1884). In it he proposed a basic belief among faith-healers: Jesus' saving work was not only for the soul but for the body as well. Carter's book, and many others like it, harked back to the New Testament emphasis on healing as a work that Christ bequeathed to His followers.

460. A. J. Gordon (1836–95)

A. J. stood for Adoniram Judson, the name of a noteworthy missionary. Gordon was a Baptist pastor in Boston at a church known for both evangelism and charitable work. He helped establish a missionary training school, which evolved into what is today Gordon College. Gordon died before the remarkable outpourings of the Spirit under Charles Parham and the Azusa Street Mission, but he had seen the Spirit at work in his life, especially in the area of healing.

He wrote several books on healing, including one that rattled people who claimed that divine healing no longer occurred. It was *The Ministry of Healing: Miracles of Cure in All Ages* (1882). Gordon surveyed history and saw that faith-healing had never completely vanished from the church, even though people had become skeptical and said that miraculous healing was confined to the age of the apostles.

461. Charles H. Spurgeon (1834–92)

The Prince of the Pulpiteers was Spurgeon, one of the great preachers of Victorian England. The huge Metropolitan Tabernacle in London was built to accommodate the crowds that came to hear him. Thousands of divine healings were reported at the Metropolitan Tabernacle, and many others through Spurgeon's paying pastoral calls to church members who were ill.

462. John L. Nevius (1829–93)

A Presbyterian missionary to China, he is remembered for his Nevius method of planting churches abroad. Nevius insisted that mission churches overseas be self-supporting, self-propagating, and self-governing—in other words, as little dependent as possible on the nation sending out the missionaries. He outlined his method in *The Planting and Development of Missionary Churches,* which was widely studied by missionary students in the late 1800s.

463. Johann Tobias Beck (1804–78)

Beck was a respected Lutheran theologian and Bible scholar who struggled with the great question, In what way is the Bible divinely inspired? He understood the Bible as showing the history of the Spirit's work progressing toward man's salvation and revealing the kingdom of God as a supernatural reality in history.

464. D. L. Moody (1837–99)

One of the great evangelists of all time, Dwight Lyman Moody was a former shoe salesman and was never ordained. Yet he was a phenomenal preacher, and his revivals in the U.S. and Britain reached millions. He also founded a conference center, a boys' home, a girls' home, and the Chicago Evangelization Society (now the Moody Bible Institute). Moody's ministry preceded the Pentecostal and charismatic revivals, and he did not emphasize spiritual gifts in his preaching. Even so, during his tour of England in 1873 he addressed a group of young men at a YMCA (which at that time was genuinely *Christian*), and witnesses affirmed that the men's group was later found prophesying and speaking in tongues. More than once, Moody had told people, "Get full of the Holy Ghost!"

465. Gerard Manley Hopkins (1844–89)

English poet and also a Catholic priest, Hopkins never published poems in his lifetime, but he is now recognized as one of the most unique poets in the Christian tradition. There has never been Christian poetry quite like his. One of his most famous poems is "God's Grandeur," which concludes with its mention of the Holy Ghost, which "over the bent / World broods with warm breast and ah! bright wings." Hopkins was recalling Genesis 1:2, with the image of the Spirit hovering over the waters of creation, but also the image of the Spirit as a dove.

466. Swedish Mission Church

In 1892 the Swedish Mission Church in North Morehead, Minnesota, witnessed an outpouring of the Spirit, with remarkable healings and people falling to the floor and speaking in tongues. One woman, Augusta Johnson, prophesied and felt the Spirit calling her to Africa, where she was a missionary more than thirty years.

467. John Alexander Dowie (1847–1907)

Not many religious figures have built cities, but Dowie did: Zion City, north of Chicago. Dowie had a noted healing ministry in Australia and, with his family, immigrated to America in 1888. During the 1893 World's Fair in Chicago, he conducted healing services nearby, drawing crowds and having people attest to being healed. Eventually, his ministry established itself north of Chicago in Zion City, home to his eight-thousand-seat tabernacle.

Zion City was to be a community run on Christian principles. His followers, known as the Doweyites, were officially the Christian Catholic Church. Dowie was First Apostle in the community, which he ruled strictly, banning alcohol, tobacco, drugs, and pork. Zion City grew, but its leader became eccentric, believing he was the prophesied Elijah and the apostle sent to renew the church for the end times. He planned to launch Zions in other locations, but a stroke, followed by his death in 1907, prevented the expansion.

Dowie's attitude toward healing was not shared by all faith-healers. He insisted that people coming to him for healing give up all medicines. He is a textbook case of a good man led astray by his eccentricity. Even so, his influence on many of the early Pentecostal leaders was immense.

468. the Two Chains

The best-known healing evangelist at the turn of the century was John Alexander Dowie, famed as the founder of Zion City, Illinois, and for the many later Pentecostal leaders he influenced. In Dowie's healing ministry he stated that he believed in the Two Chains—the Chain of Good, from Christ, that brings salvation in soul and body, and the Chain of Evil, from Satan, that leads to sin, disease, death, and finally hell. Like most faith-healers in the late 1800s (and today), Dowie emphasized that Christ had come not just to save the soul eternally but to bring health in this life.

469. healing or tongues, or both?

The renewal movement of the twentieth century has its roots (or some of them) in the Holiness movement of the 1800s. One of the leading Holiness evangelists, and its most famous healer, was John Alexander Dowie, certainly the most renowned healing evangelist of the century. His ministry prepared a large audience to accept divine healing as a reality. Dowie was not a Pentecostal; he flatly rejected speaking in tongues as evidence of baptism of the Spirit. But his nationwide ministry laid the groundwork for the Pentecostal evangelists who followed, people who preached healing *and* tongues, as well as other gifts of the Spirit. Many early Pentecostal leaders had been connected with Dowie's ministry.

470. Adventists

Ellen Gould White (1827–1915) traveled as an evangelist in the northeastern U.S., and a typical part of her meetings was anointing the sick with oil, laying hands on them, and praying for deliverance. In those days she taught that reliance on medical science was a denial of the power of the

Spirit. Over time she downplayed the role of faith in healing and shifted the emphasis to good nutrition and personal hygiene. The various Adventist churches are descended from White's followers.

471. Father John of Kronstadt (1829–1909)

He was a noted healer in Russia, with reports of deliverance from people on whom he had laid hands and prayed. He traveled frequently and was widely regarded for the saintliness of his life.

472. Cherokee County, North Carolina, revival

In 1896 along the Tennessee–North Carolina border came an unexpected outpouring of the Spirit. Three lay evangelists—one Methodist, two Baptists—conducted a revival in a schoolhouse, resulting in numerous conversions to Christ. They continued in the North Carolina home of W. F. Bryant, where many adults and children began to speak in tongues and show other signs of the Spirit's filling. This took everyone by surprise (it was before the better-known revivals in Kansas and Los Angeles), but the people searched the Bible and found that the Christians in the book of Acts had had just such experiences. In the summer-long revival 130 people were filled with the Spirit and spoke in tongues. Healings were also reported, and many conversions were made. The revival is amazing in that no one had talked it up beforehand—that is, no one there *expected* to be baptized in the Spirit or speak in tongues.

473. *On the Holy Spirit*

In 1897 Pope Leo XIII issued the document *On the Holy Spirit*, drawing all Catholics' attention to the gifts of the Spirit and asking Catholics to pray to the Spirit before Pentecost Sunday each year.

10

Key People, 1900 to 1940

474. Aimee Semple McPherson (1890–1944)

Sister Aimee was a religious superstar of the 1920s and 1930s, broadcasting via radio from her five-thousand-seat Angelus Temple in Los Angeles. The huge Pentecostal church was the base of her own denomination, the International Church of the Foursquare Gospel. She emphasized Christ as Savior and Healer, baptism of the Holy Spirit, and speaking in tongues.

This attractive and amazing woman wrote and preached more than twenty sermons per week in her heyday. *Preached* is perhaps too narrow a word since Aimee, a theatrical figure, was noted for acting out her sermons, dressing in costumes, and even bringing in circus animals and props from nearby Hollywood movie studios. Critics sneered, and so did many Christians, but Sister believed it was important to reach people with the gospel in a dramatic way. Cynical and worldly celebrities such as Charlie Chaplin and Tallulah Bankhead attended her services, studying and admiring her stage technique even while they rejected the faith itself. The brassy Texas Guinan, a noted New York speakeasy queen, graciously introduced Sister at her club—surely a rare case of a charismatic Christian being made *welcome* in a speakeasy. Like Billy Graham, in her own day Sister could hobnob with the famous without lowering her standards. And Sister was far more than a showman. She led the church in relief efforts during the depression and during natural disasters. Though she never advertised herself as a faith-healer, a number of remarkable healings occurred at her services.

A noted controversy she engendered involved her alleged "kidnapping" in 1926. She claimed she was abducted from a beach and held captive for five weeks, but a grand jury (and many people in the media) suspected she had run off for a brief fling with a male admirer. The jury eventually dismissed the case, and the world will probably never know whether Sister was genuinely kidnapped or simply fell into a brief bout of sin. Certainly, she was a woman with a real heart for the gospel and for people. The denomination she founded survives and thrives, as does the Angelus Temple (see 151 [Foursquare Gospel Church]; 52 [Angelus Temple]; 620 [Rolf McPherson]; 888 [Robert Semple]).

475. J. Wilbur Chapman (1859–1918)

A Presbyterian evangelist, Chapman was influenced by D. L. Moody, and under his counsel Chapman received a filling with the Spirit. Evangelistic tours took him to major U.S. cities, and he worked with Moody at the 1893 World's Fair revival meetings. At age fifty-three he calculated that he had preached about fifty thousand sermons to sixty million people. One of his books was *Received Ye the Holy Ghost?*

476. Charles F. Parham (1873–1929)

Parham is a pivotal figure in Christian history, particularly in connection with spiritual renewal. Caught up in the Holiness movement, young Parham had preached and managed a faith home in Kansas. Impressed with Frank Sandford's Shiloh fellowship in Maine (see 222), he believed his ministry still lacked something special. While serving as the head of a Bible school in Topeka, Kansas, in 1900, Parham asked his students to study the biblical evidence for the baptism of the Holy Spirit. On January 1, 1901, one student, Agnes Ozman, requested prayer and laying on of hands from Parham. He did so, and she began to speak in tongues. On January 3, Parham and other students had the same experience.

Word spread, although the novelty of speaking in tongues provoked ridicule. Even so, Parham believed he had found the true Apostolic Faith. He evangelized and healed widely. A 1903 revival in Galena, Kansas, sparked interest in the movement, and many converts were made. Parham established a number of Apostolic Faith churches in

Texas. While teaching in Houston, Parham had as a student William J. Seymour, a black Holiness evangelist who carried the Pentecostal message to Los Angeles, resulting later in the famed Azusa Street revival.

After the experience at Parham's Bible school, Pentecostalism as we now know it took shape. The baptism of the Spirit was believed to be a demonstrable experience, and speaking in tongues was the initial evidence of it.

Parham, with the title of Projector of the Apostolic Faith congregations, preached throughout the U.S. Over the course of his life he was credited with 200,000 conversions. A scandal in 1907 blackened Parham's reputation and permanently removed him from any further influence on the Pentecostal movement. He was charged with sodomy in San Antonio, Texas, and though the authorities eventually dropped the charges with no explanation, the damage was done. Parham would not elaborate, though he apparently expected his followers to see the matter as a frame-up. At the time of his death, a new generation of Pentecostals hardly even knew of the existence of this amazing man.

477. Agnes Ozman (1870–1937)

Charles Parham (see 476), head of Bethel Bible College in Topeka, Kansas, had taught that speaking in tongues was evidence of baptism in the Spirit. Agnes Ozman was the first student there to speak in tongues. On January 1, 1901, she asked Parham to lay hands on her and pray. She wrote later that "as his hands were upon my head the Holy Spirit fell upon me and I began to speak in tongues, glorifying God. I talked several languages, and it was clearly manifest when a new dialect was spoken . . . It was as if rivers of living waters were proceeding from my innermost being." Her experience that night in 1901 has been called by some "the beginning of modern Pentecost." Ozman worked as a city missionary for a time and later married a Pentecostal pastor.

478. A. B. Simpson (1844–1919)

Simpson founded the group known as the Christian and Missionary Alliance (see 192), which, true to its name, sends out missionaries worldwide. In its early days (but less so today), the group emphasized such manifestations of the Spirit as healing and sanctification. Like many sensitive Christians, Simpson believed the book of Acts wasn't just history but was a model of what the church still could be. Simpson was intrigued with the matter of speaking in tongues and took a middle position, neither opposing it nor claiming it should be encouraged. Simpson wrote, "This gift is one of many gifts and is given to some for the benefit of all. The attitude toward the gift of tongues held by pastor and people should be 'Seek not, forbid not.'"

479. John Salmon (1831–1918)

Born in Scotland, Salmon was a Congregationalist minister who was healed of a kidney disease at an A. B. Simpson meeting in 1885. He became interested in divine healing and several years later received the baptism in the Spirit and the gift of tongues. He was a founding member of the Christian and Missionary Alliance in the U.S. and in Canada.

480. William J. Seymour (1870-1922)

America's Pentecost was the famous Azusa Street revival that began in 1906 (see 674). The man pastoring the Azusa Street Mission at that time was the son of former slaves. An illness left him blind in one eye, and while reflecting on this misfortune, he felt a call to preach. In Houston, he attended for about five weeks a Bible school where Charles F. Parham taught. Seymour accepted Parham's teaching that tongues was a sign of the baptism in the Spirit. A woman from a Holiness church in Los Angeles invited Seymour to pastor there, but Seymour found himself locked out of it after preaching about tongues.

Without a church building, he led a group at a private home on Bonnie Brae Street (see 673), which eventually moved to the Azusa Street Mission, a former church that had been used as a warehouse. Seymour held his first service at Azusa Street on April 14, 1906. In a few days the Los Angeles *Times* had reported the "wild scenes" and "babble of tongues" at the mission, and hundreds of people flocked to the mission. Speaking in tongues was certainly the most notable feature. Seymour was in charge, but did not dominate—indeed, he was certain that the Spirit was presiding.

The revival continued, and visitors from around the country came. Many of them were filled with excitement about the new Pentecost taking place. Seymour was humble throughout the revival. He published a magazine, *Apostolic Faith,* which went out to fifty thousand subscribers.

481. Jennie Evans Moore (1883–1936)

While attending the Bonnie Brae prayer meetings (see 673) in 1906, she became the first woman in Los Angeles to speak in tongues. She also sang in tongues at that time and played the piano, claiming she had never had lessons. The following Sunday she gave her testimony at her home church and spoke in tongues. She became active at the Azusa Street Mission, where she led the singing and became an evangelist, traveling as far as Chicago. She married William J. Seymour (see 480), and the two lived on the second floor above the Azusa Street Mission, where Jennie stayed on as a pastor after Seymour's death in 1922.

482. "Mother" Crawford (1872–1936)

The child of atheists, Florence Crawford visited the Azusa Street Mission in 1906 and was baptized in the Spirit and healed of spinal meningitis. She took an active role at Azusa Street, although her newfound faith led to a separation from her unbelieving husband. She eventually parted company with Azusa Street pastor William J. Seymour because she disapproved of his marriage. She opened the Apostolic Faith Mission in Portland, Oregon, in 1907, becoming known as "Mother" Crawford. (See 190 [Apostolic Faith Mission].)

483. Frank Bartleman (1871–1936)

A farm boy, son of a German Catholic father, Frank Bartleman was converted in 1893. He entered the ministry and served under various denominations. Around 1907 he became involved in the Azusa Street revival, then began his life as an international evangelist. Bartleman was not only an evangelist but also the first Pentecostal to write a popular history of the movement. In books such as *How Pentecost Came to Los Angeles* and *Around the World by Faith,* he helped spread the news about the outpourings of the Spirit around the world. An opinionated man, Bartleman criticized many church practices: national flags in church buildings, denominational bureaucracies, and Christian political involvement.

484. Jonathan Paul (1853–1931)

Christians in the renewal movement had more of a reputation as evangelists and missionaries than as Bible translators. But Jonathan Paul, a German, was one of a group that made the first modern German translation of the New Testament. (The classic was the beloved translation by Martin Luther.) Paul was active in ministry to industrial workers, preaching his message of full salvation and, in 1907, becoming a Pentecostal believer.

485. E. N. Bell (1866–1923)

Eudorus N. Bell had been a Baptist pastor for seventeen years but, after his baptism in the Spirit, became an Assemblies of God pastor, eventually becoming the denomination's general superintendent. His baptism in the Spirit came in 1908 following a leave of absence from his Baptist church in Fort Worth, Texas. Moving to Arkansas, he published a paper, *Word and Witness,* that issued a "call" that resulted in founding the Assemblies of God. He gave the paper to the new denomination, then returned to the pastorate and also editorship of *Pentecostal Evangel,* which ran a regular column in which Bell answered readers' questions. He was named general chairman of the Assemblies in 1920.

486. H. M. Turney (1850–1920)

A former alcoholic, Turney was converted to Christ and in 1897 experienced sanctification. At the Azusa Street Mission in Los Angeles he was baptized in the Spirit in 1906. Turney founded the Apostolic Faith Mission in San Jose the same year and later took the gospel across the U.S., to England, and finally to South Africa, where he and his wife were noted evangelists in the Assemblies of God.

487. A. A. Boddy (1854–1930)

Alexander Alfred Boddy was son of a Church of England minister and was himself ordained in that church. He was deeply concerned about the spiritual life of his congregation and began to study the Welsh revival and the 1907 revival in Norway. Thomas Barratt (see 886) visited his parish, and several people experienced the baptism of the Spirit. Boddy hosted the Annual Whitsuntide Pentecostal Conventions from 1908 to 1914, drawing speakers from various nations. (Whitsuntide is the Church of England's name for Pentecost.) Boddy is remembered as the first Pentecostal in the Church of England, but his movement made little headway at the time. Historians refer to it as the "renewal that failed."

488. Mary Boddy (d. 1928)

The wife of A. A. Boddy, she, too, was a child of a Church of England minister. She assisted in A. A.'s revival services and married him in 1891. God healed her of asthma, and she began a healing ministry. Her two daughters spoke in tongues. Mary was noted for helping lead people into the baptism of the Spirit. In later life she became an invalid even while she conducted her healing ministry to others.

489. F. F. Bosworth (1877–1958)

Fred Francis Bosworth's Pentecostal roots went back to Zion City, Illinois, where he was baptized in the Holy Spirit after Charles F. Parham brought the Pentecostal message. Moving to Dallas, Bosworth opened a church in 1910, and it began to draw people from across the U.S. because of its healing services. Bosworth affiliated with the Assemblies of God, but broke with them because of his view that speaking in tongues was only one of many evidences of being baptized in the Spirit. He and his brother B. B. Bosworth held healing services in major cities in the U.S. and Canada, with thousands in attendance. At one 1921 meeting a woman was healed of blindness. As with many Pentecostal revivals, there was mixing of the races. Late in life he worked with African missions.

490. A. S. Worrell (1831–1908)

A Confederate army veteran and later a Baptist evangelist, Worrell was a respected scholar of Greek and published his own translation of the New Testament. After a long ministry he looked closely at the emerging Pentecostal movement and gave it his wholehearted approval.

491. Finis Yoakum (1851–1920)

A doctor who gives up his lucrative practice to become a faith-healer? Yes, it does make a good story. Like many people in the healing movement, he had been healed miraculously. He was hit by a drunk driver (of a buggy—it was 1894) and was given no hope of survival. A man prayed over him, and though he was not healed instantly, he did recover with amazing speed. Yoakum closed his medical practice, lived in a tent, wore hand-me-down clothes, and dedicated his life to ministering to sick and destitute people. He healed people at a tabernacle and also maintained an office in Los Angeles, where he laid hands on the sick and prayed for them. His compassion resulted in the numerous Pisgah charities. (See 921 [Pisgah Home].)

492. Maria Woodworth-Etter (1884–1924)

A well-known healing evangelist, she claimed that God had called her to preach when she was a child. As an adult, she seemed to have her hands full with six children, but five of them died. She began preaching in local revivals, then took to the sawdust trail and became known throughout the

U.S. Her revival tent, seating eight thousand, was often inadequate for the crowds. In her meetings, lasting sometimes five hours, many people were "slain in the Spirit," and many conversions occurred. Healings were almost always reported when she came to town.

When the Pentecostal movement got into full swing after the Azusa Street revival, Woodworth-Etter happily joined. Most Pentecostals were pleased to have the renowned evangelist as part of the movement. However, during her long ministry, she aroused controversy. She would "come under the power" and go into trances that might last for hours. Critics called her the trance evangelist, and some people tried to have her committed to an asylum. Her name, by the way, stems from her two marriages. She divorced P. H. Woodworth (he had supposedly committed adultery) and married Samuel Etter.

493. Warren Fay Carothers (1872–1953)

He was a Texas lawyer who became a noted lay preacher in the Methodist church until contact with Charles Parham's ministry brought him into the Pentecostal movement. Carothers became Parham's field director in the Apostolic Faith movement, and in that position he helped train pastors and evangelists. He wrote *The Baptism with the Holy Spirit* in 1906. Parham and Carothers split in 1912.

494. G. B. Cashwell (1862–1916)

Born in North Carolina, Gaston Barnabas Cashwell was a Methodist minister but left the Methodists to join the

Holiness Church of North Carolina, in which he reached out to both blacks and whites in his tent meetings. After hearing of the Azusa Street revival in California, Cashwell borrowed money to travel to L.A. His first reaction was that the Azusa services seemed "fanatical," but he eventually accepted the revival as God's work. After pastor William Seymour and other members laid hands on him, he received the baptism in the Spirit and, he said, proceeded to speak in English, French, and German.

The Azusa Street people paid for his return to North Carolina, where he worked to involve other Holiness churches in the Pentecostal movement. So great was the interest that he rented out an enormous tobacco warehouse to accommodate the crowds. The meetings in North Carolina were the southeastern spin-off from Azusa Street. Through his tent meetings, Cashwell became the most noted Pentecostal revivalist in the southern U.S.

495. Ivey Campbell (1874–1918)

Brought up in a strict Presbyterian home, Campbell was a seamstress who, sometime around 1900, claimed to receive sanctification during an evangelistic service. She and some like-minded believers formed the Broadway Mission in East Liverpool, Ohio. While visiting relatives in Los Angeles in 1906, she went to the Azusa Street Mission, where she received the baptism of the Spirit. She returned to Ohio and began holding services at the Union Gospel Mission in Akron, Ohio. She worked with other Pentecostal leaders in a huge camp meeting in Alliance, Ohio, which helped spread Pentecostalism in that part of America.

496. Elmer Kirk Fisher (1866–1919)

His story has many duplicates: Baptist pastor receives baptism in the Spirit, then changes denominations. In Fisher's case, under the influence of the Azusa Street revival, he founded his own church, the Upper Room Mission in Los Angeles. Fisher later turned the mission over to his son-in-law and did evangelistic work. Fisher was criticized as not being a true Pentecostal because in his meetings he was not open to letting people speak just because they claimed to be moved by the Spirit.

497. Lucy Farrow (early 1900s)

A former slave from Virginia, Lucy Farrow was the link between Pentecostal pioneers Charles Parham and William Seymour. She experienced the baptism of the Spirit and speaking in tongues while employed with Parham. William Seymour, a friend, was intrigued with the story of her experience, and thanks to her, he became a student of Parham (see 476).

At the time of the Azusa Street revival, Seymour sent money for her to come to Los Angeles to serve as an "anointed handmaid" in the Lord's work in that city. Through her ministry of laying on of hands, many people received the gift of tongues. She later held meetings in her native Virginia, with about two hundred people reporting that they received the baptism of the Spirit during her meetings. Then she went as a missionary to Liberia, the African nation settled by ex-slaves from the U.S.

498. Minnie Draper (1858–1921)

Minnie Draper was living as an invalid, getting no help at all from her physicians, when relief came after being anointed and prayed for at A. B. Simpson's Gospel Tabernacle. She claimed that she was not only healed but also received the Spirit at that time. She became an associate of Simpson and became known for praying for the sick. She was curious about the new Pentecostal movement in 1906, then testified that the Lord had appeared to her in her own room and that she found herself speaking in a language she had never learned. After that she identified with the Pentecostal movement.

499. William Durham (1873–1912)

Like many notables in the Pentecostal movement, Durham was deeply influenced by the Azusa Street revival in Los Angeles. He visited there in 1907 and received the baptism of the Spirit and spoke in tongues. William J. Seymour prophesied that wherever Durham preached, the Spirit would fall upon people. Back at his home church, North Avenue Mission in Chicago, Durham led a Pentecostal revival, with crowded meetings that sometimes lasted until daybreak. Aimee Semple, before she became a McPherson, was healed instantly of a broken ankle at one of Durham's meetings. In contrast to the Holiness teaching that sanctification is an all-at-once experience later than justification, Durham insisted that sanctification is spread out over the Christian life, not concentrated at one moment. (See 218 [finished work controversy].)

500. A. B. Crumpler (1863–1952)

His biography could be titled *Am I a Methodist or What?* Ambrose Blackman Crumpler, North Carolina born, was a Methodist pastor who in 1890 experienced entire sanctification. He preached the Holiness message in tent revivals, watching as people experienced the second blessing that he himself had received. The Methodists frowned on Holiness people within their fold, so Crumpler left to form the Pentecostal Holiness Church, a new denomination.

His church grew, but in 1906 faced a controversy. One of its ministers, G. B. Cashwell (see **494**), had led the church's entire leadership in receiving the baptism in the Spirit, evidenced by speaking in tongues. Crumpler opposed those who insisted that tongues was the only initial evidence of Spirit baptism. He found himself in the minority in the church he had established. He returned to the Methodist church and remained there.

501. George Floyd Taylor (1881–1934)

While a pastor in North Carolina, Taylor got caught up in the Pentecostal revival led by G. B. Cashwell (see **494**). Taylor spoke in tongues in 1907 and published a defense of the Pentecostal experience, *The Spirit and the Bride*. He became head of the Pentecostal Holiness Church (PHC) in 1913 and helped found what became the PHC's liberal arts school, Emmanuel College, where he later was a faculty member.

502. Frank J. Ewart (1876–1947)

Ewart was a multinational preacher, beginning as a bush missionary in his native Australia, then a Baptist pastor in Canada, and finally a Pentecostal pastor in the U.S. (The Baptists in Canada dismissed him after he testified to being baptized in the Spirit.) He became assistant to noted pastor William Durham (see 499), then senior pastor on Durham's untimely death.

Ewart is associated with Oneness Pentecostalism (see 216)—in brief, emphasis on "Jesus only" instead of the traditional Trinity (Father, Son, Holy Spirit). Ewart and like-minded Pentecostals began to insist on being *rebaptized* in the name of Jesus only. He affiliated with a Oneness denomination, the United Pentecostal Church. Ewart authored several popular books, including *The Revelation of Jesus Christ* and *The Phenomenon of Pentecost*.

503. Rachel Sizelove (1864–1941)

The nation's largest Pentecostal denomination, the Assemblies of God, has its headquarters in Springfield, Missouri. The woman evangelist who did a lot to bring that about was herself introduced to Pentecostal belief in Springfield. Rachel Sizelove had received the baptism of the Spirit at the Azusa Street Mission in Los Angeles. Returning to Springfield, she had a vision of a beautiful fountain in the middle of Springfield, which proceeded to water the entire land. The Assemblies of God had not even been formed yet, but five years later Sizelove's vision became a reality.

504. Glenn A. Cook (1867–1948)

Working as a newspaperman in Los Angeles, Cook came under the influence of the Pentecostal revival connected with William J. Seymour. He left his job to work with Seymour, handling the finances of the Azusa Street Mission. In 1907 he took the fire of the Azusa Street revival to Indianapolis. Cook conducted evangelistic campaigns in Arkansas, Oklahoma, and Missouri. After 1914 he preached the "Jesus Only" message (see 216 [Oneness Pentecostalism]).

505. A. G. Garr Sr. (1874–1944)

He was pastoring the Burning Bush Mission in Los Angeles when he heard of the Azusa Street Mission revival, which led to his receiving baptism in the Spirit and speaking in tongues in 1906—notably, the first *white* pastor to receive that at Azusa. His own church refused to accept his baptism in the Spirit, and Garr resigned. Afterward he felt called to India as a missionary. He believed that the experience of speaking in tongues had equipped him and his wife to minister abroad in languages they had not learned. That notion failed, but the Garrs remained in India, working through interpreters. Their ministry moved to Hong Kong, Japan, and China, then back to the U.S. where A. G. became known as a healing evangelist. Settled in Charlotte, North Carolina, he pastored a large congregation in an old auditorium, later known as the Garr Auditorium, one of the largest Pentecostal churches in the South.

506. Frederick A. Graves (1856-1927)

Throughout his youth Graves suffered from epilepsy but was permanently healed after encountering healing evangelist John Alexander Dowie. The healing was a milestone on his spiritual journey. Graves moved his family to the Christian community Dowie had founded, Zion City, north of Chicago. He was ordained (at the ripe age of sixty-two) in the Assemblies of God. Graves is best known as a songwriter, particularly for two perennially popular songs, "He'll Never Forget to Keep Me" and "Honey in the Rock."

507. Joseph H. King (1869-1946)

King was founder and first bishop of the Pentecostal Holiness Church (PHC). From a poor Georgia family, he was a Methodist, converted at a camp meeting in 1882. Having experienced the second blessing of entire sanctification, he became disenchanted with the Methodists' negative attitude toward the Holiness movement. He gladly joined with B. H. Irwin's Fire-Baptized Holiness Church (FBHC) (see 148), which taught the "fire" experience after sanctification.

When Irwin left the denomination after confessing to "gross sin," King became the church's leader. Soon after the pivotal Azusa Street revival in Los Angeles, most of King's pastors became Pentecostals, as did King himself, who spoke in tongues. He immediately moved the FBHC toward Pentecostalism, believing that the baptism of the Spirit, evidenced by speaking in tongues, was the baptism of fire that he had earlier taught. The FBHC merged with the

Pentecostal Holiness Church, and in a few years he was elected its head, given the honorary title of bishop. King's 1911 book *From Passover to Pentecost* was a key work in the early Pentecostal movement.

An interesting personal note: King married in 1911, but his wife deserted him, not wanting to be a minister's wife. Not believing in divorce and remarriage, he would not remarry until he learned in 1920 that his first wife had died.

508. Albert Ernest Robinson (1877–1950)

Rarely does a denomination have a layman serving as its head, but Robinson, who helped organize the Pentecostal Holiness Church (PHC), served as its general secretary from 1911 to 1925. He had been a printer and came to know the Fire-Baptized Holiness Church while printing its literature. Along with printing the PHC's Sunday school curriculum, Robinson wrote a book popular with his denomination, *A Layman and the Book*.

509. G. T. Haywood (1880–1931)

Garfield Thomas Haywood was an Indianapolis high school dropout when, in 1906, news of the Azusa Street revival in California began to spread. A Pentecostal pastor named Henry Prentiss, fresh from the Azusa Street revival, started a church in Indianapolis and led Haywood into the baptism of the Spirit. Haywood succeeded Prentiss as pastor, and the church grew rapidly. Around 1915 he swung over to the Oneness position (see 216), and his congregation followed suit, pastor and parish all being rebaptized in the name of Jesus only.

The noted black pastor and speaker wrote and illustrated (he had been a cartoonist) several books, including *The Finest of the Wheat* and *Before the Foundation of the World*. He was also a noted songwriter, producing such still-popular songs as "Jesus the Son of God."

510. Elizabeth Sisson (1843–1934)

Sisson claimed that she received her ordination to the ministry after she had attended an Episcopal ordination service. Christ appeared to her in a vision and said, "I ordain you." She became missionary to both Hindus and Muslims in India, but left the mission field because of illness. Back in the U.S. she became a noted evangelist and author, affiliating with the Assemblies of God. Many of her articles in Pentecostal magazines were reprinted as tracts.

511. Joseph Smale (1867–1926)

A Baptist pastor from England, Smale moved to the United States and became pastor of a Los Angeles church in 1895. But he returned to Britain after hearing of the Welsh revival, and then he returned to Los Angeles praying for an outpouring of the Spirit like what he had seen in Wales. It happened, and it crossed denominational lines. Baptist authorities were not pleased, and Smale formed his independent New Testament Church in 1906. There on Easter 1906 occurred the church's first case of speaking in tongues.

Smale's church crossed racial and socioeconomic lines, and services were packed. Meetings often lasted well into the night, and people spoke in tongues, shouted, and were "slain in the Spirit." Curiously, Smale himself never experienced tongues or the baptism of the Spirit.

512. George Jeffreys (1889–1962)

Born in Wales, he turned out to be one of Britain's greatest evangelists. Converted to Christ in 1904, George suffered from a speech disability and facial paralysis. In 1911 he was baptized in the Spirit and healed of his ailments. He preached in his native Wales and was scheduled to preach in Ireland until his sponsors canceled his engagement because they found out he was a Pentecostal.

He and some like-minded friends formed the Elim Pentecostal Alliance, and George established churches in Ireland and England. Huge crowds were drawn to his preaching, and new churches were founded wherever he went. He spent a few months evangelizing in the U.S. and Canada, and also in Switzerland, Sweden, France, and the Netherlands. George's older brother Stephen (see 513) was also a notable evangelist.

513. Stephen Jeffreys (1876–1943)

The brother of evangelist George Jeffreys (see 512), Stephen was working as a coal miner when he was converted during the Welsh revival. After his son Edward received the baptism in the Spirit, Stephen sought the experience also, as did George. Through George's urging,

Stephen became an evangelist and left his mining job. Both brothers preached in Wales, then later in London. In 1914 Stephen saw a vision while preaching: the face of a lamb, which changed to the face of the Man of Sorrows. People in the church also saw the vision, which was reported in the newspapers. Like George, Stephen was a popular preacher, and his work contributed to the growth of the Assemblies of God in Britain. His warmth and simplicity contributed to his popular appeal.

514. Charles H. Mason (1866–1961)

The son of former slaves in Tennessee, Mason fell seriously ill at age fourteen and was miraculously healed. He became a lay preacher, testifying to his healing at churches and in camp meetings. His Baptist denomination eventually expelled him for his Holiness views, and he became the founder of the Church of God in Christ (CGIC) (see 177), which became one of the largest black denominations. New Holiness churches under the CGIC banner were established throughout the South and Southwest.

Under the ministry of William Seymour (see 480), Mason received the baptism of the Spirit, and the Pentecostal experience was added to the CGIC's formula. Mason was widely loved and respected, not only by his own denomination but also by the many white Pentecostals who were impressed by his saintliness. He is buried at the Mason Temple, the headquarters of the CGIC in Memphis.

515. Lizzie Roberson (1860–1945)

Charles Mason, founder of the predominantly black Church of God in Christ (CGIC), asked her to head the CGIC's women's department. She did so, and she was a gifted organizer, also noted as an excellent teacher. She is one of countless examples of vibrant, Spirit-filled women filling leadership roles in the renewal movement.

516. Amanda Smith (1839–1915)

She was a beloved Holiness evangelist in the South, teaching sanctification and dependence upon the Lord. Her influence was even wider than her evangelistic travels, for her autobiography, *The Story of the Lord's Dealing with Mrs. Amanda Smith, the Colored Evangelist,* was widely read, particularly among blacks. Many blacks became involved in the Holiness movement because of the book's effect on them.

517. Herbert Buffum (1879–1939)

Imagine writing more than ten thousand songs. Buffum did—and with no formal musical training whatsoever. The King of Gospel Song Writers was called to the ministry at age eighteen in the Church of the Nazarene and became a noted evangelist, in the meantime writing songs based on the Bible and his own experiences. "I'm Going Higher Some Day," "The Old-Fashioned Meeting," and "My Sheep Know My Voice" were only a tiny part of his tremen-

˙dous output. He wrote songs out of love for the Lord, not money, for most of them sold for only a pittance.

518. Carrie Judd Montgomery (1858–1946)

Like many people of faith, she came to believe in divine healing when she was healed. Suffering a fall while young, she became an invalid but was miraculously healed in 1880 and gave her testimony in the book *The Prayer of Faith*. The book brought her to the forefront of the healing movement. She wrote several other books but was mostly influential through her magazine, *Triumphs of Faith*, which she began in 1881 and edited for sixty-five years. Nondenominational, the magazine helped the dialogue among people from various Holiness and Pentecostal churches. After being baptized in the Spirit and speaking in tongues, she introduced a Pentecostal vein to her writing, while still adhering to Holiness teaching and an emphasis on divine healing. She spoke in tongues, but worked to build bridges between those who had had the experience and those who had not.

519. Smith Wigglesworth (1859–1947)

Jesus was a carpenter, and evangelist Smith Wigglesworth was a plumber. Having to work to support his family from an early age, he received little education and later claimed that when he finally learned to read, he read only the Bible. (Books published under his name were, he said, his sermons that others had written down.) He was healed of a ruptured appendix, which led to his dynamic healing ministry. In

1907 he was baptized in the Spirit, and after that his evangelistic meetings focused on healing the sick and calling believers to seek the baptism of the Spirit. He was still active in the ministry when he died at age eighty-seven.

520. Virginia E. Moss (1875–1919)

Always in frail health, Virginia fell on ice when she was thirteen, leaving her to face a spreading paralysis until she was completely healed in 1904. The healing led to her commitment to Christian ministry, although her home church did not receive her testimony with pleasure. She began home prayer meetings, which led to founding the Door of Hope mission in 1906. After a 1907 Pentecostal meeting in Nyack, New York, she received the baptism of the Spirit and spoke in tongues. Several healings were reported at the mission. Seeing the need to train missionaries, the assembly opened its Bible and Missionary Training School in 1912. The school founded by "Mother" Moss was noted for the many distinguished missionaries among its graduates.

521. Thomas Myerscough (1858–1932)

A gifted teacher of the Bible, Myerscough was baptized in the Spirit in 1909. His Bible classes evolved into the Pentecostal Missionary Union Bible School, influencing many pastors and evangelists. He was one of the founders of the Assemblies of God in Britain.

522. Daniel Opperman (1872–1926)

Like many early Pentecostal leaders, Opperman had an association with the sometimes controversial John Alexander Dowie (see 467). Opperman was education director for Dowie's Zion City in Illinois but later moved to Texas, where he met Charles Parham and, in 1908, experienced the baptism of the Spirit. He was noted for conducting short-term Bible institutes and was a founder of the Assemblies of God (AG). He left the AG to head a Oneness denomination (see 216).

523. Charles S. Price (1887–1947)

Born in England, Price was pastoring a Congregational church in California when some of his church members convinced him to attend a service led by Aimee Semple McPherson. He went full of skepticism, but ended up responding to an altar call and later experiencing the baptism in the Holy Spirit. Price returned to his congregation where "the power of God commenced to fall." The Congregationalist authorities objected, so Price started an independent congregation. He traveled as an evangelist in the Pacific Northwest, drawing huge crowds at meetings where healings were reported. During a campaign in Belleville, Illinois, more than one thousand conversions per day were reported.

524. Saint Samuel (ca. 1934)

With a colorful name, he was a colorful evangelist of his time. A minister in the Church of God in Christ, he sometimes led worship at the denomination's annual conventions in Memphis. While speaking he would "wrestle with the devil," stamping his feet and rebuking Satan with such phrases as, "Get out of here, you fool!"

525. John Schaepe (1870–1939)

His biography seems made for Hollywood: a German boy who ran away from home, worked as a sailor, became a gaucho in Argentina, worked as a cowboy in the U.S., fled to Hawaii to escape justice, and converted to Christ after stumbling into a Salvation Army mission. Schaepe claimed that after leaving the mission, he returned to his hotel room where he was baptized in the Spirit, speaking in Japanese, Chinese, and Korean.

The man with the colorful life became an advocate for the Oneness doctrine (see 216). He attended a camp meeting where the preacher noted that in the book of Acts all baptisms were done in the name of Jesus only, not in the Father-Son-Spirit formula that Jesus stated in Matthew 28:19. Schaepe became obsessed with this, shouting out his "revelation" to the camp: baptisms had to be in Jesus' name only, and people who had been baptized in the old way had to be rebaptized. Out of Schaepe's "revelation" grew the Oneness movement.

526. "Mother" Barnes (1854–1939)

Known as "Mother" Barnes, Leonore Barnes was conducting a revival meeting in Missouri when some thugs threatened to kill the evangelists. They didn't, and the six-week-long revival resulted in many converts and people who experienced baptism in the Spirit. When the Assemblies of God was founded in 1914, she was a charter member.

527. John Chalmers Sinclair (1863–1936)

There is an independent streak among charismatics and Pentecostals—or, put another way, a bias against denominations. That was evident in the ministry of Sinclair, a Scottish minister who pastored a Chicago church and was reputed to be the first person in the city to be baptized in the Spirit. He was one of the first executives in the Assemblies of God (AG) when the AG was established in 1914, but he left the AG and, in a few years, became head of the newly founded Pentecostal Church of God, which he later left. Always the independent, Sinclair continued his evangelistic ministry outside the boundaries of denominations.

528. Wesley R. Steelberg (1902–52)

The son of Swedish immigrants to the U.S., Wesley had spinal meningitis as a child but was miraculously healed. After receiving the baptism of the Spirit, he began preaching at age sixteen and was ordained at seventeen. Based in California, he was a noted evangelist and became general superintendent of the Assemblies of God.

529. George B. Studd (1859–1945)

A renowned English cricket player, Studd helped establish Peniel Hall, a Holiness church in Los Angeles. He was noted for his contributions to Pentecostal missions.

530. A. J. Tomlinson (1865–1943)

A former Bible salesman, Ambrose Jessup Tomlinson is credited with establishing several Pentecostal denominations. Most notable was the Church of God (Cleveland, Tennessee) (see 146), which Tomlinson served as overseer from 1907 to 1923. He preached that speaking in tongues was the initial evidence of baptism in the Spirit, even though at that time he had not experienced it himself. In a Sunday service in 1908 he fell to the floor and spoke in tongues (in ten different languages).

Tomlinson traveled widely, preaching at churches and camp meetings, helping establish the Church of God publishing house in 1913. He also pushed for a Bible Training School and an orphanage, both of which came to pass. But the Church of God grew restless under his leadership (there were questions about his handling of finances). Though he was supposed to be general overseer for life, the council of elders ousted him. He departed, with his faction taking the name "Church of God, over which A. J. Tomlinson is general overseer"; it became the Church of God of Prophecy. One of his sons was the extremely colorful Homer Tomlinson (see 223).

531. Flavius J. Lee (1875–1928)

The Church of God (Cleveland, Tennessee) named its undergraduate school, Lee College, after the CG's second head, Flavius Josephus Lee, who happened to have been born in Cleveland. Lee received the baptism of the Spirit at a revival led by CG pastor A. J. Tomlinson, and Lee became a pastor. Tomlinson was the CG's first general overseer, and Lee became his right-hand man. The CG became restless under Tomlinson's heavy-handed leadership. The denomination ousted him and replaced him with Lee, who, much to the church's regret, died after only five years. Lee believed strongly in divine healing and would not accept medical treatment for his cancer. The CG renamed its school Lee College in 1947.

532. E. W. Kenyon (1867–1948)

Essek William Kenyon is known for his teaching on positive confession (see 785). He started out as a fairly conventional pastor in Los Angeles, moving into radio with *Kenyon's Church of the Air*. He was also a traveling evangelist, but his greatest influence has been through his books, widely read by charismatics and Pentecostals (even though Kenyon was neither).

533. F. B. Meyer (1847–1929)

He was not a Pentecostal or charismatic, but his writings helped pave the way for the movement. A noted Baptist pastor in England, he was a popular evangelist and helped launch an American evangelist who became even more famous, D. L. Moody. Meyer's sermons and books helped spread the idea of the overcoming life of victory over sin and sadness. He wrote many devotional studies on Bible characters that were widely read by Pentecostals.

534. Oswald Chambers (1874–1917)

The talented devotional writer was born in Scotland but traveled widely. He was a missionary for the Pentecostal League of Prayer and in his last years ministered to British troops during World War I. He is best known for *My Utmost for His Highest,* but he also wrote *He Shall Glorify Me: Talks on the Holy Spirit.*

535. Myer Pearlman (1898–1943)

He was passing by the Glad Tidings Mission in San Francisco and was drawn inside to the singing. This Jewish man began attending the church, was converted, and received the baptism in the Spirit. He graduated from the Assemblies of God Central Bible College and joined its faculty, also publishing curriculum for the Gospel Publishing House. Pearlman wrote a widely used summary of theology, *Knowing the Doctrines of the Bible.*

536. John Martin Pike (1840–1932)

Born in Newfoundland, Canada, Pike became a Methodist minister in South Carolina where he was active in the Holiness movement. From 1890, he published *The Way of*

Faith, a weekly magazine with a healing-Holiness slant. In the magazine Pike published articles to spread the word about the 1906 Azusa Street revival in Los Angeles. Pike also published the autobiography of Pentecostal leader Frank Bartleman (see 483).

537. Robert J. Craig (1872–1941)

A Methodist minister based in San Francisco, Craig received the baptism of the Spirit and joined the Assemblies of God. He opened the small Glad Tidings Temple in San Francisco in 1913, and it grew into an enormous church hosting prominent evangelists.

538. Anna Larssen Bjorner (1875–1955)

A famous actress in her native Denmark, she was baptized in the Spirit in 1908 and hosted Pentecostal gatherings in her spacious home. She retired from the stage in 1909, then married. She and her husband became leading figures in the renewal movement in Denmark. She and he were booted out of the national Lutheran church of Denmark after they were rebaptized by immersion.

539. William H. Piper (1868–1911)

Both he and his wife were healed under the ministry of John Alexander Dowie (see 467), and both went to live in Dowie's Christian city, Zion City, Illinois. Piper became disillusioned with Zion City in 1906 and left to found the Stone Church in Chicago, many of his church people being former Zion City residents. Piper invited three Pentecostals to speak at his church in 1907. The congregation responded with enthusiasm, and the church grew. His wife was baptized in the Spirit that year, and Piper had the experience in 1908. The Stone Church began to publish a monthly magazine, *The Latter Rain Evangel*, which Piper edited. He died in 1911, with his wife continuing as pastor of the Stone Church, which later affiliated with the Assemblies of God.

540. M. M. Pinson (1873–1953)

A Georgian from a large farm family, Pinson was converted at a Baptist revival in 1893 and became an evangelist in the South. He learned about the Azusa Street revival from evangelist G. B. Cashwell but was skeptical. He decided to seek the baptism of the Spirit and received it in 1907 while praying in bed. Pinson started his own Pentecostal newspaper, *Word and Witness*. At the formation of the Assemblies of God, Pinson was selected as keynote speaker and an executive presbyter.

541. Stanley H. Frodsham (1882–1969)

We think of the YMCA today as a place to exercise, but it really was a *Christian* association in its early days. Stanley Frodsham accepted Christ at the London YMCA, though he was still seeking a deeper spiritual experience. He found it in 1908 when he received baptism in the Holy Spirit. After moving to America, he became a minister with the Assemblies of God, but is best remembered as editor of its publications, including the magazine *Pentecostal Evangel*. He wrote *With Signs Following: The Story of the Pentecostal Revival in the Twentieth Century*.

542. Robert Brown (1872–1948) and Marie Brown (1880–1971)

Robert had been a bobby, one of London's police. Following his conversion, he became a Wesleyan Methodist minister, then moved to New York in 1898. A few years later, while he was working by day and serving as an evangelist in his spare hours, he met Marie Burgess, a Pentecostal evangelist in Manhattan, sent there by Charles F. Parham (see 476). She had been converted through the ministry of healing evangelist John Dowie in Illinois, where she also met Parham.

Robert became a Pentecostal in 1908 and married Marie the following year. Their storefront mission in Manhattan outgrew its site and moved to roomier quarters, which it also outgrew. By 1921 the congregation had moved into a former Baptist building, which was rechristened the Glad Tidings Tabernacle, one of the best-known Pentecostal churches on the East Coast.

543. Emma Cotton (1877–1952)

At Azusa Street in 1907 Emma was healed of a lung ailment and cancer. Having a husband whose job took him away from home frequently, Emma had time to conduct divine healing services throughout California. Through the 1920s she was active in establishing new Pentecostal churches in

California. During the 1930s "Mother" Cotton became friends with the famous Aimee Semple McPherson. With Sister Aimee's encouragement, Mother Cotton built the Azusa Temple in Los Angeles.

544. John G. Lake (1870–1935)

A noted faith-healer in his day, Lake had good reason to believe in the power of the Spirit to heal: he had seen his wife cured instantaneously from tuberculosis. Hers was only one of several healings he had witnessed, and it led him to seek the baptism of the Spirit, which finally came. Having been a success in the business world, he felt God calling him to South Africa, where he went in 1908, his wife and seven children in tow. Later he made the Pacific Northwest his base, and in the 1920s and 1930s numerous healings were reported in his ministry.

545. Donald Gee (1891–1966)

His father was a sign painter and so was he, but he became a world leader in the Pentecostal movement. Gee became a Pentecostal believer in 1913 and became pastor of the Bonnington Toll Chapel near Edinburgh, Scotland. He was not only a noted pastor and speaker, but also a musician. He produced the *Redemption Tidings Hymn Book* in 1924. His first book, *Concerning Spiritual Gifts*, was published in 1928.

Gee became known as the "Apostle of Balance," working to build bridges among Spirit-led Christians instead of sowing divisiveness. He noted that like the early Christians,

Spirit-led Christians in the twentieth century were too quick to quarrel when they should have been seeking common ground. He wrote an early history of the movement, *Upon All Flesh* (1935), observing that the movement of the Spirit was a global phenomenon. He lectured widely in Europe, the U.S., and Australia, and was widely read because of his more than thirty books.

546. J. Roswell Flower (1888–1970) and Alice Reynolds Flower (1890–1991)

The Flowers have been called Mr. and Mrs. Assemblies of God, since so much of their history is the history of that denomination. When the Assemblies of God (AG) organized in 1914, the couple were deeply involved. J. Roswell served the denomination in several key national offices and also left extensive notes that became the first history of the AG. He helped the AG link up with the National Association of Evangelicals and the Pentecostal Fellowship of North America. Alice, whom he married in 1911, was a noted speaker and author, producing such devotional books as *Open Windows, Threads of God, Grace for Grace,* and many others.

547. Raymond T. Richey (1893–1968)

Richey led a wild youth but changed dramatically after his failing eyesight was restored at a revival meeting in 1911. He became a noted evangelist, setting up a revival tabernacle near an army camp during World War I, leading to hundreds of conversions. He contracted tuberculosis but was miraculously healed in 1919. The following year his healing ministry began. He took his crusades to large auditoriums all over the U.S. One crusade in Tulsa reported eleven thousand conversions, and those who had been healed paraded through the streets. During World War II, Richey reached out again to servicemen, traveling with his distinctive red, white, and blue revival tent.

548. Thoro Harris (1874–1955)

Pop singer Ray Stevens introduced his hit "Everything Is Beautiful" with a verse from the old gospel song "Jesus Loves the Little Children." The music for the gospel was a 1921 composition of the prolific songwriter Thoro Harris, who also wrote the music for "All That Thrills My Soul Is Jesus," "He's Coming Soon," "More Abundantly," and many others. Harris was a child musical prodigy whose songs became widely used in Holiness and Pentecostal churches.

549. James Eustace Purdie (1880–1977)

As an Anglican pastor in Canada, he became known for his healing ministry. In 1919 he received the baptism of the Holy Spirit and speaking in tongues. His experiences led to contact with the Pentecostal Assemblies of Canada, and he became head of the denomination's Pentecostal Bible College in 1925, a position he held until retirement. His theological writings were widely used in his college and in other Pentecostal colleges.

550. Ernest S. Williams (1885–1981)

Williams was working at a Colorado ranch when his mother wrote him about the Azusa Street revival in Los Angeles. He headed to California and, following a visit to Azusa Street, was baptized in the Spirit. Like many Azusa alumni, he felt called to the ministry. He pastored several Pentecostal churches in the eastern U.S. The Highway Mission Tabernacle in Philadelphia grew tremendously during his pastorate. He caught the attention of the Assemblies of God, which called him to be the general superintendent in 1929, and he held that position for twenty years.

551. Karl Barth (1886–1968)

One of the great theologians of the twentieth century, Barth, a Swiss pastor, is best known for his multivolume theological work *Church Dogmatics*. After his lifelong study of the New Testament, Barth concluded that healing by faith was a reality, one too long neglected by the churches. He harked back to the healing ministry of Johann Blumhardt in the 1800s (see 939) and noted that Blumhardt's understanding of sickness as a struggle with evil powers was the view of the Bible.

552. Ralph Riggs (1895–1971)

Riggs was converted at age ten and baptized in the Spirit at age fourteen. He joined the Assemblies of God (AG) when it was founded and was ordained as an AG pastor. He and his wife were missionaries in South Africa, where they traveled by donkey cart.

The family settled in Springfield, Missouri, where Ralph became pastor at Central Assembly, the home church for the AG headquarters. He served six years as superintendent of the AG, watching the denomination grow and overseeing the founding of its first liberal arts college, Evangel College. Riggs wrote several books, including *The Spirit Himself.*

553. John Richey (1899–1984) and Louise Richey (1894–1986)

Coevangelists, the Richeys had been ministers in the International Church of the Foursquare Gospel, but in 1932 joined with other ministers to form the Open Bible Evangelistic Association. Louise experienced a divine healing under the ministry of Maria Woodworth-Etter.

11

Key People, 1940 to Now

MEDIA FACES AND VOICES

554. Billy Graham (b. 1918)

Graham's place in Christian history is assured, not only as one of the most dynamic evangelists of all time, but also as a committed evangelical who has steered clear of divisiveness and controversy. In his 1978 book *The Holy Spirit: Activating God's Power in Your Life,* the great communicator explains the Bible's teaching on the Spirit. In the delicate area of the sign gifts (tongues, healing, miracles) he is careful to say that such gifts are indeed still exercised. In regard to tongues, he states his view that tongues are not necessarily a sign of being baptized in the Spirit. And he adds that tongues have been overemphasized both by advocates and by critics.

As always, Graham is a bridge builder, not a wall builder. Graham's crusades have been widely supported by Spirit-led Christians. Curiously, this connection with Pentecostals has blackened Graham's reputation in the eyes of some fundamentalists (Bob Jones, for example), who claim that true believers should not fellowship with "fanatics."

555. James Robison (b. 1945)

With Billy Graham's encouragement, Robison began his TV ministry years ago and now has a daily talk show, *Life Today*, cohosted by his wife, Betty. Robison has been preaching for years, including a stint at the huge First Baptist Church in Dallas. He developed his James Robison Evangelistic Association (now LIFE Outreach International) based in Fort Worth. Robison has seen the power of the Spirit at work in his own life, delivering him from demons and healing him and family members from sickness. He clearly emphasizes the power of the Spirit, though he maintains his Southern Baptist connection and (tactfully) does not blatantly identify himself as a charismatic (or deny being one).

556. Pat Robertson (b. 1930)

Marion Gordon "Pat" Robertson turned a small TV station in Portsmouth, Virginia, into the worldwide Christian Broadcasting Network (CBN), with its still-running daily program the *700 Club*, plus prayer counselors, Regent

University (see 946), and various related ministries. Robertson positioned CBN as a nondenominational entity that largely attracts (but is not limited to) charismatics from all churches and social backgrounds. He founded the Christian Coalition, a conservative political-religious organization that is now probably better known than CBN itself.

557. Marilyn Hickey (b. 1931)

Thanks to the power of television, she is probably one of the best-known women Bible teachers in the world. She was teaching a Bible class in her home when, in 1976, the Lord called her to "cover the earth with the Word." She began radio broadcasts and is now broadcast in more than 30 TV markets and 120 radio stations. The magazine published by Marilyn Hickey Ministries has a circulation of 200,000. Beyond teaching via TV and radio, she has helped raise money to feed hungry people in Ethiopia, Haiti, Bangladesh, and other Third World countries.

558. David Mainse (b. 1936)

He is probably Canada's best-known religious TV personality, thanks to the many U.S. cable systems that carry his program *100 Huntley Street*. Born in the province of Quebec, he pastored Pentecostal churches and in 1962 began his television ministry that evolved into Crossroads Christian Communications. The program *100 Huntley Street*, based in Toronto, is broadcast in ten languages.

Mainse has published *100 Huntley Street, God Keep Our Land,* and *Past, Present, and Promise.*

559. Oral Roberts (b. 1918)

The son of a Pentecostal preacher, Granville Oral Roberts was ordained at age seventeen. His ministry of preaching and healing, much of it televised, made him one of the most widely known ministers in America. He founded Oral Roberts University, which includes a medical school, in Tulsa, Oklahoma. His many books have included *Don't Give Up* and *If You Need Healing, Do These Things.* His autobiography, *Expect a Miracle,* was published in 1995. His son Richard has continued his ministry via television (see 560 [Richard Roberts]; 923 [City of Faith]; 945 [ORU]). In many ways Roberts is the grand old man of American Pentecostals.

560. Richard Roberts (b. 1948)

Son of the famous Oral Roberts, Richard is now seen more often on television than his venerable father is, and he is known as both evangelist and singer. Richard graduated from (surprise!) Oral Roberts University and married a singer in the ministry. Their divorce caused some murmuring among supporters. Richard remarried in 1980, and he and his wife, Lindsay, continue the healing ministry of Richard's father. *Something Good Today* is his daily television show. Richard is president of the Oral Roberts Evangelistic Association.

561. Senator John Ashcroft (b. 1942)

The U.S. Senate's first Pentecostal is John Ashcroft, son of Assemblies of God pastor and college president J. Robert Ashcroft. John, elected from Missouri (and former governor of the state), was an early contender for the Republican presidential candidacy in 2000. True to his roots, the senator has written and performed gospel music. In 1998 he published *Lessons from a Father to His Son*.

562. Benny Hinn (b. 1952)

Healing evangelist Hinn, author of *The Anointing* and *Good Morning, Holy Spirit*, is also host of the TV program *Benny Hinn Daily*. His crusade meetings are held in some of the largest auditoriums across the country. He gained additional fame when boxer Evander Holyfield, diagnosed with a heart problem, requested prayer at a Hinn crusade. Holyfield resumed his boxing career and made a sizable contribution to the ministry. Headquarters for Benny Hinn Ministries are in Orlando, Florida, site of his four-thousand-member Orlando Christian Center.

563. Kathryn Kuhlman (1907–76)

Her enormous revival meetings around the nation in the 1950s and 1960s were based on one of her key statements: "I believe in miracles." Despite having detractors, Kuhlman claimed that many people were healed during her revivals, and many came forward to back her claims. She gave all the credit to the Spirit for the healings. She never claimed to have spoken in tongues and did not permit tongues speaking during her miracle services.

A tall, striking redhead, Kuhlman provoked criticism from some Christians because of wearing jewels and expensive clothes, and also for being divorced. No one could deny that in the television age she was definitely "camera ready."

564. Pat Boone (b. 1934)

Charles Eugene Boone, better known as Pat, is a rarity—a former teen idol who has become a witness for Christ. A popular singer and actor in the 1950s, Boone in 1969 received baptism in the Spirit. His Church of Christ congregation booted him out, but Boone, unfazed, joined the Church on the Way and was seeing people baptized in his own swimming pool. Soon afterward he portrayed evangelist David Wilkerson in the movie *The Cross and the Switchblade*.

Boone wrote the book *A New Song* (1970) to talk about the life changes since his new dependence on the Spirit. He later wrote *A Miracle a Day Keeps the Devil Away*. Boone aroused a minor controversy in 1997 when he appeared in leather garb to promote a new album, *In a Metal Mood*. Kinder critics knew that it was a publicity stunt and that the squeaky-clean singer had not changed a bit.

565. Mother Angelica (b. 1923)

There are several Christian cable networks, but the only one started by a Catholic nun is Eternal Word Television

Network, launched in 1981. Founder of Our Lady of the Angels monastery in Birmingham, Alabama, Mother Angelica's presentations focus on the "straight gospel" and intercessory prayer. She has surprised many with her fellowship with (and support from) non-Catholic charismatics. She threw out a quotable tidbit in 1995: "I'm tired of you, liberal church. You're sick."

566. Rex Humbard (b. 1919)

Alpha Rex Emmanuel Humbard was for many years head of the Cathedral of Tomorrow in Akron, Ohio, and, thanks to its television broadcasts, a familiar figure in American Christianity. The Cathedral (noted for its Cathedral Singers) and its founder had their heyday in the 1950s and 1960s, but Humbard's ministry has continued, with headquarters now in Florida. Although the Cathedral did not position itself as a Pentecostal church, Humbard's services have included prayer for the sick and anointing with oil. Humbard has evangelized frequently in Latin America.

567. Kenneth Copeland (b. 1937)

Thanks to his TV ministry, Copeland is probably one of the best-known preachers in America. He and his wife, Gloria, founded his evangelistic association in Fort Worth, Texas, in 1968. In 1973 they began publishing *The Believer's Voice of Victory*. The next year they began radio broadcasts, and in 1979 launched the daily television show that has gained them an international following. Copeland's ministry has reported many healings, and it has managed to avoid the scandals that have seemed to plague too many televangelists. Copeland's associate, Jerry Savelle, has become a prominent face in the TV broadcasts.

568. Ben Kinchlow (b. 1936)

Harvey Ben Kinchlow had been an "angry young man," deeply affected by the teachings of Black Muslim leader Malcolm X. Under the direction of John Corcoran, a white pastor, the anger gave way to a deep love for the Lord. The converted Kinchlow opened His Place for teenage runaways and, later, Christian Farms for drug and alcohol rehabilitation. He was also ordained in the AME church. But he is perhaps most famous as cohost for the *700 Club* with Pat Robertson for several years in the 1980s and 1990s.

569. John Osteen (1921–99)

Osteen was serving as a Southern Baptist minister in Houston when he received the baptism in the Spirit, occurring about the time his daughter was healed of cerebral palsy. His church charged him with heresy because of speaking in tongues, so he left and founded Lakewood Baptist Church in Houston, which has since become the charismatic Lakewood Church, with about twenty thousand members. Osteen was told by the Lord to "lift up your voice like an archangel and prophesy to my people in the valley of dry bones." Osteen published several books and was known through his television ministry.

570. Andrae Crouch (b. 1940)

One of America's best-known gospel singers and songwriters, Crouch became a Christian at the age of nine and decided to use his considerable musical gifts for the Lord. He began recording in 1971 and has appeared in concerts all over the world, as well as being a guest on secular and Christian television shows. Many of his songs are contemporary reworkings of songs he knew and loved as a child. He has won several Grammy and Dove Awards.

571. C. Morse Ward (1909–96)

Morse was a familiar radio voice for many years, beginning in 1953 when he began his stint with the Assemblies of God program *Revivaltime*. From then until 1978 he preached more than 1,300 radio sermons and wrote articles and tracts to accompany them.

AND SOME OTHER CELEBRITIES

572. John Wimber (1934–97)

The founder of the Vineyard Christian Fellowship of Anaheim, California, had been a successful jazz musician and an unbeliever. Converted in 1963, he became a pastor at a Friends (Quaker) church in California. Enrolled in a church growth course at Fuller Theological Seminary, Wimber became intrigued by the writings of C. Peter Wagner and other authors on spiritual gifts. Studying the Gospels, Wimber observed that Jesus combined His preaching with healing the sick and casting out demons. He concluded that evangelism should shift from *proclamation* (preaching in the traditional style) to *demonstration* of spiritual gifts in conjunction with preaching. Wimber believed that the miracles and phenomenal church growth in the Third World might be possible in the U.S. Wimber and his wife, Carol, began a worship and Bible study group in their home, which grew to two hundred people meeting in a high school gym. The group later connected with the Vineyard Christian Fellowship of West Los Angeles.

Wimber's initial experience with power evangelism was not positive. He preached for many months on signs and wonders, but no one in the church was healed, and many people left. Finally, feeling dejected, he prayed for a woman with a life-threatening illness, and she was healed. Many more healings followed. His church grew to 5,000 and expanded into more than 480 Vineyard churches around the U.S. and in 24 countries.

Wimber believed that the Holy Spirit enters the believer's life at conversion, and that no second work of grace is needed for empowerment. He believed that any of the spiritual gifts can potentially be manifested by any believer, as the Spirit wills, and that the gifts are not necessarily permanent possessions. Wimber became a key figure in the renewal movement. His books include *Power Evangelism, Power Healing, Power Encounters,* and *Power Points.*

573. Dennis Bennett (1917–91)

The Episcopal church is noted for its dignified worship rituals. Hardly anyone expected that a key figure in the charismatic movement would be an Episcopal minister. London-born Bennett was pastor of St. Mark's Episcopal Church in Van Nuys, California. One Sunday in 1960 he announced that he and several members were baptized in the Spirit and spoke in tongues. (An assistant minister threw off his robes and marched down the aisle as a gesture of resignation.) *Time* and *Newsweek* ran stories on the episode. Bennett's overseer, the Episcopal bishop of Los Angeles, announced a ban on speaking in tongues in churches under his authority.

Bennett moved to Seattle and transformed the inner-city St. Luke's Episcopal Church into a two-thousand-member charismatic congregation. With his wife, Rita, he formed Christian Renewal Association, a transdenominational agency for evangelization, healing, and church renewal. The two authored several books, including *The Holy Spirit and You* (1971). A much-respected figure, he is widely regarded as the lead-off man of the twentieth-century charismatic revival. (See 830 [Jean Stone Willans].)

574. C. Peter Wagner (b. 1930)

Wagner is "Mr. Church Growth," the professor of that subject at Fuller Theological Seminary in California and author of countless books and articles on growing churches. Once an understudy to church growth specialist Donald McGavran, Wagner has traveled widely (South America in particular) observing what makes churches grow or decline. He persuaded John Wimber to join Fuller's Institute of Evangelism and Church Growth, and he and Wimber taught the popular (and controversial) MC510, the signs and wonders course (see 221 [MC510]).

In 1985 he was founding president of the North American Society for Church Growth. He coined the term *Third Wave* to refer to evangelicals (like Wimber and himself) who had admired Pentecostals and charismatics from a distance but who were now willing to seek the power of the Spirit in their own ministries. His books include *Warfare Prayer, What Are We Missing?, Your Spiritual Gifts Can Help Your Church Grow, Strategies for Church Growth, Church Growth and the Whole Gospel,* and many others.

575. David Wilkerson (b. 1931)

Author of *The Cross and the Switchblade,* Wilkerson first gained fame with his 1958 trip to New York City to talk with seven young men on trial for murdering a disabled person. The court would not grant him permission to visit the men, and he was ejected from the court, gaining him a front-page story in a New York newspaper.

This experience in court made him "the guy the cops don't like," which gave him status in the eyes of New York gangs. He launched his Teen Challenge ministry, which he still heads. It reaches out to gang members and substance abusers and provides both evangelism and discipling. Many of his converts have entered the ministry.

God moves in mysterious ways: the growth of Teen Challenge and the publicity it produced gave exposure to being filled with the Spirit. Wilkerson mentioned tongues in *The Cross and the Switchblade,* which some say led to the Catholic renewal at Duquesne University. Other people who were baptized in the Spirit say that Wilkerson's book had led them to seek the experience. Wilkerson has published many other books, including *Parents on Trial*, *The Untapped Generation*, and *Rebel's Bible*.

576. Nicky Cruz (b. 1938)

Many men would be proud to have been portrayed on screen by heartthrob Erik Estrada. Puerto Rican–born Cruz was, in the movie *The Cross and the Switchblade*. He came to New York in his teens and, as the movie shows, was part of the barbarous Mau Mau gang. The movie was based on David Wilkerson's book of the same title, which told the dramatic story of Cruz's conversion, further related in Cruz's own book, *Run, Baby, Run*. Cruz had been a vicious knife fighter and had perpetrated sixteen stabbings. His conversion was an inspiration to other urban ministries reaching out to alienated youth. Cruz has been active in Wilkerson's Teen Challenge ministry.

577. David du Plessis (1905–87)

The man known as "Mr. Pentecost" was a key figure in twentieth-century Christianity but was not a household name. Born in South Africa, he received the Holy Spirit at age thirteen at a meeting led by an English evangelist. He was active in the Apostolic Faith Mission in South Africa. After some time in America, he introduced the camp meeting to South African Christianity.

He became deeply involved in the worldwide outreach of Pentecostal Christianity, an obsession throughout his life. He traveled widely, affiliated with the Assemblies of God, and worked for dialogue between Pentecostals and

Catholics. And he did a rare thing: tried to build bridges to the World Council of Churches, with its aura of liberalism. Some Pentecostals criticized such "consorting with the enemy," just as they criticized the way he urged new Spirit-led believers to stay in their own denominations rather than migrating to Pentecostal denominations. But many believers applauded du Plessis' willingness to be a sensible, sane ambassador for the Pentecostal movement.

578. Demos Shakarian (1913–93)

Born in Armenia, he lived past childhood because a Pentecostal prophet warned his family of the coming Armenian holocaust. His family fled to America, and not surprisingly, he grew up in an Armenian Pentecostal church and became a Christian at a young age. He received the baptism of the Spirit and was also miraculously healed of a hearing problem. His sister, seriously injured in an automobile accident, was expected to die, but Dr. Charles Price laid hands on her, and (as X rays revealed) her crushed bones were completely restored.

Shakarian was a highly successful businessman, but also a noted supporter of such evangelists as Oral Roberts. His most notable achievement was the founding of the Full Gospel Business Men's Fellowship in 1951. Roberts was present at its first meeting and asked the Lord to anoint the group and make it a force for spreading the gospel. Shakarian asked the Lord to lead him to the individuals who would give personal testimonies in the meetings. The Fellowship (see 140) has indeed proved to be an effective means for reaching people with the Lord's Word.

579. Kenneth Hagin (b. 1917)

As author Hagin reports in *I Went to Hell*, he literally did. In 1933, during one ten-minute period his vital signs failed three times, each time leading him to see hell. The event resulted in his conversion, and a year later, he was healed of his ailments. The former invalid was baptized in the Spirit in 1937 and began a Pentecostal ministry in Texas. Later he had several visions of Christ, in one of which he was granted the power to pray effectively for people who were sick. Hagin wrote that under the power of the Spirit, he has been enabled to know things supernaturally about people and places. Sometimes while preaching he would see visions concerning a person in the congregation.

Hagin settled his ministry headquarters in Oklahoma, and he founded Rhema Bible Training Center. There are probably sixteen thousand Rhema graduates in the world, many of them ministers. He hosted a daily radio program, *Faith Seminar of the Air*, broadcast nationwide, with perhaps three million listeners. He has written several books, including *He Gave Gifts Unto Man, How You Can Be Led by the Spirit of God*, and *I Believe in Visions*.

580. Harald Bredesen (b. 1918)

A noted speaker, Bredesen was ordained a Lutheran in 1944 but baptized in the Spirit at a Pentecostal camp in 1946. His Lutheran superiors would not accept his resignation from the denomination, so he remained within that church but not as a pastor. Later, in 1957, he became pastor of a Dutch Reformed church in New York and conducted a charismatic prayer meeting.

Bredesen supposedly coined the term *charismatic renewal*, which has since passed into common usage. He has traveled widely, often under the auspices of the Full Gospel Business Men's Fellowship. Bredesen retired from his New York church pastorate and pastored at Trinity Christian Center in Victoria, British Columbia, Canada, for several years. He continues as a popular and effective charismatic speaker in the U.S. and abroad.

581. Leon-Joseph Suenens (1904–96)

Suenens, who was made a cardinal in 1962, was probably the highest-ranking Catholic to be actively involved in the charismatic movement. He had participated in the planning of the historic Vatican II Council (see 41), which aided in the Catholic church's openness to the renewal movement. He came into contact with Catholic charismatics in the U.S. in 1972 and hosted a conference in his native Belgium to evaluate the movement, which resulted in *Theological and Pastoral Guidelines on the Catholic Charismatic Renewal* (1974). In effect he was for many years the middleman between the Vatican and the Catholic renewal movement. He published several books, including *A New Pentecost?*, *Ways of the Spirit, Renewal and the Powers of Darkness,* and *Come, Holy Spirit.*

582. Chuck Smith (b. 1927)

Smith was the well-known pastor of the famous Calvary Chapel (see 69) in Costa Mesa, California. In the hippie era the church became known for its outreach to hippies and drug abusers and other societal dropouts. Smith received media attention for his baptisms at the California beaches and will probably be forever identified with the Jesus People movement of the early 1970s. He is the author of *Charisma vs. Charismania* and *The Reproducers: New Life for Thousands.*

583. George Carey

Britain's archbishop of Canterbury is head of the Church of England and, in a broad sense, father figure to the various Anglican churches around the globe (churches that have descended from the Church of England, that is). Carey became archbishop in 1991 and marks a breakthrough, the Church of England's first charismatic head. This is perhaps appropriate, since the church's only real growth in recent years has been among its charismatics.

584. John Paul II

The Polish cardinal who became pope in 1978 has given a warm reception to Catholic charismatics. In 1981 he addressed a gathering of their leaders in Rome and stated that priests should adopt a "welcoming attitude" toward the charismatic renewal.

585. Paul VI (1897–1978)

Pope Paul watched several dramatic developments in the Catholic church, including the Vatican II conference in the early 1960s and the Catholic charismatic movement in the 1970s. He received warmly the leaders of the charismatic conference held in 1973 and gave an encouraging address to another charismatic conference in 1975.

THE EVANGELISTS

586. Morris Cerullo (b. 1931)

The Christian woman who gave young Morris Cerullo a New Testament at the Orthodox Jewish orphanage where he was raised got a reward for her action: she was dismissed. But at age fourteen he was led by divine guidance to find this woman, who took him into her home. After attending church he was baptized in the Spirit and was ordained by the Assemblies of God. By 1956 he had a healing ministry and was associated with the Voice of Healing organization. He founded his own organization, World Evangelism, based in San Diego, California. He is a well-known evangelist in the U.S. and abroad.

587. Lester Sumrall (b. 1913)

Sumrall experienced a divine healing from tuberculosis and soon after began preaching. Ordained by the Assemblies of God (though he later became an independent), he evangelized around the world, including a revival campaign in

Canada while on his honeymoon. He was particularly effective in the Philippines, with thousands of conversions and the founding of what was then the largest church in the country. In 1963 he settled in South Bend, Indiana, where he pastors the large Christian Center Cathedral of Praise. He purchased several radio stations that he organized as World Harvest Radio International. His many books include *Gifts and Ministries of the Holy Spirit.*

588. John Bertolucci (b. 1937)

He is one of the most notable figures in the Catholic renewal movement. Born in Albany, New York, Bertolucci, a priest, taught in Catholic schools for years and, in 1969, was baptized in the Spirit at a charismatic meeting. By the 1970s his bishop recognized his gifts as a popular evangelist. Bertolucci has taught theology at the University of Steubenville in Ohio and established the St. Francis Association for Catholic Evangelism (FACE) to support his radio and TV ministry. He has written several books, including *On Fire with the Spirit* and *Healing: God's Work Among Us.*

589. Warren Black (b. 1927)

Can a stammering man preach the gospel? Black stammered badly and suffered from a lung condition and a hernia. God healed him of all these conditions, and Black went on to a healing and counseling ministry. He worked for the Nazarene Publishing House and sang in the Showers of Blessing radio choir for the Nazarene radio shows. Reared in the Church of the Nazarene, Black is now an officer in the Wesleyan Holiness Charismatic Fellowship.

590. Gerald Derstine (b. 1928)

Like many pastors who have had Pentecostal experiences, Gerald Derstine, a Mennonite, was asked to leave his church. But he had good reason to believe in the power of the Spirit: he had been healed of stuttering shortly after his conversion. When he and several of his church members reported Pentecostal experiences, he lost his pastorate in Minnesota. He became an evangelist with Gospel Crusade, a nondenominational organization, and later founded the Christian Retreat Center in Bradenton, Florida.

591. Tom Rees (1911–70)

English evangelist Rees has been sadly forgotten today. Converted in his teens, he was active in evangelism and worked with poor youth, organizing camps for boys from the London slums. His evangelistic rallies in the huge Albert Hall in London drew thousands and made many converts. Rees said of the Spirit, "On the very day you committed your life to Jesus Christ, God sealed you by giving you the gift of his Holy Spirit. Every child of God bears the same seal, and is indwelt by the same Holy Spirit."

592. Richard W. Culpepper (b. 1921)

The Spirit can come upon a person anywhere—even in a haystack. Culpepper was baptized in the Spirit while stationed in England during World War II. He happened to be with a group of Pentecostal soldiers in a haystack at the time. After the war he became a healing evangelist. With several other men he formed the World Convention of Deliverance Evangelists. Culpepper's ministry supports missionaries in Africa, India, the Philippines, and Jamaica.

593. David C. K. Watson (1933–84)

A gifted English evangelist, Watson was baptized in the Spirit while serving a church in Cambridge. In a period when Church of England congregations were dwindling in size, he saw his churches grow. He reached out to college students and enlisted creative artists in his evangelistic campaigns. He died of cancer in 1984, after the archbishop of Canterbury had visited him to thank him for his contributions to Christianity in England. He wrote several popular books, including *I Believe in Evangelism, I Believe in the Church, One in the Spirit,* and the story of his battle with cancer, *Fear No Evil.*

594. Percy S. Brewster (1908–80)

The London-born Brewster was converted under the ministry of evangelist George Jeffreys (see 512). He had a vision of a hall filled with people, and at a crusade in Neath, Wales, he found that the crusade hall was the one he had seen in the vision. The crusade, and others, led to the establishment of new churches. He became pastor in 1939 of the large Cardiff City Temple, where he ministered until 1974.

He also conducted crusades throughout Britain and was a popular speaker in the U.S. and elsewhere.

595. Robert W. Schambach (b. 1926)

A healing evangelist, Schambach was an associate of A. A. Allen (see 231) but in 1959 began his own ministry, Schambach Miracle Revivals. Despite changes in American culture, he has stuck firmly to old-style revivalism, using a tent in his meetings.

596. Ray H. Hughes (b. 1924)

A pastor and pastor's son in the Church of God (Cleveland, Tennessee), Hughes is a respected evangelist as well as an executive in the CG. He spoke at a Pentecostal youth rally held at the Hollywood Bowl in 1946 and has spoken more than once at meetings of British Pentecostals in London's Royal Albert Hall. His books include *Pentecostal Preaching, The Outpouring of the Spirit,* and *What Is Pentecost?*

597. Herbert Mjorud (b. 1910)

While pastoring a Lutheran church in Alaska, Mjorud experienced miracles of healing, and at the parish of Dennis Bennett (see 573) he received the gift of tongues. His zeal for the charismatic message did not go over well with his denomination (the American Lutheran Church), which refused to renew his credentials as an evangelist. He formed an independent ministry and in 1968 toured the world as an evangelist, focusing on the Asian nation of Sri Lanka.

Expected to die of cancer in 1981, he was miraculously healed.

598. Jim Kaseman (b. 1943)

Kaseman was an alcoholic with suicidal tendencies before he met the Lord at a Bible study in 1972. Since then he has had a remarkable career as a pastor and evangelist and, perhaps most notable, as a smuggler of Christian books into the Soviet Union when the practice was illegal. Kaseman helped establish numerous churches on his evangelistic travels in the Dakotas and Minnesota, then he took the word of the Lord to, of all places, Finland. He relates that in 1982 God told him to arrange the translation of Christian books and smuggle them into Russia.

599. H. Richard Hall (b. 1920)

Hall is a healing evangelist of Pentecostal background but has positioned himself as a sort of renegade, uncomfortable in any denomination. Like many mavericks, he started his own association, the United Christian Ministerial Association, for issuing credentials to independent ministers and churches. Unique among Pentecostal evangelists during the hippie era, Hall did attempt to relate to the alienated youth subculture.

600. Clifton Erickson (b. 1915)

A noted healing evangelist, Erickson states that his baptism in the Spirit came about in a curious way. Four years after his conversion, the Lord revealed to him that he would be baptized in the Spirit at a specific time, following three days of prayer and fasting. It happened exactly as prophesied. God also revealed that he would have a ministry of healing and miracles. Both he and his wife experienced divine healing, and when Oral Roberts laid hands on him, he felt the healing power that would come out through his ministry. Erickson, born to Norwegian immigrants, has had a worldwide ministry, notably in Chile, where he drew a crowd of 75,000, and in the Philippines, site of another amazing revival.

601. Richard Vinyard (b. 1913)

While an Assemblies of God pastor in Kansas City, Vinyard wondered why his own ministry had not borne the fruit that visiting evangelist William Branham bore. Vinyard claims he was awakened early one morning and told by God that he would be a healer. Reporting this to his church, several people were healed, and Vinyard took his healing ministry across the U.S. and abroad.

602. Tommy Tyson (b. 1922)

A well-known evangelist in recent years, Tyson was and is a United Methodist, though his ministry cuts across denominational lines. Baptized in the Spirit in 1952, he has traveled widely but has always been a North Carolina man, living now at the Aqueduct, a Christian conference center at Chapel Hill.

603. Francesco Toppi (b. 1928)

Yes, Italy has long been a Catholic country, but Protestants have been active in evangelism there. One of the most active is Toppi, who was ordained in the Assemblies of God (AG) in 1949. A noted evangelist, Toppi became head of the Italian AG, supervising more than nine hundred churches along with radio stations and other ministries. The Italian AG is the largest Protestant denomination in Italy.

604. Edgar J. Trout (1912–68)

An English Methodist lay preacher, Trout was baptized in the Spirit in 1958, afterward forming the All for Christ Fellowship and spreading the Pentecostal message over Britain. Many miracles were associated with Trout's revivals.

605. Don Stewart (b. 1939)

Stewart was an associate evangelist with A. A. Allen (see 231) and, sometime after Allen's death, successor to Allen's ministry, which is now the Don Stewart Evangelistic Association. The ministry is a huge operation, and Stewart is known for his emphasis on both healing and prosperity. He has published several books, including *Fakes, Frauds, and Fools.*

606. Argue family

A. H. Argue (1868–1959), a Canadian, experienced the baptism of the Spirit while in Chicago. He became an evangelist in the U.S. and Canada, and his son and daughter were also noted evangelists. Watson Argue (1904–85) filled the pulpit at Angelus Temple when Aimee Semple McPherson mysteriously disappeared in 1926. He pastored two large and dynamic churches, both named Calvary Temple, one in Winnipeg, Manitoba, the other in Seattle, Washington. His sister, Zelma Argue (1900–1980), traveled as an evangelist with her father and was a noted writer, publishing *Contending for the Faith*, *Garments of Strength*, *Practical Christian Living*, and many other books and articles.

607. Frederick H. Squire (1904–62)

A healer and evangelist in England, Squire was with the Assemblies of God (AG). He eventually left the AG and formed his many converts into a new denomination, the Full Gospel Testimony. This Pentecostal group eventually disbanded, but Squire's International Bible Training Institute continues.

608. Vernon Byrd (b. 1931)

Byrd, a pastor in the black African Methodist Episcopal (AME) Church, began preaching at age thirteen and was ordained at seventeen. He became an AME bishop in 1984. Baptized in the Spirit at a Kathryn Kuhlman meeting, he has become a noted evangelist and is one of the key figures in the black charismatic movement.

609. Robert DeWeese (b. 1910)

The most noted associate of Oral Roberts (other than his son, Richard) is probably DeWeese, an evangelist who was active in the International Church of the Foursquare Gospel. He became a manager and afternoon warm-up speaker for Oral Roberts crusades and is now a trustee for the Oral Roberts Evangelistic Association. He and his wife, Charlotte, have attested to divine healing from leukemia and heart troubles.

610. Happy Hunters

Charles Hunter (b. 1920) and his wife, Frances (b. 1916), are known for their "healing explosions" in the U.S. and abroad. Both were from the Church of God (Anderson, Indiana), a non-Pentecostal denomination, but both experienced baptism in the Holy Spirit. They have coauthored several books.

611. Little David

David Dalillo Walker (b. 1934) was the son of evangelists, and he and they had experienced miraculous healings. Healed of blindness that had been caused by an eye infection, he was baptized in the Spirit, leading to his preaching ministry that began at age nine. He took his healing ministry through the western U.S., Mexico, France, and England.

where he was preaching at age fourteen at the Albert Hall. He founded a church at age seventeen and served as its pastor, but was soon back on the road evangelizing.

612. W. V. Grant Sr. (1913–83)

Evangelists and faith-healers are often accused of trying to bilk followers out of their money. That was hardly the case with Grant, who was already a successful businessman when he became an Assemblies of God minister and healer in the 1940s. Grant associated with the Voice of Healing organization and was a noted author on healing, with such popular books as *Raising the Dead, Power to Detect Demons,* and *Must I Pray for a Miracle?* He launched the *Voice of Deliverance* magazine in 1962, and it had a huge circulation.

613. Tommy Lee Osborn (b. 1923)

In the 1960s, healing evangelist Osborn looked more like the young people he was trying to reach than the typical "starchy" evangelist. He had already been a healing evangelist for many years, having heard voices at a William Branham healing service telling him, "You can do that." In 1948 he and his wife, Daisy, began their ministry in Jamaica, then went back to the U.S., where they worked with William Branham, F. F. Bosworth, and Gordon Lindsay. They led highly successful crusades in Puerto Rico, Cuba, Chile, Guatemala, and Venezuela, where Catholic priests and physicians arranged to have him arrested for witchcraft. The opposition did not slow them down, however. They also held meetings with thousands of converts in the Far East. Tommy Lee also established the Association for Native Evangelism to help indigenous peoples spread the gospel. His Osborn Foundation continues to produce tapes and literature to spread the gospel.

614. Ralph DiOrio (b. 1930)

From an Italian family, DiOrio was serving as a priest in Massachusetts in 1976 when he came in contact with the healing services led by another priest, Edward McDonough. He felt God's power for healing flowing through him, leading to a healing ministry in his parish, which became known as the Apostolate of Prayer for Healing Evangelism. Involved full-time in this Catholic-approved ministry, he has told his story in such books as *Called to Heal*.

PLANTING AND MAINTAINING THE CHURCHES

615. James H. Brown (1912–87)

Brown was a Presbyterian pastor and a graduate of Princeton Theological Seminary, but like many mainline Christians, his conversion experience occurred in a Pentecostal setting. He was baptized in the Spirit sometime in the 1950s, and thereafter his Presbyterian church in Parkesburg, Pennsylvania, was a center of charismatic renewal. It became known for its prayer and praise services

held on Saturday evenings, and the church drew people
from around the world.

616. Howard P. Courtney (b. 1911)

In the International Church of the Foursquare Gospel
founded by Aimee Semple McPherson, Courtney was the
first nonfamily member to be the head. After Sister Aimee's
death, her son, Rolf, headed the church, while Courtney
was general supervisor and also copastor of the huge
Angelus Temple. Courtney helped the church affiliate with
the Pentecostal Fellowship of North America as well as the
National Association of Evangelicals. He resigned as general
supervisor of the denomination but served as the temple's
senior pastor until 1981.

617. William E. Fuller (1875–1958)

Jesus grew up in a working-class home, and so did many
noted church leaders. Fuller was the son of South Carolina
sharecroppers but became a leader in the Fire-Baptized
Holiness Church, an interracial group that elected Fuller to
its executive board. He was a skilled leader, organizing
more than fifty churches in South Carolina and Georgia.
For some reason Fuller chose to organize a separate black
denomination, which became known as the Colored Fire-
Baptized Holiness Church. This group moved its headquarters to Atlanta and took the (even longer) name
Fire-Baptized Holiness Church of God of the Americas.

618. Howard Goss (1883–1964)

The Spirit's movements are unpredictable. Howard Goss received the baptism of the Spirit while riding a train in 1906. For a while he was an associate of Charles Parham, then split from him and became an evangelist and church planter in the Southwest and Midwest. With E. N. Bell, Goss organized the Assemblies of God (AG) in 1914. Later Goss identified with the Oneness movement (see 216) and left the AG. As many Oneness followers formed the United Pentecostal Church (see 163) in 1945, Goss became its general superintendent. With his wife, Ethel, he wrote *The Winds of God* (1958), a valuable history of the Pentecostal movement.

619. Ivan Q. Spencer (1888–1970)

While in seminary, Spencer fell ill with typhoid fever; he was instantly healed while returning home on a train. He received the baptism of the Holy Spirit in 1913 and became an Assemblies of God pastor. Later he founded the Elim Bible Institute in New York State to train Pentecostal ministers.

620. Rolf McPherson (b. 1913)

He is the son and successor of Aimee Semple McPherson and her International Church of the Foursquare Gospel (see 474 and 151). He became vice president of the ICFG in 1944, the year of his mother's death, and became president after that. He proved to be a skilled administrator, and the ICFG grew from 492 churches in 1944 to more than 12,000 by the 1980s, with more than a million adherents worldwide. The ICFG joined with the National Association of Evangelicals and the Pentecostal Fellowship of North America, and McPherson served on the boards of both. He retired as president of ICFG in 1988 but remains as a member of its board of directors.

621. Joseph A. Synan (1905–84)

From a family of thirteen children, Synan was converted at a Virginia tent revival in 1921. He became a pastor in the Pentecostal Holiness Church (PHC) and founded churches in eastern Virginia. He became the PHC's general superintendent in 1945, and the PHC grew considerably during his years as its head. Vinson Synan (see 646) is one of his sons.

622. Milton Tomlinson (1906–95)

"Tony," youngest son of A. J. Tomlinson (see 530), was baptized in the Spirit in 1927. His father, head of the Church of God of Prophecy (CGP), died in 1943, and a tongues message told the CGP overseers to "bring forth the younger son" as the new head. Some CGP leaders compared him to Joshua taking up where Moses left off.

623. Nathaniel A. Urshan (b. 1920)

He was son of the Persian evangelist Andrew D. Urshan, but, unlike his Iranian-born father, he was born in the U.S.

Nathaniel pastored the huge Calvary Temple in Indianapolis and was a speaker on the United Pentecostal Church's *Harvestime* radio show. He became the general superintendent of the UPC in 1978.

624. Clint Utterbach (b. 1931) and Sarah Utterbach (b. 1937)

The Utterbachs founded the Redeeming Love Christian Center in their home, moving to its present location in Nanuet, New York, in 1985. It is one of the largest independent black charismatic fellowships in the eastern U.S. Not surprisingly (considering their connections with Kenneth Copeland and Kenneth Hagin), they stress prosperity (financial as well as spiritual), solid family life, and teaching based on the Bible.

625. Juan L. Lugo (1890–1984)

Born in Puerto Rico, Lugo was converted in his youth and began his ministry in the mainland U.S. With the support of an Anglo church in Los Angeles he returned to Puerto Rico. He and his associates established eight Assemblies of God congregations in two years. The churches and those that followed eventually adopted the name Iglesia de Dios Pentecostal (Pentecostal Church of God).

626. P. H. Walker (1901–75)

Born in North Dakota, Paul Haven Walker began his ministry in 1919 with the Church of God (Cleveland,

Tennessee) and planted churches in several states and in ten mission fields on four continents. He published his autobiography, *Paths of a Pioneer*, and *The Baptism with the Holy Ghost and the Evidence*. His son, Paul Laverne Walker, is general overseer of the Church of God.

627. Joseph Wannenmacher (1895–1989) and Helen Wannenmacher (1890–1985)

Joseph had tuberculosis in his youth but received healing and the baptism of the Spirit at a Pentecostal meeting in 1917. He frequently appeared at revival meetings, giving his testimony and playing the violin, at which he excelled. Born in Hungary, he helped establish a Hungarian church in Milwaukee, with him and his wife leading services in Hungarian and English. The church grew into Calvary Assembly of God.

628. Ralph Wilkerson (b. 1927)

The megachurch Melodyland Christian Center was founded in 1961 by Wilkerson, an Assemblies of God pastor. Wilkerson saw the church grow tremendously, with ministries such as a delinquency prevention hot line, a theology school, and a college. He has published several books, including *Satellites of the Spirit*, *Success from Stress*, and *Loneliness: The World's Number One Killer*.

629. Myrtle Beall (1896–1979)

If Christians are to wear the "whole armor of God" (Eph. 6), then a church might be considered an armory. This is what Myrtle Beall called her three-thousand-seat Bethesda Missionary Temple in Detroit, completed in 1949. The armory was a center for the Latter Rain movement (see 224).

630. Elmer Erickson (1896–1980)

Erickson was from a Swedish family that settled in Wisconsin. The entire family converted to Pentecostalism during his childhood, and they began hosting Pentecostal meetings in the home. He became an Assemblies of God minister but had strong feelings about local churches holding to their independence, so he organized a loose affiliation known as the Independent Assemblies of God, now known as the Fellowship of Christian Assemblies. He pastored a large Pentecostal fellowship, the Duluth Gospel Tabernacle.

631. Bob Weiner (b. 1948)

Weiner is best known as founder of the Maranatha Campus Ministries (see 197), at one time associated with more than 150 colleges. Weiner is also founder of World Ambassadors, a ministry for teaching foreign students in U.S. colleges. His TV program *Forerunner* was broadcast via satellite.

632. Howard Conatser (1926–78)

There *are* charismatics in the Southern Baptist Convention. Howard Conatser was one of the most prominent, being pastor of the enormous Beverly Hills Church in Dallas. His ministry received criticism from the venerable W. A. Criswell of Dallas's First Baptist Church, but Conatser's church grew anyway. The church grew so large that for a time it held services in the local Bronco Bowl. Conatser was a featured speaker at the Southern Baptist charismatics' first national conference in 1976. After his death, the Beverly Hills Church left the Southern Baptist Convention.

633. T. F. Zimmerman (1912–91)

The gap between Pentecostals and evangelicals has narrowed considerably from the early days. One of the "narrowers" was Thomas Fletcher Zimmerman, for many years the general superintendent of the Assemblies of God and also the first Pentecostal to serve as president of the National Association of Evangelicals. More important, during his twenty-six years as superintendent of the Assemblies of God, the denomination more than doubled in size. He was one of the founders of the National Religious Broadcasters (see 803), and he had a background in radio as host of the weekly program *Sermons in Song*.

AUTHORS AND TEACHERS

634. Jamie Buckingham (1932–92)

James William Buckingham II was one of the best-known Baptist charismatic leaders in the U.S., but admitted that his earlier life as a pastor had its sinful moments, including sexual immorality, which led to his being ousted from two churches. He attended a Full Gospel Business Men's Fellowship meeting and there experienced the filling of the Spirit. Following that, he formed the Tabernacle Church in Melbourne, Florida, where he was senior pastor. The nondenominational church—called "the Tab" by locals—has a membership of four thousand. Buckingham was a noted author and columnist, known for *Power for Living, Summer of Miracles,* and other books.

635. Merlin Carothers (b. 1924)

Prison to Praise, Carothers's 1970 book, is still widely read among charismatics, and on its initial publication it focused the public's attention on praise as a key factor in renewal. Carothers was a pastor and an army chaplain in Vietnam. His other books include *Praise Works* and *Bringing Heaven into Hell.*

636. A. W. Tozer (1897–1963)

A noted devotional writer, Tozer was affiliated with the Christian and Missionary Alliance (CMA). *The Divine Conquest* was one of his many excellent books. Like many sensitive Christians, Tozer was appalled at how churches neglected teaching about the Holy Spirit: "The idea of the Spirit held by the average church member is so vague as to be nearly nonexistent."

637. Judith C. Tydings (b. 1935)

Married and mother of four, she was baptized in the Spirit around 1966 and became a key figure among Catholic charismatics. She and Edith Difato started the charismatic prayer group that evolved into the Mother of God community. True to her Catholic heritage, she is the author of *Gathering a People: Catholic Saints in Charismatic Perspective*.

638. Gordon Lindsay (1906–73)

Gordon Lindsay was an associate of healing evangelist John G. Lake (see 544) and then began his own ministries in California and Oregon. He joined the William Branham campaign as manager and began publishing the magazine *Voice of Healing*. Branham did not approve of the magazine reporting on the work of other evangelists, so he and Lindsay split. Lindsay continued the magazine in order to report on and encourage healing movements throughout the U.S.

In addition to working on the magazine, which was published until 1967, Lindsay became a historian and leading author on the healing movement. He combined writing and editing with various ministries all under the umbrella of Voice of Healing, based in Dallas. The various enterprises were reorganized as Christ for the Nations, which is also the name of the magazine published since 1967. Christ for the Nations Institute opened in 1970 with a view toward spiritual formation in the Pentecostal and charismatic movements. Gordon died in 1973, and his son Dennis has taken his place as head of the institute.

639. George M. Flattery (b. 1936)

Flattery serves the Assemblies of God headquarters as the denomination's president of the International Correspondence Institute (ICI), a means of receiving theological education via mail. The ICI offers a college degree in ministerial training as well as programs in evangelism. It is probably one of the world's best-known programs in theological training by extension.

640. Vep Ellis (1917–88)

Vesphew Benton Ellis was pastor of the Harvest Temple Church of God (Cleveland, Tennessee) in Largo, Florida, near Clearwater, a ministry that included TV and radio broadcasts. He had been a music director for Oral Roberts crusades, but is probably best known as a songwriter, publishing more than five hundred in his lifetime. He was also a noted singer, recording several albums and singles.

641. Russell P. Spittler (b. 1931)

A noted Bible scholar, Spittler has served as professor of New Testament at Fuller Theological Seminary and has published many books, including *The Church*, *God the Father*, and *Perspectives on the New Pentecostalism*.

642. Ira Stanphill (1914–93)

Songwriters are, in some ways, more influential in the long run than preachers, for their songs live on. Stanphill, who wrote both words and music, was one of the best-known songwriters in the gospel tradition, being the author of "Happiness Is the Lord," "Room at the Cross," "I Know Who Holds Tomorrow," "Mansion Over the Hilltop," and other favorites. His autobiography is *This Side of Heaven*.

643. William W. Menzies (b. 1931)

Menzies is a respected teacher and author in the Assemblies of God (AG). His 1971 book *Anointed to Serve*, a history of the AG, is an adaptation of his doctoral dissertation at the University of Iowa. He has also published *Bible Doctrines: A Pentecostal Perspective*, *Understanding the Times of Christ*, and *Understanding Our Doctrine*.

644. Watson Early Mills (b. 1939)

A respected scholar, Mills is not part of the renewal movement, but his many books have furthered Christian understanding of the movement. Among his books are *Charismatic Religion in Modern Research*, *A Theological/ Exegetical Approach to Glossolalia*, and *Speaking in Tongues: A Classified Bibliography*. He is Southern Baptist by affiliation.

645. Robert Earl Cooley (b. 1930)

Archaeology is not a field where Pentecostals have made much of an impression, but Cooley is both an Assemblies of God minister and a respected archaeologist. He has taught archaeology at several colleges and was the first Pentecostal elected president of the Evangelical Theological Society.

646. Vinson Synan (b. 1934)

A pastor in the Pentecostal Holiness Church, Synan wrote a history of the denomination, *The Old-Time Power*. He is even better known for *The Holiness-Pentecostal Movement in the United States* and also such lay-level books as *Charismatic Bridges, Azusa Street,* and *The Twentieth-Century Pentecostal Explosion*.

647. G. H. Montgomery (1903–66)

Ghostwriters have received recognition in recent years, and Montgomery is now known as the author of most of Oral Roberts's many books. Roberts hired him in 1952, both men being members of the Pentecostal Holiness Church at that time. He left Roberts in 1961 and became editor of the *Christian Challenge,* causing some controversy with articles that criticized certain aspects of the healing movement. Under his own name, Montgomery published *Practical Holiness* and *After Armageddon—What?*

648. James D. G. Dunn (b. 1939)

A Scot, Dunn is the author of several notable books, including *Jesus and the Spirit, The Evidence for Jesus,* and his commentary on Acts. But he is best known for his doctoral dissertation, *Baptism in the Holy Spirit,* which is required reading for all scholars interested in the subject. Dunn claimed that his book was intended to introduce pastors and scholars to the most distinctive item of Pentecostal teaching, baptism in the Spirit. Although the book is hardly anti-Pentecostal, it challenges the belief that baptism in the Spirit is an event subsequent to salvation. Some Pentecostal authors responded with books of their own, encouraging a lively debate about this vital subject.

649. Robert A. Walker (b. 1912)

Walker was founding editor of the Inter-Varsity Christian Fellowship's *HIS Magazine* and for more than forty years edited *Christian Life,* an evangelical-charismatic monthly. In 1987 it merged with the renewal magazine *Charisma.*

650. Howard M. Ervin (b. 1915)

Like David du Plessis, Ervin has been a key figure in the dialogue between Roman Catholics and Pentecostals. But he is best known as an author of several books on the charismatic and Pentecostal experiences, including *Spirit Baptism: A Biblical Investigation* and *This Which Ye See and Hear.* He is a widely respected scholar and taught for many years at Oral Roberts University.

651. Robert C. Frost (b. 1926)

No, not the New England poet, but a scientist who, much to his surprise, became a noted author and teacher on the Spirit-filled life. Frost has published such books as *Set My Spirit Free, Overflowing Life,* and *Aglow with the Spirit,* and he has taught at several colleges, including Oral Roberts University.

652. Michael C. Harper (b. 1931)

Ordained in the Church of England, Harper served at one of England's best-known evangelical churches, All Souls, Langham Place, under its famous minister-author John Stott. In 1963 Harper received baptism in the Spirit and the gift of tongues, and afterward he became a major figure in the renewal movement in the Church of England. He resigned from All Souls and became general secretary of the Fountain Trust. He left the Church of England in 1995 and affiliated with the Orthodox church. He has been a globe-trotting speaker but is probably better known as the author of many books, including *Power for the Body of Christ, Spiritual Warfare,* and *Let My People Grow.*

653. Gordon Fee (b. 1934)

Fee is a respected New Testament scholar, having taught at Gordon-Conwell Seminary and authored such books as *How to Read the Bible for All It's Worth* and *God's Empowering Presence,* as well as scholarly Bible commentaries. He is also an ordained Assemblies of God minister and a dedicated

Pentecostal with a deep commitment to the Spirit-led Christian life. He and his wife are active in overseas missions.

654. John Sherrill (b. 1923) and Elizabeth Sherrill (b. 1928)

Sometimes our jobs lead us to unexpected places. John Sherrill, editor with the popular *Guideposts* magazine in the 1960s, asked Harald Bredesen to write an article on speaking in tongues. It grew too large for an article, and Sherrill became Bredesen's ghostwriter for a book on the subject. It became the popular book *They Speak with Other Tongues* (1964), and somewhere in the process Sherrill was baptized in the Spirit. John and his wife, Elizabeth, became notable ghostwriters for several other charismatic best-sellers, including David Wilkerson's *The Cross and the Switchblade*, Brother Andrew's *God's Smuggler*, and Corrie ten Boom's *The Hiding Place*.

655. Leanne Payne (b. 1932)

Having experienced a healing, Payne is noted for her healing ministry, working through Pastoral Care Ministries, founded in Milwaukee in 1982. Her books include *Real Presence, Crisis in Masculinity*, and *The Broken Image: Restoring Personal Wholeness Through Healing Prayer*.

656. Barbara Leahy Shlemon (b. 1936)

Known for her healing ministry, she received the baptism of the Spirit in 1965 and, working with Francis McNutt, began a healing ministry. For several years she edited the *Journal of Christian Healing* and authored such books as *Healing Prayer* and *Healing the Hidden Self.*

657. Betty Malz (b. 1929)

My Glimpse of Eternity, Betty Malz's first book, spoke of her death experience (clinically dead for twenty-eight minutes and in a coma for more than a month). The book was a best-seller, published in several languages. She has also written *Touching the Unseen World, Prayers That Are Answered, Angels Watching Over Me,* and other books. She is a popular conference speaker.

658. Catherine Marshall (1914–83)

Her books *A Man Called Peter* and *Christy* were phenomenal best-sellers. The first book was a biography of her first husband, the noted Presbyterian pastor Peter Marshall, who died in 1949. She worked for *Christian Herald* magazine for a time and for *Guideposts* after marrying its editor in 1959. She and her second husband founded Chosen Books, a Christian publisher.

While married to Peter Marshall, Catherine was stricken with tuberculosis. She had a vision of Jesus and was miraculously healed.

659. John Wright Follette (1883–1966)

Some people have accused Christians, particularly charismatics and Pentecostals, of being antiart. That could not be said of Follette, who was a poet, painter, and musician. He was a noted speaker at Assemblies of God gatherings and also a teacher, but is best remembered for such books as *Broken Bread*, *A Christmas Wreath*, and *This Wonderful Venture Called Christian Living*.

660. Agnes Sanford (1897–1982)

After dealing with depression for many years, she claimed that she was divinely healed of it and that she had the gift of healing. In 1947 she published *The Healing Light*, which became a best-seller. Sometime around 1953 she believed she had been greatly empowered by the Spirit, receiving the gift of tongues. She and her husband, an Episcopal minister, opened the School of Pastoral Care, hosting conferences on healing for ministers and medical workers. Her books include *The Healing Gifts of the Spirit* and *The Healing Power of the Bible*.

661. Walter J. Hollenweger (b. 1927)

An ordained pastor in the Swiss Reformed Church, he is a noted author and expert on missions. He has written extensively on the growth of charismatic and Pentecostal churches across the globe and argues that the movements succeed when they focus on spiritual renewal rather than on maintaining their organizational structures—in other words, when they lose their emphasis on the work of the Spirit and focus instead on themselves as institutions that have to be maintained. Among his books is *Pentecostalism: Origins and Developments Worldwide* (1997).

662. Stanley M. Horton (b. 1916)

The Pentecostal and charismatic tradition is better known for its preachers than its theologians, but it has in this century produced some notable theological scholars. Horton is one. Ordained in the Assemblies of God in 1946, Horton jumped through the right hoops in education, taking degrees at Harvard, the University of California, and several other schools. He has taught since 1978 at the Assemblies of God Theological Seminary in Springfield, Missouri. He has written numerous books, including *Into All Truth* and *What the Bible Says About the Holy Spirit*.

663. Thomas A. Smail (b. 1928)

Ordained in the Church of Scotland, Smail received the baptism of the Spirit under the ministry of Dennis Bennett. He became head of the Fountain Trust and edited *Renewal* and, later, *Theological Renewal*. While he is committed to charismatic renewal, he has insisted on building a solid theological foundation for spiritual revival.

664. Carl Brumback (1917–87)

The Oneness movement in Pentecostalism has caused numerous splits and controversies. Brumback, a Pentecostal dedicated to traditional teaching on the Trinity, authored *God in Three Persons* (1959), a widely read response to the Oneness movement. Like most Pentecostals, Brumback opposed the Oneness insistence on baptizing people in the name of Jesus only. He also published *What Meaneth This?*, a defense of the Pentecostal movement.

665. Charles E. Capps (b. 1934)

Capps wrote the popular book *The Tongue, a Creative Force* (1976), which reflects his ties to Kenneth Hagin, Kenneth Copeland, and other Faith Movement leaders. His book carries the Faith Movement's basic teaching that what the mouth confesses can be brought into being by faith.

666. Richard A. Quebedeaux (b. 1944)

Scholar Quebedeaux is more of an observer than a fellow traveler. He has written several books on new developments in the Christian churches. He examined the growing evangelical movement in *The New Evangelicals* (1974) and *The Worldly Evangelicals* (1978). He applied his skills as a sociologist to the renewal movement in *The New Charismatics* (1976) and *The New Charismatics II* (1983).

667. Simon Tugwell (b. 1943)

Though he has not identified with the renewal movement recently, Tugwell, an English Catholic scholar, wrote some influential books that aided the movement. They include *Did You Receive the Spirit?* and *Prayer*.

668. Charles Farah Jr. (b. 1926)

Farah was educated at Fuller Seminary and the University of Edinburgh, but received the baptism of the Spirit only after listening to a tape by Episcopal charismatic leader Dennis Bennett. Later he taught theology at Oral Roberts University in Oklahoma. His book *From the Pinnacle of the Temple* is an interesting study of faith-healing.

669. Tony Campolo

The bald, jovial, sometimes provocative evangelical speaker-author published *How to Be a Pentecostal Without Speaking in Tongues* in 1992. On the whole it is a balanced view of renewal Christianity and a hopeful sign that the old line between evangelicals and charismatics is becoming increasingly blurred. The number of people who consider themselves both is growing every day.

670. Ruth Carter Stapleton (1929–83)

A Baptist, she was known for her healing ministry even before her brother was elected president in 1976. But his public office and their relationship provided her ministry and books wider publicity. Stapleton stressed the power of the Spirit to heal both physical and mental ailments. Her books include *The Gift of Inner Healing* and *The Experience of Inner Healing*. She died of cancer, having refused to accept medical treatment.

12

Some Landmark Events

671. Welsh revival

Evan Roberts (1878–1951) was a coal miner's son in Wales, going to the mines himself at age twelve. He felt called to preach, and in 1904 he kept being awakened in the early morning by a sense of God's presence. He told a friend that God would give him 100,000 souls in Wales. He began holding young people's meetings, accompanied by a group of young women, the Singing Sisters. Roberts and another preacher, Seth Joshua, made many converts, and the revival spread. Visitors came from England, France, Germany, and Russia to observe the revival.

The revival had some interesting features: praying in concert, extended singing sessions (which the Welsh love), spontaneous praise, and emphasis on the baptism in the Spirit. Roberts, a layman, had the aid of ministers such as

A. A. Boddy (see 487). Roberts's vision became a reality: 100,000 had been converted.

The revival spread to western England and was publicized around the world. Observers noted that gambling and drinking decreased and that the ponies working in the Welsh mines grew confused because the men driving them weren't swearing at them as they had before. Several American witnesses of the Welsh revival took the news back to Los Angeles, where it no doubt influenced the historic Azusa Street revival of 1906.

672. Topeka outpouring, 1901

Charles F. Parham (see 476) was the father of the Apostolic Faith movement and a key figure in the renewal movement in the twentieth century. Essentially a self-taught lay preacher, Parham had established several ministries in Topeka, Kansas: a faith home, a mission, and a small publishing firm. He emphasized healing and prayer for the sick, and he called his message "living Christianity" and "the Apostolic Faith." He began publishing biweekly the *Apostolic Faith* and worked to reestablish a vibrant Christianity like that of the apostles—"the faith once delivered to the saints."

Parham opened his Bethel Bible School, with one text (the Bible) and one teacher (the Spirit, speaking through Parham). Students prayed, worshiped, studied the Bible intently, and evangelized. On January 1, 1901, one student, Agnes Ozman (see 477), asked for the laying on of hands. Parham laid hands on her and prayed over her. She spoke in tongues and was unable to speak English for three days.

Shortly afterward, Parham and twelve students had the same experience. Parham believed he had found the true Apostolic Faith, the name he gave to his movement. The zealous students went out to spread the word but met with opposition and ridicule.

Parham shifted his focus from tongues back to healing again, and his many evangelistic meetings in Kansas produced a harvest of both converts and healings. The Apostolic Faith (AF) spread into neighboring states. In Houston he taught William J. Seymour, who carried the movement's message (and the AF name) back to Los Angeles, where he played a role in the Azusa Street revival. The AF movement and the name spread widely, although no one felt obliged to treat Parham as the head of the movement.

After Parham's arrest on a sodomy charge, he lost credibility, but the AF name continued. (Parham insisted that *his* AF ministry was the true one.) In time the name "Pentecostal" came to replace "Apostolic Faith" for the broad movement.

673. Bonnie Brae Street cottage

The Los Angeles home of Richard and Ruth Asberry, a janitor and his wife, was the site of the prelude to the Azusa Street revival of 1906. A group of black Christians met at the home on North Bonnie Brae Street for Bible study and prayer. The group grew too large for the home and moved to a storefront mission. William Seymour came to serve as pastor of the group, but a leader in the church had Seymour

locked out for teaching that speaking in tongues would follow baptism in the Spirit.

Seymour then led his services at a private home, and
when the group grew too large for that home, they moved
to the Asberry home on Bonnie Brae Street. At a meeting
there in April 1906 several people began to speak in
tongues. One woman improvised a melody on the piano
and accompanied the tongues speaking. The meeting lasted
several hours, and word of it spread widely. Crowds began
to gather at the front of the home for services, and at one
point the porch collapsed from the weight of the people.
Meetings then moved to 312 Azusa Street. (See 674.)

674. Azusa Street revival, 1906

"Breathing strange utterances and mouthing a creed which
it would seem no sane mortal could understand, the newest
religious sect has started in Los Angeles." Thus did the _L.A._
Times report in April 1906, noting that "meetings are held
in a tumble-down shack on Azusa Street," where the people "work themselves into a state of mad excitement."
Negative publicity, yes, but it drew crowds. The people at
the "tumble-down shack" (actually a two-story wood
building) knew that they weren't working themselves into
mad excitement—the Spirit was doing it.

Watching and leading the revival (though he would have
said that the Spirit was doing all the leading) was William J.
Seymour, a black pastor who had been a promising student
at a Houston Bible school founded by Charles F. Parham
(see 476). A woman from Los Angeles visited the Houston
school and was baptized in the Spirit. Returning home, she

urged her Nazarene mission church to call Seymour as associate pastor. Ironically, Seymour's emphasis on Spirit baptism and especially tongues speaking offended some members, and he was denied access to the church. For a while he held meetings in a home (see 673 [Bonnie Brae]), but as more people came, more space was required.

Eventually, he held meetings at a former church on 312 Azusa Street. There, sitting (and even standing) on pews made of planks, amid building supplies, the people of various races continued their Spirit-filled worship. Seymour preached, and people prayed, spoke in tongues, wept, and sang in "heavenly chorus." There was no offering taken or any advertising, yet the crowds grew. The church was christened the Apostolic Faith Gospel Mission. For three years the site was the hub of a growing Pentecostal movement. People from across the country and even overseas visited and took home with them what they had found there. There is no event mentioned more often in this book than the Azusa Street revival.

675. the healing of Upshaw

In the eyes of God, each person is precious, but in the eyes of the public, some are more precious—or at least more interesting—than others. William Branham's healing ministry in the 1940s made him world renowned, and his growing fame got a boost in 1951 when William Upshaw, a California congressman disabled from birth, was healed. This healing of a notable figure gave credibility to the divine healing movement.

676. Duquesne Weekend

Duquesne, a Catholic university in Pittsburgh, was the focus of an amazing revival in 1967. In the fall of 1966, some devout laymen on the faculty prayed that the Spirit would renew them. They studied the New Testament, and they studied David Wilkerson's *The Cross and the Switch-blade*, which led them to believe that the Spirit's gifts were not limited to the age of the apostles.

In February 1967 about thirty faculty members and students went to an inn called the Ark and the Dove for a spiritual retreat. One student went to the chapel to pray, others followed, and while they prayed, the Spirit was poured out on them. With no human direction of the proceedings, people wept for joy and praised God in tongues. The encounter with the Spirit continued until five in the morning.

Those who were there spread the news to other Catholics in the university area. As with the Azusa Street revival years earlier, news of the Duquesne Weekend spread, leading to other outpourings of the Spirit in various locations. The phenomenal weekend is often considered the beginning of the Catholic charismatic renewal in the U.S.

677. Notre Dame retreat

In 1967 word of the Duquesne Weekend (see 676) spread among Catholics. In April, forty-five students and faculty members from Michigan State University joined forty from the University of Notre Dame for a weekend retreat on the Notre Dame campus. They shared their recent experiences of being filled with the Spirit. The press took an interest and helped publicize these new Catholic Pentecostals.

678. Kansas City Conference, 1977

With the rise of the charismatic movement in the 1960s it was inevitable that charismatics from the mainline denominations would eventually stage a national conference. This took place July 20–24, 1977, in Kansas City, Missouri. The various denominations held their separate meetings during the day, while each evening the groups gathered at Arrowhead Stadium. The conference included mainliners, Pentecostals, messianic Jews, and various nondenominational groups that defined themselves as charismatic and/or Pentecostal. Many Catholic charismatics were present, including Cardinal Suenens of Belgium, the papal link to the Catholic charismatic movement. "Jesus Is Lord" was the conference theme, and the conference emphasized unity and cooperation among the people represented there. About fifty thousand people were registered—at the time, the largest ecumenical conference ever held in the U.S.

679. Jesus '78

Held on Pentecost Sunday in 1978, the first Jesus Rally was in Meadowlands, New Jersey, and drew an interdenominational crowd of fifty-five thousand people. Although the gathering was not limited to charismatic believers, they were a vital force in it and a sign to the world of the grassroots appeal of the movement.

680. New Orleans conference, 1986

More than seven thousand leaders from more than forty denominations and other groups gathered in New Orleans on October 8–11, 1986, for the first North American Congress on the Holy Spirit and World Evangelization. The conference featured several notables, including John Wimber, who taught workshops on Signs and Wonders. A Southern Baptist renewal group was formed, as was another renewal group for the Churches of Christ, Disciples of Christ, and Christian Church. The conference honored Demos Shakarian, Oral Roberts, and David du Plessis, among others.

681. New Orleans conference, 1987

The New Orleans conference on the Holy Spirit and World Evangelization, 1986 (see 680), had been for leaders, while the 1987 gathering was for all believers. And large it was, with more than forty thousand people attending. Held July 22–26, 1987, the conference focused on evangelization and personal holiness and featured 110 workshops, taught by such notables as Dennis Bennett, Marilyn Hickey, and James Robison. True to the emphasis on evangelism, the conference witnessed thousands of people responding to altar calls. Evangelist Reinhard Bonnke received an amazing response to his altar calls, and healings were also reported under his ministry.

682. Indianapolis '90

Has the day of enormous Holy Spirit conferences come and gone? The second North American Congress on the Holy Spirit and World Evangelization drew 40,000 attenders, while the 1990 Congress in Indianapolis drew only 23,000—"only"? Isn't 23,000 still a huge number? The 1995 Congress in Orlando had even fewer, but there is no sign that the renewal movement at large is slipping.

683. Brighton conference, 1991

Brighton '91 was the International Charismatic Consultat-ion on World Evangelism, held in Brighton, England. More than three thousand leaders from one hundred nations gathered to affirm unity in Christ and commit to world evangelization. George Carey, archbishop of Canterbury, spoke on the importance of theology for the charismatic renewal, emphasizing that theology and experience had to work together. Because of the international flavor of the gathering, delegates from China, Eastern Europe, and Iran spoke of how Christians fare under persecution.

684. 1991 WCC conference

Held in Canberra, Australia, the World Council of Churches (WCC) conference took as its theme "Come, Holy Spirit—Renew the Whole Creation." It sounded promising, but a few critics sniped that liberals in the WCC liked to focus on the Spirit because God the Father and God the Son seemed so "sexist."

13

Critics, Naysayers, and Persecutors

685. Holy Rollers

Holiness and Pentecostal Christians have been dubbed *Holy Rollers*, a derogatory term referring to movement (dancing, swaying, etc.) during worship. Christians who believed in a more restrained worship style were as likely to use the term *Holy Rollers* as unbelievers were. The term has fallen out of use as upper-class charismatics have made "rolling" seem respectable.

686. *Charismatic Chaos*

Published in 1992, this book by John F. MacArthur Jr. is critical of many aspects of the charismatic movement. MacArthur made some valid points, but he has been accused of picking the most grotesque examples of charismatic practices and using them to smear the entire movement. He has stated that charismatics are too fixated on their own experiences and do not feel compelled to measure their experiences by the standards of the Bible. This is no doubt true of some individuals, but certainly not true of the whole movement.

687. Benjamin B. Warfield (1851–1921)

He was one of the most respected evangelical theologians, a staunch defender of Calvinist teaching. Warfield was a defender of the Bible and Christian belief, yet he could be hostile to what he considered subjective Christianity, such as the Pentecostal movement. In his view, subjective movements substituted religious experience for the objective truth found in the Bible. Warfield held the traditional view that tongues and other spiritual gifts were used by the apostles to authenticate their preaching, but the gifts were no longer in operation. Warfield's negative attitude toward spiritual gifts still affects many Christians who fear the subjective nature of spiritual gifts.

688. *Counterfeit Miracles*

B. B. Warfield (see 687) was a noted evangelical theologian, but also one of the most influential critics of the Pentecostal movement. His 1918 book *Counterfeit Miracles* was a powerful influence in closing the minds of many evangelicals and fundamentalists to the new movement of renewal.

Warfield clung to the traditional view that the spiritual gifts had ceased with the age of the apostles.

689. R. A. Torrey (1856–1928)

Torrey was an associate of noted evangelist D. L. Moody and became the first head of Moody Bible Institute in Chicago. He wrote many books, one of the most-loved being *The Person and Work of the Holy Spirit*. Torrey was suspicious of the Pentecostal movement and declared it was "not of God," since the gifts of healing, prophecy, and tongues had ended (so he believed) with the first-century Christians.

690. *The Confusion of Tongues*

Charles W. Ferguson published this book in 1929, criticizing Pentecostals and referring to "the modern Babel." He was critical not only of speaking in tongues (Babel— or maybe "babble") but also of the multitude of new denominations.

691. Mr. Fundamentalist

In 1940 Carl McIntire (b. 1906) organized the fundamentalist association the American Council of Christian Churches, basically as a counter to the Federal Council of Churches (now known as the National Council of Churches), which many conservative Christians believed was too liberal. McIntire's intentions were good: he wanted to preserve historic Christian belief in the modern world. But in his paper the *Christian Beacon*, McIntire published articles in 1944 criticizing the Pentecostal movement, particularly the practice of speaking in tongues, which he said was a sign of apostasy, not of having the Spirit. The National Association of Evangelicals (NAE) had shown some openness to Pentecostals, but McIntire said that he could not merge his group with the NAE as long as the NAE tolerated "tongues groups."

692. "heresy in embryo"

Episcopal bishop James A. Pike was one of the more controversial liberals of the 1960s, casting aside traditional beliefs and dabbling in communication with the dead. Oddly enough, the bishop's response to the charismatic movement was to call it "heresy in embryo." (It wasn't a heresy, and it certainly isn't an embryo anymore.) Pike issued a letter prohibiting all 125 churches under his supervision from speaking in tongues. The Spirit was not so easily quenched.

693. devil in the radio?

Pentecostals and evangelicals have made wide use of radio in ministry, but in the early days of radio many Pentecostals were suspicious of it. Ephesians 2:2 refers to Satan as the "prince of the power of the air," and some believers have applied this to radio, since it is an "air" form of communication. Because radio then and now was seen as mostly a form of entertainment—*worldly* entertainment to boot—many believers felt that Christians should avoid it altogether. The same criticism was later applied to TV. Most Christians today are happy to use both radio and TV to spread the faith.

694. Ronald A. Knox (1888–1957)

An English Catholic scholar, Knox did a one-man translation of the Bible. He also published the book *Enthusiasm*, in which he critiqued (and mostly condemned) groups such as the Methodists, Quakers, and others he considered "heretics." In the book he wrote, "To speak with tongues you had never possessed was, and is, a recognized symptom in cases of alleged diabolical possession."

695. Satan and tongues

More than a few Christian scholars have stated that speaking in tongues is the work of the devil. Possible? Perhaps, for Paul warned the early Christians that Satan masquerades as "an angel of light" (2 Cor. 11:14). Thus Satan could, in theory, cause counterfeit spiritual gifts, even including tongues. But Paul and the other New Testament writers did not suggest that tongues was the work of the devil. True, tongues could be faked, but what would Satan have to gain from it? Paul, Peter, and other apostles warned against false *teaching*, but never mentioned what evil (if any) might result from speaking in tongues.

696. *The Seduction of Christianity*

Dave Hunt and T. A. McMahon published this book in 1985 to inform people about how New Age beliefs were influencing churches. Their criticisms of the occult, pantheism, and the "I love me" philosophy were on target; however, they also criticized some Christians who teach inner healing and suggested that these Christians had been influenced by pagan teachings. It is true that some Christians use a term such as *visualization,* which is also used by New Age gurus. That in itself should not condemn them. Christians are wise to "test the spirits," but also to do so in a spirit of charity.

697. World's Christian Fundamentals Association

This was the fundamentalist counterpart (or alternative) to the World Council of Churches, which was perceived as being too liberal. The association exhibited the usual fundamentalist reaction to the rising Pentecostal movement: in 1928 it officially rejected any Pentecostals, referred to as "the tongues movement" with its "wave of fanatical and unscriptural healing," which was a "menace in many churches and a real injury to sane testimony of Fundamental Christians."

698. Bob Jones (1883–1968)

Fundamentalists, particularly such leaders as Carl McIntire, denounced Pentecostals from the beginning (because of speaking in tongues and because the fundamentalists rejected healing and other miracles in the present-day church). Evangelicals have been more accepting, generally, as evidenced by the presence of Pentecostals and charismatics in the National Association of Evangelicals. Bob Jones, famous preacher and founder of the university that bears his name, was one of many fundamentalist leaders who have denounced evangelicals (such as Billy Graham) for fellowshipping with Pentecostals.

699. "windsucking, chattering, jabbering"

Christians can sometimes be unkind. Charles F. Parham, an early renewal leader, took affront at the publicity given to William J. Seymour and the Azusa Street revival in 1906. Parham (who had taught Seymour) insisted that the Pentecostal movement had its origins in Parham's Kansas revival in 1901. He accused the Azusa Street revival of being fanatical, and he said that all the "windsucking, chattering, jabbering, trance, bodyshaking originating in Azusa will fall." Historians have a more balanced view: the revivals in Kansas and at Azusa Street were both outpourings of the Spirit.

700. Parham's student naysayer

Charles F. Parham beheld a miraculous outpouring of the Spirit at his Kansas Bible school in 1901, and some have called this the start of the modern Pentecost. Most of his students were caught up in the revival, but not all were. One, S. J. Riggins, withdrew from the school a few days after the revival began. In an interview with a Topeka newspaper, he claimed that the school was a "fake." He was the only student there who actually voiced a criticism of the revival.

701. Berlin Declaration

Some of the strongest opposition to the Pentecostal movement has come not from unbelievers but from Christians. In 1909, fifty-six leaders in the German Lutheran church met to condemn the Pentecostal movement. They called themselves the Gnadau Alliance, and they represented the Pietist-Holiness strain in German Christianity. Their Berlin Declaration claimed that the Pentecostal movement was "from below, not from on high," that Satan and demons were using the movement to lead people astray. Many Germans became the *Gegner* (opponents) of Pentecostalism, though many people were also neutral on the issue, open to the possibility of fellowship with Pentecostals.

702. "a doctrine of demons"

The Holiness movement and Pentecostalism overlap in many ways, but at times there has been hostility between the two movements. B. H. Irwin, founder of the Fire-Baptized Holiness Church in 1895, had been a Holiness pastor but caused a stir with his teaching about the third blessing, the baptism of fire that followed salvation and sanctification. Supporters of the Holiness movement called this the "third blessing heresy"—"a doctrine of demons"—and distanced themselves from Irwin. It was a sort of preview of how the Holiness movement would deal with Pentecostals' emphasis on baptism in the Spirit.

703. *Demons and Tongues*

Published in 1912, this book by Alma White summarized the reaction of many Holiness Christians to the Pentecostal movement. The book put forward the common view that speaking in tongues was caused by demons, not by the Spirit.

704. Marjoe Gortner (b. 1944)

He is what unbelievers love: a former preacher who turns his back on Christianity and says it was all a sham. In his youth he was billed as "the world's youngest ordained preacher." Being a preacher was in the family, since his grandfather was noted preacher J. Narver Gortner, and his parents were Pentecostal preachers. Marjoe was prepared for public ministry practically from the cradle. While still a child he performed a wedding in California and was noted as a colorful and dramatic preacher.

But the boy preacher "retired" at age thirteen. He tried several other vocations, returned for a while to evangelism, then briefly became a media darling for his denunciation of evangelists. Attempting life as an actor, he portrayed himself in the 1972 movie *Marjoe*, but the novelty of the turncoat evangelist soon wore off.

705. Lutheran Church–Missouri Synod (LCMS)

This conservative branch of Lutherans is noted for holding to its orthodox beliefs while other Lutheran branches have become liberal. The denomination as a whole has not been receptive to the renewal movement, even though many laymen and pastors participate. An official church commission reported that though charismatic gifts *might* still be available to believers today, they were mainly for the age of the apostles. A few LCMS congregations have become known as centers of charismatic worship.

706. Charles Hodge (1797–1878)

One of the most influential American theologians of the 1800s, Hodge affected generations of evangelical pastors, particularly his own denomination, the Presbyterians. Hodge's enormous three-volume *Systematic Theology,* widely used as a seminary textbook, devoted only a few pages to the subject of spiritual gifts. Hodge stated flatly that the spiritual gifts of the New Testament were for that time only, designed to jump-start the early church, but no longer needed.

707. enthusiasm

We use the word in a positive way, but in England in the 1700s it was a negative thing, at least in religion. England, like most countries in Europe, had witnessed centuries of Christians fighting over doctrine, and people were tired of it. The Church of England had settled into a bland orthodoxy—intellectually believing the right doctrine and having (in general) Christian morals, but with none of the joy and dynamism seen in the Bible.

Enthusiasm was the sneering word used to refer to Christians who prayed spontaneously or witnessed to their faith or seemed joyous about their faith. John Wesley's original Methodists were accused of enthusiasm, as were the Evangelicals (a party within the Church of England) a little later. Christians no longer use the word *enthusiasm* as a slur word to refer to Spirit-filled believers, but the attitude lingers.

708. non-Pentecostal

There are literally dozens of denominations with some form of "Church of God" in their official name. One of the largest is the Holiness body known as the Church of God (Anderson, Indiana). For many years its congregations would often designate themselves non-Pentecostal to avoid confusion with the "other" large Church of God group, the one with headquarters in Cleveland, Tennessee (which definitely *is* Pentecostal).

709. the Enlightenment

Europe had been (in theory, anyway) Christian for many centuries. But in the 1700s many people, particularly intellectuals, began to put more faith in human ability than in Christianity. Enlightenment philosophers stressed mankind's rationality, which could serve as a better guide to life than the Bible and the church, which were "superstitious."

Many Enlightenment leaders called themselves *deists,* believers in one God, but a God that pretty much left mankind to itself. Christ was seen as a moral teacher, but not the Savior. There was no place in Enlightenment thought for spiritual gifts since they could not be explained scientifically. Enthusiasm in religion was regarded as primitive, unenlightened (see 707 [enthusiasm]). The Enlightenment had—and still has—a powerful effect on human thought, particularly the educated elites.

710. Thomas Jefferson (1743–1826)

America's third president, author of the Declaration of Independence, and noted political philosopher, Jefferson had no use for traditional Christianity. Like many educated men of his day, he was a deist, believing in a God who pretty much left man to his own affairs. Jefferson edited his own version of the Gospels, *The Life and Morals of Jesus of Nazareth,* in which he deleted all the miracles. Jefferson deleted references to the Holy Spirit, even in the story of Jesus' conception and His baptism.

711. David Hume (1711–76)

The brilliant Scottish philosopher is remembered for his attacks on miracles and on the supernatural in general. Although probably not an atheist, he certainly did his best to discredit Christianity. Oddly enough, in his *Enquiry Concerning Human Understanding,* Hume attacked people's reasons for believing in miracles—not the miracles themselves. He stated that he did not rule out the possibility that some people might believe in a miracle "by the immediate operation of the Holy Spirit."

712. the Schwarmer

The German word *Schwarmer* means "fanatics." In the 1500s both Protestants and Catholics used it to refer to Christians who wanted to experience the Christian life deeply, not just have it spoon-fed to them by the clergy. The Protestant Reformation was a much-needed break from the dead traditions and ritualism of Catholic life, but the Protestant leaders were so devoted to the Bible (and rightly so) that they feared any "private interpretation" of it would lead to problems. Some of the *Schwarmer* probably were misguided people, some of them perhaps not even Christian. But no doubt some of them were sincere believers wanting a deeper Christian experience than could be found in most churches of that day.

713. Church of the Nazarene

A Holiness denomination made up of groups that broke away from the Methodists in the 1800s, this was originally known as the Pentecostal Church of the Nazarene. However, when the Pentecostal movement got under way in California, and the word *Pentecostal* suggested "those who speak in tongues," the Nazarenes dropped the "Pentecostal" from their name. This occurred in 1919.

714. the noncritic, Gamaliel

Tolerance wasn't highly valued in the ancient world. Most people believed their god or gods were the true ones, and everyone else's were not. The Jews were intolerant, but so were most other people in those days. It was no surprise to the first Christians that the Jews (and most of the first Christians had been Jews themselves) persecuted them for their religion.

Acts 5 describes how the apostles were dragged in before the Jewish leaders and told to stop preaching the new faith. One Jewish leader was the wise and tolerant Gamaliel, who advised the other Jewish leaders to leave the Christians alone, "for if this plan or this work is of men, it will come to nothing; but if it is of God, you cannot overthrow it" (Acts 5:38–39). His speech had an effect—sort of. The Jewish leaders released the Christians after having them flogged.

Many Christians have been persecuted by religious establishments, but there have been "Gamaliels" in the various churches who take a "wait and see" attitude instead of a "condemn them without giving them a chance" attitude.

715. Southern Baptist Convention

The convention is hardly "Southern" anymore, since it has churches in all fifty states and around the world. America's largest Protestant denomination has been, many say, lukewarm in its attitude toward the renewal movement, even though as many as 20 percent of Southern Baptists in the U.S. consider themselves charismatics. The convention's various national boards have issued statements discouraging or prohibiting speaking in tongues or public faith-healing services.

Even so, many pastors have declared themselves or their congregations to be fulness churches (see 783) that are open to the exercise of spiritual gifts. And some of the stars in the charismatic movement today are, or were, Southern Baptists—James Robison, Pat Robertson, John Osteen, and Larry Lea, to name a few. More than a few Southern Baptist laymen have relocated in Pentecostal fellowships or independent churches that are more positive toward the renewal movement.

716. hands off

A sixty-foot bronze, *Praying Hands*, was the most noted landmark of the various Oral Roberts properties in Tulsa, Oklahoma. It graced the City of Faith healing complex, and when financial difficulties forced the sale of the City of Faith in 1989, the sculpture was moved to the campus of Oral Roberts University. Realtors claimed that getting the religious sculpture off the property of the City of Faith would make the site more marketable.

TRUE PERSECUTION

717. the Soviets and the Pentecostals

The Communists who brought about the Russian Revolution in 1917 were atheists who hated all churches. But because they particularly hated the national church, the

Orthodox, they allowed a certain freedom to Russia's Protestants in the hope of undermining the Orthodox. Briefly, Russian Pentecostals had a mission field day, having freedom to evangelize that they had not had under the czar's government. Hundreds of fellowships were planted in the 1920s. Then the Communists began to crack down on all religions, but the movement endured despite harsh persecution.

718. "harmful to health"

The Soviet leaders of Russia were anti-Christian in general, but particularly hostile to Russian Pentecostals. They often condemned Pentecostals on the ground that speaking in tongues was "harmful to health." Pentecostals were also persecuted because many of them were pacifists, refusing to serve in the Soviet military.

719. "registered" churches under communism

Life was not easy for Christians in the former Soviet Union and the nations it dominated in Eastern Europe. The Communists did not close all churches, yet they thought it wise to monitor them to make sure no one spoke out against the government. Pentecostal groups had two choices: register with the government (which meant government supervision, including moles who would spy on the church), or not register and gather underground (which risked punishment for illegal association). The stories of the bravery of both registered and unregistered Christians under communism are still being told.

720. Julio Cesar Ruibal

In December 1995 evangelist Ruibal was killed by two bullets in Cali, Colombia. The criminal element in Colombia regarded Ruibal as a threat since he not only won converts to Christ but also worked to end drug trafficking. He was forty-two years old.

721. Teddi Hodgson (1898–1960)

Hodgson was a tireless missionary worker in Africa with the Congo Evangelistic Mission, known for manual skills that proved useful in building churches. As proof that martyrdom of Christians is not a thing of the past, Hodgson was murdered in the Congo in 1960.

722. Siberian Seven

Seven people from Russian peasant families became some of the world's most famous Pentecostals when they attempted to flee religious persecution in the Soviet Union by taking refuge in the U.S. embassy in Moscow. Their story began in 1963 when Augustina Vashchenko and thirty-one other Pentecostals requested exit visas from the U.S. embassy. Legally, the embassy could not grant the visas, and the petitioners went home and endured years of prison, labor camps, and discrimination.

Some tried again in 1978 for visas, and seven of them refused to leave the embassy. The refugees gained the attention of the media, and their plight was discussed in the halls of Congress, drawing needed attention to the persecutions of Pentecostals in Russia and other locales. In 1983 Mrs. Vashchenko and four of the other seven left for Israel, and the other two refugees left soon after.

723. J. W. Tucker (1915–64)

Christian martyrdom did not end with the Roman persecutions in the Colosseum. Tucker, an Assemblies of God missionary, was beaten to death by Congo rebels who saw white Americans as threats to their revolution. The rebels spared his wife and three children.

724. pipe bombs and Satan

Anti-Christian forces are alive and well in America, as attested by the pipe bomb that exploded during a Sunday service at First Assembly of God in Danville, Illinois, May 1998. Thirteen people were injured, but the congregation continued meeting at a local auditorium. The pastor stated, "Satan meant to blow us off the block and destroy us all, but all he did was raise up a defiant church."

725. martyr in Iran

A native of Iran, Hossein Soodmand had been an Assemblies of God pastor there for twenty-four years, during which time he was arrested and beaten several times. Determined to plant another congregation, he was finally executed by hanging in 1997. Iran has (in theory) freedom of religion.

726. Congo Evangelistic Mission

In the 1950s and 1960s most of the African nations that had been under European rule achieved independence. Regrettably, the change in government sometimes resulted in the persecution or even murder of missionaries. Some of them were Pentecostals in the Belgian Congo. The Congo Evangelistic Mission was mostly comprised of English missionaries, who between 1919 and 1960 established 950 congregations with about 40,000 members. What is now known as the Pentecostal Church of Zaire has about 3,000 congregations with 190,000 members. See if you can keep track of the nation's name: Belgian Congo, Republic of the Congo, Zaire, and now (but probably not permanently) Democratic Republic of Congo.

727. the Klan

The Ku Klux Klan is usually portrayed as an antiblack organization, but in times past some Klansmen harassed Pentecostals, sometimes taking them into the woods, flogging them to unconsciousness, and leaving them to find their way home by night.

728. Maria Atkinson (1879–1963)

Born in Mexico, she married an American man in 1920 and in 1924 was healed of cancer and baptized in the Spirit. She began a ministry of healing and praying for the sick in Arizona and her native Mexico. Her missions were the foundations for the Mexican branch of the Church of God

(Cleveland, Tennessee). The much-loved Maria Atkinson ministered until her death at age eighty-four, and she was called *La Madre de Mexico* ("the mother of Mexico"). Like many people of faith, she endured persecution. Mexican officials responded to ridiculous accusations that she was a witch, a dope peddler, demon-possessed, a sinister hypnotist, and more.

729. church burnings

Or, in some cases, *tent* burnings. Many Pentecostals and Holiness Christians have (in the past, but today as well) found their churches vandalized, burned to the ground, even dynamited. Pentecostal revival preachers sometimes had their tents burned.

730. stoning

It sounds like a biblical punishment, but in the past century Christians have indeed been stoned by hostile mobs. It has occurred in America (notably in the early 1900s in the South), but has been particularly noted in (surprise!) the Middle East—the homeland of Christianity and the place where the first Christian martyr, Stephen, was stoned to death.

14

Ideas and Terms

731. Pentecostals

Pentecostals take their name from Acts 2, with its description of the outpouring of the Holy Spirit on Jesus' disciples at Pentecost. For Pentecostals, this outpouring of the Spirit is essential in the life of each Christian, more important than the symbolic baptism in water. In 1 Corinthians 12, Paul described the various "spiritual gifts" of Christians, including speaking in tongues. These gifts are important to Pentecostals and are evidence of having been baptized in the Spirit. Many denominations consider themselves Pentecostals, including the fast-growing Assemblies of God. Pentecostals are similar in many ways to charismatics (see 732).

732. charismatics

The name comes from the Greek *charismata,* meaning "gifts." The "spiritual gifts" are bestowed upon Christians through the working of the Holy Spirit. Paul listed and described the various gifts in 1 Corinthians 12; 14; and Romans 12:6–8. Churches have often become so mired in ritual and social issues that they neglect teaching about spiritual gifts, including speaking in tongues. The charismatic movement in American churches began in the 1960s as people sought a more emotional spiritual life and deeper intimacy with God. Charismatics are similar in many ways to Pentecostals (see 731), and it is possible to be both. But Pentecostals tend to form their own denominations, while charismatics are scattered throughout many denominations, including Catholics. There are also many new independent charismatic churches.

733. charismata

The New Testament uses the Greek word *charisma* to mean "gift"—more specifically, a gift from God. (The plural of *charisma* is *charismata.*) The apostle Paul used the term several times to refer to gifts given to believers by the Holy Spirit. The Bible's basic teaching on *charismata* is found in Paul's instructions in Romans 12:6–8; Ephesians 4:7–12; and 1 Corinthians 12. The purpose of all the *charismata* was the building up of faith in the individual and, more important, in the community of believers. The word *charismata* is the basis of the modern term *charismatic,* used to refer to Christians who emphasize the gifts of the Spirit.

734. glossolalia

Speaking in tongues appears in the New Testament in two forms: speaking in languages one does not know (see 31 [xenolalia]), and speaking in a special spirit language under the influence of the Holy Spirit. At Pentecost, Jesus' apostles were filled with the Spirit and began to "speak with other tongues." They could be understood by people from other nations (Acts 2:1–12). But more often the New Testament refers to the second meaning of "speaking in tongues," an "unknown tongue" as a way of prophesying or praising God. Acts mentions this several times (e.g., Acts 10:46; 19:6), and Paul stated he had spoken in tongues many times. In 1 Corinthians 12, we learn that the Christians at Corinth placed a high value on speaking in tongues. Paul told the Corinthians that the practice was fine, but that it was only one of many gifts from the Holy Spirit, and not everyone should expect the same gifts.

Pentecostals and charismatic Christians place a high value on gifts of the Spirit, including speaking in tongues. It has been a subject of much controversy, as will be evident in many of the other entries in this volume.

735. pneumatology

Theologians and Bible scholars use this word to mean "study of the Holy Spirit." The name comes from the Greek word *pneuma*, "Spirit."

736. Trinity

The idea of God as three-in-one and one-in-three is present in the Bible, though the word *Trinity* is not. In His Great Commission to His disciples, Jesus told them to baptize people "in the name of the Father and of the Son and of the Holy Spirit" (Matt. 28:19), and baptisms still use that formula. Paul referred to God the Father, Son, and Spirit in the same verse (Gal. 4:6). The Oneness Pentecostals (see 216) baptize in the name of Jesus only.

737. Christian freedom

Paul, the former Pharisee who had been obsessed with following the many regulations of the Jewish law, rejoiced that Christianity gave more freedom—not freedom to be immoral, but freedom from fastidious details. Chapter 5 of his epistle to the Galatians is the Bible's great freedom chapter. Paul affirmed that Christians please God by being led by the Spirit, not by obeying rules. He told the Galatians: "Through love serve one another. For all the law is fulfilled in one word, even in this: 'You shall love your neighbor as yourself'" (5:13–14). Paul was saying that loving one's neighbor is made easier thanks to the power of the Spirit.

738. holy

We talk of the *Holy* Spirit. Just what does it mean to be holy? In Isaiah 55:8–9, God said, "My thoughts are not your thoughts, nor are your ways My ways . . . For as the heavens are higher than the earth, so are My ways higher than your ways." This is *holiness:* God is distinct from, greater than, His creation. The Bible speaks again and again of God as holy. He was greater than the fertility gods of the pagan peoples, gods who were powerful, but not moral. Israel's God was all-powerful *and* righteous. God's chosen people, the Israelites, were to be like Him: "You shall be holy; for I am holy" (Lev. 11:44). The people were to practice a higher morality than the idol-worshiping peoples around them. They were to worship only one righteous God, not forces of nature.

The New Testament continues the idea of a holy God and His holy people, but the holy people are no longer only the Jews, but anyone who puts his faith in Christ, the Holy One of God. The idea of being holy is related to the whole process of sanctification (see 739).

739. sanctification

It means "to make holy" or "to make pure." The Bible continually contrasts God's holiness with human sin. The New Testament speaks of this process as something God does—but also something we do. Paul told believers, "I beseech you therefore, brethren, . . . present your bodies a living sacrifice, holy, acceptable to God" (Rom. 12:1). Paul also pointed to the role Christ and the Spirit play in sanctifying the believer: "You were washed . . . you were sanctified . . . you were justified in the name of the Lord Jesus and by the Spirit of our God" (1 Cor. 6:11). Sanctification has two sides: God sanctifies us, *but* as believers, we must continually strive to keep ourselves morally pure. Sanctification is a deep concern of Holiness and Pentecostal Christians and is mentioned in many other entries in this book.

740. full gospel

How is the *full* gospel different from the gospel? In the early 1900s, the Pentecostal movement in America began to emphasize Christian teachings that had been long neglected—baptism in the Holy Spirit, divine healing, and expectation of the Lord's return. The full gospel meant that Pentecostals taught the usual gospel (man's sin, salvation through faith in Christ) *plus* the neglected teachings— thus a full gospel. Many churches built by Pentecostals called themselves Full Gospel tabernacles. The Full Gospel Business Men's Fellowship is a well-known group.

741. "pouring out" the Spirit

Most Old Testament references to the Spirit describe Him as empowering particular individuals for a great task. But later in the Old Testament period, the prophets of Israel looked forward to a time when the workings of the Spirit would be expanded. Several of the prophets described the Spirit as being "poured out" on all of Israel (Isa. 32:15; 44:3; Ezek. 36:27; Joel 2:28–29). The early Christians applied these prophecies to themselves—that is, the Spirit would not be poured out on the literal nation of Israel, but on the "spiritual" Israel, all who put their faith in Christ.

742. He, not It

The Bible, in its original Hebrew and Greek, consistently refers to the Holy Spirit as a personal being—*He*, never *It*. The Spirit is a personal He just as God is always described as He. To some people the distinction may seem unimportant, but clearly, a He is more important and more personal than an It. The Spirit is the presence of God Himself in the world—the Almighty among us. It would hardly be appropriate to call the presence of God an It.

743. Holy Ghost

Holy Ghost has pretty much been replaced by *Holy Spirit*, though both have the same meaning. Older English translations, such as the much-loved King James Version, used *Holy Ghost*. In earlier times, the Anglo-Saxon *ghost* meant the same as the Bible's Greek word *pneuma*—"breath" or "spirit."

744. tarrying

It means "hanging around" or "waiting in anticipation." Pentecostals of the early twentieth century encouraged tarrying meetings at which, after the main worship was ended, people would tarry and strive to open themselves to the baptism of the Spirit. The word is no longer widely used, but the idea of opening oneself to the Spirit is still very much alive.

745. conversion

Jesus told His disciples, "Unless you are converted and become as little children, you will by no means enter the kingdom of heaven" (Matt. 18:3). It is the same idea He expressed to Nicodemus: "You must be born again" (John 3:7). Conversion, or new birth, is tied to the Holy Spirit, as Jesus made clear to Nicodemus: "Unless one is born of water and the Spirit, he cannot enter the kingdom of God" (John 3:5).

Is conversion sudden or gradual? There is no doubt that the Spirit, guiding a person toward repentance and faith in Christ, can act quickly upon one person, more gradually upon another. And conversion is not completion. Even the most saintly believers desire to grow, and the Spirit is involved here as well. (See 739 [sanctification].)

746. assurance

This refers to assurance of being saved, the certainty of heaven after death. The New Testament is clear that believers can have assurance. Paul spoke often of assurance, and so did John in his epistles, where he connected assurance with the working of the Spirit: "By this we know that we abide in Him, and He in us, because He has given us of His Spirit" (1 John 4:13).

747. backsliding

The word does not occur in the New Testament, but the concept of a believer slipping back into sin is there. During

Jesus' earthly ministry, His disciples, notably Peter, were guilty of it (Matt. 26:56, 69–75), and the New Testament refers to Christians who forsook their faith (2 Cor. 12:20–21; Rev. 2:4). The early Christians believed that this relapse into the sinful life grieved the Holy Spirit (Eph. 4:30). But the Spirit was also the seal of the believer's eternal union with Christ (Eph. 1:13–14), so there is always hope for the wayward Christian.

748. slain in the Spirit

Observers with no religious belief might call this falling down or passing out. It is a common phenomenon in many evangelistic crusades, and charismatics and Pentecostals use a variety of phrases to describe it, such as "being overcome by the Spirit" or "falling under the power." It is not new. During the field preaching of John Wesley, people sometimes fell to the ground as if they had been knocked down, and other evangelists saw similar occurrences. In some cases the people did not move or speak for several hours. Being slain in the Spirit was very common in the evangelistic meetings of Maria Woodworth-Etter in the 1880s, and it has also been associated with Kathryn Kuhlman, Kenneth Hagin, the Happy Hunters, and others.

Those who are "slain" seem to experience a loss of feeling, and they collapse. Evangelists typically provide "catchers" nearby so that the persons do not injure themselves when they fall. The experience is positive, not unpleasant, and many people come to the platform at evangelistic rallies in the hope of having the experience.

Paul seemed to have been "out" following his conversion (Acts 9), but Acts does not indicate that it happened to other believers.

749. circumcision, spiritually

In Bible times circumcision was more than a surgical procedure. It was a visible sign to the people of Israel that they were God's chosen people. According to Genesis 17, God commanded Abraham that every male child must be circumcised when eight days old—a practice that Jews still observe.

Later in the Old Testament, the prophets warned the people of Israel that outward signs of religion were not enough: a person's heart had to be right with God and with others. More than one of the prophets spoke of the necessity of being circumcised inside—the important change of the heart turning to God. The prophet Jeremiah told the men to circumcise their hearts (Jer. 4:4).

A change occurred with Christianity. All the first Christians were Jews, but the faith began to spread to non-Jews, many of whom were not circumcised. A question arose, Must males be circumcised to be Christians? A council in Jerusalem (see Acts 15) decided that, no, circumcision was not a requirement for Christians. The apostle Paul was interested in the discussion, since he was eager to spread the faith to non-Jews. Writing to Christians in Rome, he said that "circumcision is that of the heart, in the Spirit" (Rom. 2:29).

750. pacifism

The issues of nonviolence, the "just war," and such have puzzled and divided Christians for centuries. Historically, most Pentecostals were pacifists, unwilling to be in the military or, at least, in combat. That changed somewhat with World War II, and it has changed even more as Pentecostals and evangelicals (it is possible to be both, of course) have engaged in dialogue. Evangelicals as a group have not been pacifists. As Pentecostals have become more open to serving in the military, there are now Pentecostals serving as military chaplains.

751. military chaplaincy

Historically, many Pentecostals were pacifists (see 750 [pacifism]), so there were almost no Pentecostal chaplains in the military. This situation has changed considerably, not only the pacifism but the Pentagon's attitude toward Pentecostal and charismatic churches. Many of them are independent, but in 1984 the Pentagon officially recognized them so that they could supply military chaplains. The Chaplaincy of Full Gospel Churches has supplied several men to the military.

752. the "no makeup" look

Strict morality may depend on where you live. Many Pentecostal women in Europe refuse to wear makeup but will drink wine at a church supper, while among American Pentecostal women, the reverse is more likely true. Strictly speaking, the Bible doesn't provide a strong "No!" to either activity. Rather, it gives warnings against worldliness, which Christians through the ages have interpreted differently.

Up until the 1970s most Pentecostal women were known for not wearing any makeup, along with wearing simple clothing and little or no jewelry. Consider 1 Peter 3:3–4: "Do not let your adornment be merely outward—arranging the hair, wearing gold, or putting on fine apparel—rather let it be the hidden person of the heart, with the incorruptible beauty of a gentle and quiet spirit, which is very precious in the sight of God." Many Pentecostal and charismatic women today would say, "Yes, but . . ."

The subject is still debated, though most have come down on the side of at least mildly conforming to the general trend of society. Occasionally, the face of an aged, wrinkled, but spiritually beautiful woman—such as the late Mother Teresa of India—reminds us of the truth of the words in 1 Peter.

753. cutting women's hair

Along with the "no makeup look," many women in Spirit-filled churches were known for not cutting their hair (meaning, in practice, usually wearing it pulled back tightly in a bun). Pentecostals cited Paul's words in 1 Corinthians 11:15: "If a woman has long hair, it is a glory to her." Like the no-makeup look, this practice is not as common as it once was, and many charismatic women are probably not even aware that the custom existed.

754. "enduement of power"

This phrase is no longer used much, but in the earlier days of the Pentecostal renewal it was frequently mentioned as something the believer ought to seek following conversion. The Spirit was to endue (endow, bestow) His power upon the believer. But endue can also mean "put on" (as in putting on clothes), so the Spirit-baptized person "puts on" the Holy Spirit.

755. "the foolishness of God"

The human mind is one of God's magnificent gifts, and we should all make the most of what we have. But the modern world exalts the mind, often to the neglect of other aspects of human nature. The apostle Paul was, as his letters show, an extremely intelligent man and well educated for his day. Yet having experienced the Spirit, he knew that the mind and rationality were not capable of grasping the fullness of God. Speaking in tongues is, as he knew, nonrational—not to be explained by any rational process, but real nonetheless. He told the Corinthians that "the foolishness of God is wiser than men," having noted that the Gentiles sought "wisdom" but regarded the message of Christ as "foolishness" (1 Cor. 1:22–25). Should Christians be anti-intellectual? No. Should they be open to things that are beyond the mind? The answer is obvious.

756. not peace, but a sword

No one has kept count of the denominations and individual congregations that have been split over the issue of charismatic renewal. No one could, for there have been so many. Critics point this out, calling the movement divisive, opposed to Christian unity. But Jesus said that He had come to bring not peace, but a sword, and that His teaching would result in division, even within families (Matt. 10:34–36). In a sense, every revival causes division because it causes change, which some people will not accept while others will.

757. "the second blessing"

Holiness churches as a group grew out of the Methodist church—more accurately, they formed by splitting from the Methodists, which they perceived as falling away from the ideals of founder John Wesley. He had spoken often about sanctification and Christian perfection, and he stated that a person could, after conversion, experience a "second blessing," which would enable the person to live a life governed by pure love. Wesley did not formulate the scheme as "first blessing—conversion, second blessing—entire sanctification," but many of the Holiness people did. This two-stage formula influenced the later Pentecostal movement because so many people had already come to think of a next step beyond the conversion experience. In other words, belief in the second blessing made people receptive to what we call the baptism in the Holy Spirit.

758. Spirit vs. flesh

Christians are accused of being antibody, but that isn't so. The Bible locates sin in the will and mind of man, not in the body per se. So what about all of Paul's talk concerning Spirit vs. flesh? Didn't he mean that the body is evil? Not at all. Spirit vs. flesh really means this: God's power vs. human weakness (Gal. 3:2–5). Living in the Spirit means relying on God's power, not on one's own. One is born twice (in the flesh and in the Spirit), and the two births represent living by human effort and living by the Spirit's power.

759. is spiritual really nonphysical?

Though the word *spiritual* occurs often in the English Bible, it doesn't really mean "nonphysical." The Greek word *pneumatikos* most often meant "relating to the Spirit." A spiritual person is not one who opposes or slights the physical world, but one who is connected to the Holy Spirit.

760. deliverance

Specifically, this refers to deliverance from demons, though in a broad sense it can refer to deliverance from demons, sickness, depression, and so on. Generally speaking, a person with a *deliverance ministry* has demonstrated some ability in casting out demons. It has been neglected through the centuries, particularly since modern scientific thought leads many people to believe that Satan and demons are not real. To the credit of the renewal movement—and to people's sense that there really *are* demonic forces in the world—believers are now more open to seeking divine help in deliverance from demons.

761. *daimonizomai*

This Greek word in the New Testament Gospels is usually translated "having a demon" or "demon-possessed." There are doubts about whether this is accurate. Some scholars suggest that it means something more like "demonized" or "afflicted by a demonic power." Note the difference: saying that a person is possessed suggests that the demon dwells in the person and controls him, but saying that he is afflicted by a demon suggests that the demon is causing trouble, but is not necessarily in full control. Can a Christian be demon-possessed? The Bible's answer seems to be no, since demons are under Christ's lordship. But can a Christian be *daimonizomai*, afflicted by a demon? Certainly. That is why Paul spoke about guarding against demonic influences.

762. pandemonism

The New Testament accepts the devil and demons as real and dangerous. So do most people in the renewal movement, which has made casting out demons a vital part of Christianity again. *Pandemonism* refers to the practice of "seeing devils everywhere"—that is, attributing everything unpleasant to the work of demons, including minor personal faults. Although the renewal movement often connects demonic power with serious illness (inward or outward), most Spirit-led Christians do not believe that *all* of life's minor inconveniences are caused by the powers of darkness.

763. ecumenical

Most people take this to mean "interdenominational." For years the word has had negative suggestions among more conservative Christians, who look at organizations such as the National Council of Churches and the World Council of Churches and note that *ecumenical* often means "liberal in theology and ethics." Even so, there are a National Association of Evangelicals, a Pentecostal Fellowship of North America, and various other transdenominational bodies today. More important, the renewal movement at the grassroots level cuts across denominational lines, with Christians seeking life in the Spirit turning a blind eye to the age-old competition among denominations. It is an ecumenical movement of the best sort.

764. man, the speaker

Speech is one thing that separates human beings from other living things. Animals do communicate through grunts, groans, squeaks, and so forth, but human speech has a richness of expression that no animals possess. It is inevitable that a person touched by God will speak about it. And behind speaking in tongues is the impulse to express what words cannot express. In other words, normal vocabulary does not suffice.

765. *filioque*

One of the great theological battles of the Middle Ages was over this one little Latin word in the Nicene Creed. The creed states the belief in "the Holy Spirit, the Lord, the giver of life, who proceeds from the Father." (The wording is based on John 15:26, which speaks of "the Spirit of truth who proceeds from the Father.") For some reason churches in western Europe added the Latin word *filioque,* so that the creed read "proceeds from the Father and the Son." Christians in eastern Europe claimed that this was tampering with a divine truth, and the word *filioque* ("and from the Son") became one of the major reasons why the churches divided into Catholics in western Europe and Orthodox in eastern Europe. Most Christians would reply, "Big deal—just theological hairsplitting." True. Sadly, it is also true that for hundreds of years the Holy Spirit was rarely mentioned by theologians unless they were arguing about the *filioque*. This shows the human preference for arguing instead of living a holy life.

766. "separated brethren"

For years the official position of the Catholic church was that non-Catholics were unsaved. This attitude had softened somewhat in the twentieth century, and the Vatican II Council that ended in 1965 referred to other Christians not as "heretics" but as "separated brethren." More important, the council decreed that Catholics might have something to learn from these "brethren," since "whatever is truly Christian can never conflict with the genuine interests of the faith." This openness to interaction and fellowship with Protestants has been an important part of the renewal movement among both Catholics and Protestants.

767. eschatology

This is the study of the last things, and the Greek word *eschaton* means "end" or "last." Many parts of the Bible speak of "the day of the Lord" and Jesus' return to earth sometime in the future. Eschatology is the attempt to harmonize these different parts of the Bible and make sense of them all. The book of Revelation is important in eschatology, and so are Paul's statements in 1 Corinthians 15; 1 Thessalonians 4:13–5:11; and 2 Thessalonians 2:1–12. Jesus spoke of the end times, notably in Matthew 24; Mark 13; and elsewhere. From the Old Testament, Daniel 7–12 is studied. Too many Christians neglect eschatology, believing that the present world is enough. But the early Christians clearly believed in focusing on the end as well, and it has always been a concern for the Pentecostal movement. (See 768 [Second Coming].)

768. Second Coming

The early Christians knew Jesus had ascended to heaven, and they awaited His return from heaven for His people. We refer to this expected event as the second coming of Christ (although the term is never used in the Bible). Jesus foretold His return but declared that no one could predict it (Matt. 24–25; John 14:3). Paul referred to the great hope many times (1 Cor. 15:23; Phil. 3:20; Col. 3:4; 1 Thess.

4:15–17). The New Testament authors clearly expected the event in their own lifetimes. Just as clearly, the event has not yet occurred. No doubt the New Testament authors would repeat their message: stay alert. Pentecostals believe (correctly) that since it was a key belief of the early Christians, it is important for us today.

769. trickle-up religion

Trickle-down economics may be a reality, but in the renewal movement of this past century the rule is trickle up. As with Jesus and His apostles, so with the movement of the Spirit today: the lower and lower-middle classes are renewed first, then the movement progresses upward. This has definitely been the case in Latin American churches, and it is even true of churches in the U.S. and Canada.

770. revivals

Revivalism is similar to evangelism, except that evangelism focuses on unbelievers while revivals focus on Christians whose faith needs renewing. The New Testament shows Christianity as a new faith, so it says more about evangelism than revivals. Acts 3:19 refers to "times of refreshing" that come from the Lord, and many preachers have looked upon revivals as "times of refreshing" to revitalize faith. Christian history is full of revivals, and the great movement of the Spirit in the last thirty years would certainly qualify as one.

771. dreams

People in the ancient world believed that dreams came from the gods. The Bible reports that God sent many dreams to certain people. Joseph in the Old Testament, the prophet Daniel, and Joseph, the husband of Mary, received or interpreted prophetic dreams from God. Since the 1700s people (Christians included) have become skeptical about dreams, but the early Christians definitely believed that God could make His will known through dreams. Charismatics and Pentecostals today believe this as well. They recall Joel's prophecy of the outpouring of the Spirit, predicting that "your young men shall see visions, your old men shall dream dreams" (Acts 2:17; Joel 2:28–32).

772. el movimiento

This is what Latin Americans call the astounding growth and spiritual renewal among the Pentecostal churches there. It is short for *el movimiento de renovacion*—"the renewal movement."

773. Body Life

The late Ray Stedman, pastor of Peninsula Bible Church in Palo Alto, California, published a book with this title in 1972. He was referring to the life of the church, the body of Christ, which according to Paul's epistles is a life in which all parts contribute to the whole. Stedman's book was popular among evangelicals and Pentecostals, and its title contributed a phrase to the Christian vocabulary.

774. power evangelism

This term is also the title of a popular and influential book by John Wimber (see 572). Wimber studied the Gospels and was convinced that evangelism is often ineffective because it focuses only on the message of salvation while neglecting the healings and other miracles that the apostles worked. He had observed that churches in the Third World grew because the preaching of the gospel was accompanied by signs and wonders. Wimber began to emphasize the spiritual gifts as part of effective preaching—*power evangelism*.

The 1986 book *Power Evangelism* generated controversy, mostly because some evangelicals said that Wimber was emphasizing spiritual gifts at the expense of proclamation of the gospel. A revised version of the book published in 1993 stressed that this was not so, but that preaching and demonstrating the gospel work together and reinforce each other.

775. Third Wave

Can evangelicals have the Spirit? C. Peter Wagner (see 574), who coined the phrase "the Third Wave," thought so. He referred to the Pentecostal movement in the early 1900s as the First Wave, while the charismatic renewal (mainline Protestants, Catholics, independent fellowships) in midcentury was the Second Wave. He defined the Third Wave as the moving of the Spirit among evangelicals who do not identify with either Pentecostals or charismatics. Wagner observed that the Third Wave people seldom used the old phrase "baptized in the Spirit" but preferred "empowered by the Spirit" or "filled with the Spirit." They played down—but did not rule out—speaking in tongues. The phrase "signs and wonders," popularized by John Wimber and the Vineyard Christian Fellowship, is used often by the Third Wave.

776. The Household of God

British author Lesslie Newbigin wrote several excellent books, including this one about the distinctive nature of the Pentecostal movement. Written in 1953, the book claims that the Pentecostal-charismatic form of Christianity is distinct from either Catholic or Protestant. The church, according to the Pentecostal view, is wherever the Spirit is visibly present.

777. "white for harvest"

Jesus told His disciples that the fields were "white for harvest"—meaning that the world was "ripe" with people ready to receive the gospel (John 4:35). This verse is often quoted by missionaries and evangelists, and more than a few renewal churches are named White Harvest. Approximately 1.3 billion people in the world have never heard the gospel. Pentecostals and charismatics have done much to "harvest" this huge group.

778. dunamis

This Greek word (from which we get our word *dynamic*) means "power" or "strength." The Bible sees a close connection between the Spirit and power, one example being Jesus' promise to His disciples that they would receive power when the Spirit came upon them (Acts 1:8).

779. faith-healer

This name is often applied to healing evangelists, but not one that they themselves use. Kathryn Kuhlman, for example, objected to it, saying that she was not a healer, for the true Healer was the Holy Spirit. Most healing evangelists have followed her lead in this.

780. Apostolic Faith

Before the term *Pentecostal* caught on, the new movement of the Spirit was usually referred to as *the Apostolic Faith,* a name popularized by Charles F. Parham (see 476). He gave this name to his newspaper, which circulated widely. But he had no copyright on the name, and papers and churches sprang up using the same name. The name reflected the believers' desire to get back to the basics of Jesus' apostles.

781. neo-Pentecostal

Charismatic is the general term today for Christians emphasizing the Spirit-filled life, particularly Christians in the mainline denominations (see 732 [charismatics]). When the movement became full-blown in the 1960s, people could not agree on a term to describe it. *Pentecostal* was already spoken for, so some observers applied the term *neo-Pentecostal,* which neither the Pentecostals nor the new charismatics liked much. The term was around a while, then gave way to *charismatic,* which at least is easier to say, and it also does credit to the idea of spiritual gifts (*charismata*) at work in the church.

782. restoration

This word refers to the effort to *restore* the church to what it was in the New Testament. In a sense, every new movement within the church for the last two thousand years has been an attempt to do this, with devout Christians always wanting to get back to their roots. It is a desire of the charismatic renewal movement, just as it was the desire of the Protestant Reformation in the 1500s, the followers of Francis of Assisi in the 1200s, John Wesley's Methodists in the 1700s, and so on.

783. fulness

The Southern Baptist Convention (SBC), the largest Protestant body in the U.S., has been lukewarm to the charismatic movement, though a good many Southern Baptist members attest to having been baptized in the Spirit. In the interest of maintaining a low profile (but not denying their experience), some of them prefer the term *fulness* to *charismatic.* Some SBC churches open to charismatic experience refer to themselves as "fulness churches."

784. prosperity gospel

The New Testament gives no indication that Christians will prosper in this world. In fact, Jesus and the apostles taught that persecution will come upon those who live a godly life. Nonetheless, world history shows that people leading godly lives sometimes do prosper, primarily because their life habits lead them to sobriety, thrift, and respectability, all of which lead to success. The early Methodists and Quakers are good examples: beginning among the lower classes, but leading to worldly prosperity because the members practiced clean living with little waste on bad habits.

Traditionally, Pentecostals were drawn from the lower and lower-middle classes. Charismatics, on the other hand, are often middle-class and even upper-class people. Quite a few Pentecostals and charismatics today see no conflict in leading the Christian life *and* pursuing worldly success. For this reason numerous evangelists and authors have had amazing success teaching that Christians can have both. Healing evangelist Kathryn Kuhlman was noted for living well, and of course, the Bakker scandal in the 1980s brought the matter to national attention. The issue causes heated discussions among Christian leaders and probably will continue to do so. One thing is clear: the New Testament, the ultimate authority for Christian belief, does *not* teach that people of faith will necessarily prosper in the worldly sense.

785. positive confession theology

What is sometimes called the prosperity gospel (see 784) has also been called positive confession. One of its early advocates was E. W. Kenyon (see 532), who knew his Bible but who seems to have been affected by what was called New Thought, the positive thinking movement of the 1800s. The key idea is that we can and should triumph over sickness (physical or mental), failure, and poverty. Our attitude of expectation will bring this about. Merged with Christianity, this attitude brings God into the picture: we act to succeed over obstacles and to prosper, and it is God's will that we do so. Kenyon taught the "positive confession of the Word of God." Kenyon did not actually teach that worldly prosperity is a divine right, but some of his followers did. The promise of spiritual *and* material well-being will always be popular.

786. faith to move mountains

Jesus did not intend for His followers to go around rearranging the landscape. Still, He spoke (figuratively) about faith that could move mountains: "If you have faith as small as a mustard seed, you can say to this mountain, 'Move from here to there' and it will move. Nothing will be impossible for you" (Matt. 17:20–21 NIV). This verse has been interpreted by people in the positive confession movement (also called the word of faith movement) to mean that we can and should succeed at what we do, and that God wills it—if we have the faith.

787. St. John's syndrome

The good news: churches in the renewal movement are growing. The bad news: some of them become spiritually lukewarm over time. Some who study church growth and decline call this St. John's syndrome, referring to the book of Revelation (written by John); chapters 2 and 3 show that some churches had "lost their first love" and become lazy and even corrupt. Evangelism and missions seem to be the best vaccines for St. John's syndrome.

788. righteous remnant

Throughout the Bible is the idea that the human race as a whole is terribly sinful, but there is always a "righteous remnant" that God wishes to preserve. This lies behind the saving of Noah and his family from the global flood. Later, Israel was supposed to be God's holy, righteous nation, but the nation as a whole was never righteous. Israel's prophets saw this clearly and spoke of a remnant that would be preserved by God. Spirit-led Christians, particularly when they have undergone persecution, have taken heart from the passages that refer to the remnant.

789. *ecclesiolae in ecclesia*

It's Latin for "little churches within the church." The idea of a dedicated group of Christians seeking a richer spiritual life is very old—as old as the first Christians, who experienced a deeper spirituality than they had found in the Jewish religion. As Christianity has become respectable and established, the church has become almost comatose, but there are always (as today) renewal movements. The Pietists in Germany in the 1700s sometimes referred to themselves as the *ecclesiolae in ecclesia,* since the national Lutheran church in Germany was not meeting their spiritual needs. There always will be this "church within the church" composed of believers who want more from church than "just showing up." (See 407 [Pietism]; 788 [righteous remnant].)

790. PTL

PTL was already well known before the Jim and Tammy Bakker financial scandal erupted in 1987. The name PTL meant "Praise the Lord" and "People That Love." *PTL Club*, the Bakkers' daily talk show, was broadcast from PTL headquarters in Charlotte, North Carolina.

791. state churches

Since its beginnings, America has chosen not to have an official state church. That is the real meaning of "separation of church and state" (which too many people interpret to mean "let's keep religion out of anything run by the government"). The Founding Fathers had seen the problems that arose from having a national church—dry religion, persecution of dissenters, clergy with no zeal for the gospel. So America has an "open market" on religious affiliation. Up until recently, most countries in Europe still had national churches. A key problem with a state church: it turns into a "respectable" religion that will tolerate nothing unusual, such as the exercise of spiritual gifts. No wonder the renewal movement has been slowest in nations (such as in Europe) with a long state church tradition.

792. Madison on sects

Long before he became president, James Madison wrote that religious freedom arises from "that multiplicity of sects which pervades America, and which is the best and only security for religious liberty in any society; for where there is such a variety of sects, there cannot be a majority of any one sect to oppress and persecute the rest." Such thinking explains why the Founding Fathers made sure that the Constitution forbids an establishment of a national church. This "multiplicity" made it possible for the renewal movement to proceed apace in America.

793. "the call"

Who creates ministers? God does, according to the Bible. But as denominations grow and become tradition bound, there is more and more emphasis on ministry via education. No one doubts that some churches are served by pastors who have passed all the right denominational tests but who clearly do not "have the Spirit" and who are not "called" by God to minister. Strictly speaking, *all* believers are called to minister in some way. The early Protestants called this the "priesthood of all believers." The church is healthiest when all of its members believe themselves to be called. This keeps the church more Spirit dependent and less clergy dependent.

794. vestments or Spirit?

The Old Testament describes the special garb of Israel's high priest, but the New Testament gives no hint that Christian pastors wore any distinctive clothing. Christian leaders were respected because they appeared to be led by the Spirit, not because they wore any kind of garb or called themselves "reverend" or "father" (something Jesus actually condemned, Matt. 20:26; 23:8).

795. apostolic succession

Some denominations—Catholic, Orthodox, and Episcopalian—stress the importance of qualified bishops ordaining pastors. In the rituals of ordination, the bishop (who has been ordained in his own office by other bishops) lays hands on the minister. The ritual is a symbolic (or is it real?) giving of power to the minister. And since this line of ordination goes all the way back to the apostles, every minister who is "correctly" ordained is said to be in the apostolic succession. While the denominations that believe in apostolic succession take it seriously, most Christians in the renewal movement have noted that the power of the Spirit is—or should be—operating in *all* members of the church, not just the ordained ministers.

15

The Mainline Reaction

796. mainline churches

This expression gets used often, but what exactly does it mean? It refers to the large Protestant denominations that have dominated the religious landscape in America for the past two hundred years, the "biggies" that in the twentieth century became increasingly liberal in theology and moral teaching. (A caution here: often a denomination's *leaders* become liberal, not necessarily the laymen in the pews.) While America has no national church, the mainliners represent "establishment" religion, the groups that formed the National Council of Churches and joined the World Council of Churches.

Although the mainliners have long been the largest denominations, this is becoming less true: Catholics, Southern Baptists, and Assemblies of God are now larger. Some sociologists say that the "mainline" is rapidly becoming the "sideline." Curiously, most of the mainline churches started as breakaway groups from other established churches (the Methodists, for example, broke away from the Church of England in the 1700s).

Right now *mainline* refers to the denominations that some call the "Seven Sisters": United Methodist, American Baptist, Christian (Disciples of Christ), Episcopal, Evangelical Lutheran Church in America (a merger of the American Lutheran Church and Lutheran Church in America), Presbyterian U.S.A., and United Church of Christ. All seven have been affected by the renewal movement, and all seven (some more than others) have accommodated this unexpected moving of the Spirit among mainline members.

797. Why Conservative Churches Are Growing

Dean Kelley's 1972 book with this title was like a warning call to the mainline churches: *"Wake up—you may be the establishment, but you're losing ground!"* He looked at how the mainline churches were stagnating while evangelical and Pentecostal churches were growing, sometimes amazingly. He analyzed the many reasons for the growth, including strict moral standards, belief in a fixed set of eternal truths, and a zeal for spreading the faith. Kelley observed that what people look for in churches is a satisfying explanation of "the meaning of life in ultimate terms." The churches that do not provide this have declined, and the churches that provide it have grown.

798. *The Churching of America, 1776–1990*

This is the title of a 1992 book by Roger Finke and Rodney Stark, with the subtitle *Winners and Losers in Our Religious Economy*. The book drove home the point that while mainline denominations had declined in membership and influence, more conservative churches, drawing their strength from the Bible and traditional beliefs, were growing. Writing as sociologists, not as believers, the authors observe, "Humans want their religion to be sufficiently potent, vivid, and compelling so that it can offer them rewards of great magnitude. People seek a religion that is capable of miracles and that imparts order and sanity to the human condition." They also made an interesting observation about church splits: the people who leave to form another church are usually the genuinely religious ones—meaning that the ones who remain are the least serious about their religion.

799. *The Empty Church: The Suicide of Liberal Christianity*

Professor Thomas C. Reeves of the University of Wisconsin gave this title to his 1996 book. Reeves observes that conservative churches are still growing and liberal ones are declining. He also makes an observation that applies to the charismatic renewal movement: "It is extremely unlikely that efforts to renew the mainline churches will start from the top down. Meaningful reform will no doubt have to come, as it has in the past, from the rank and file." This has already been occurring, not only in the U.S. but elsewhere. (See 769 [trickle-up religion].)

800. Orthodox churches

Unlike Catholics and Protestants, the Orthodox churches always accepted that healing, prophecy, and miracles still operate in the church's life. However, the Orthodox churches (Greek, Russian, Ukrainian, and many others) have not been much stirred by the charismatic renewals of the last few decades. Boris Zabrodsky, a Ukrainian Orthodox priest, headed a Service Committee for Orthodox Renewal, and the renewal is estimated to involve about twelve thousand participants in the U.S.

801. *Guidelines*

The United Methodist Church, like all the mainline denominations, has had to come to terms with the charismatic movement. The UM's general conference, meeting in 1976, published *Guidelines: The United Methodist Church and the Charismatic Movement*. On the whole the document takes a positive view of the movement, though it includes a statement that speaking in tongues should not be insisted upon as evidence of "a full surrender of self to the will and purpose of God."

802. convergence movement

In the 1980s, several leaders of the evangelical Campus Crusade for Christ joined the Orthodox church. They surprised many of their fellow evangelicals, but the reason for the move to Orthodoxy was a newfound reverence for the life and worship of the early church (from the New Testament period to, say, A.D. 500). This move is considered part of what has come to be called the convergence movement. Converging are pastors and laity from various denominations (Catholic, Orthodox, mainline Protestant, Pentecostal, etc.) who want to recover the style of the ancient church—an emphasis on the sacraments, but also an emphasis on the gifts of the Spirit—in short (as people in the movement might put it), the best of all possible churches. The movement has resulted in the forming of some new denominations (the Charismatic Episcopal Church is one—see 144) and may result in more. No doubt the coming years will see more congregations calling themselves "sacramental, evangelical, and charismatic."

803. National Religious Broadcasters (NRB)

Religion in American radio and television is pretty much in the hands of Pentecostals, evangelicals, fundamentalists—or Christians who might be any combination of the three. Think of the major figures of this century: Billy Graham, Pat Robertson, Oral Roberts, Kathryn Kuhlman, and Jerry Falwell. Had the mainline denominations had their way, this would not be the case.

In the 1920s the Federal Council of Churches (now the National Council) persuaded national radio networks to give them a monopoly over the free airtime given to religious groups. (This applied only to the *networks*—independent stations arose to fill the gap.) By the 1950s the mainline denominations were trying to persuade radio executives to ban paid—that is, fundamentalist and evangelical—religious broadcasting. But in 1960, the Federal Communications Commission (FCC) nixed this. The mainliners were crushed. They had no success raising necessary funds to stay on the air, but the Pentecostals, evangelicals, and fundamentalists did, and still do.

The National Religious Broadcasters group was formed in 1943 to counteract the FCC's then restrictive policies. Made up of evangelicals, fundamentalists, and Pentecostals, the NRB has been a key force in keeping American airwaves open to Christianity.

804. World Council of Churches (WCC)

Conservative Christians have long been suspicious of the WCC, fearing theological liberalism or, worse, fearing that it might try to impose one unified form of Christianity on the world. The latter is unlikely, though the former has some truth to it. The WCC, formed in 1948, has a reputation for emphasizing social action and downplaying missions and evangelism. Plus, the WCC was notoriously soft on communism. Some Pentecostal leaders, notably David du Plessis and Donald Gee, urged Pentecostals to involve themselves in the WCC. A few Pentecostal denominations joined, though most have not. This creates a sort of vacuum in the WCC: not only has the world's largest denomination, the Roman Catholic Church, not joined, but some of the most dynamic churches, the Pentecostals, are holding out as well. Men like du Plessis have a point: until Pentecostals make their voices heard in the WCC, it will not truly represent world Christianity. (See 172 [Pentecostal World Conference].)

805. National Council of Churches (NCC)

It began as the Federal Council of Churches and took its present name in 1950. Most of the largest denominations in the U.S. joined the interdenominational council, but there were some notable holdouts, including the two largest (Catholics and Southern Baptists). Conservative Christians—fundamentalists, evangelicals, Pentecostals, or people who would consider themselves all three—have hesitated to fellowship with some of the denominations that make up the NCC, mostly because those denominations' leaders (not necessarily the bulk of their membership) are theologically liberal, more committed to social gospel than to evangelism and missions. Pentecostals and charismatics find ways, officially and unofficially, to fellowship with like-spirited believers. (See 161 [Pentecostal Fellowship of North America].)

806. "bloom where you're planted"

Respected Pentecostal leader David du Plessis gave this advice to people newly baptized in the Spirit. The message meant this: if you are in a mainline church, stay there. Taken to heart, the advice no doubt had an effect on the growth of charismatics within the mainline churches.

807. the revolving door syndrome

The good news: Catholic and mainline Protestant churches are seeing more and more people declare themselves charismatics. The bad news: the commitment level is not always high. After a period of one to three years of regular attendance at worship and small group fellowship, the new charismatics become postcharismatics—going to church infrequently, moving to a noncharismatic congregation, or dropping out of church altogether. Does this mean the renewal movement is a failure? Hardly. It does mean that not everyone is in it for the long haul.

808. denominationalism or independence?

The New Testament presents us with the earliest Christian church, which faced various factions but was clearly *one* church. This situation hasn't existed for centuries, and denominationalism seems to be here to stay. Today Spirit-led Christians belong to the mainline denominations, to one of the older Pentecostal denominations, or often to an independent congregation that may not even call itself a church but perhaps a fellowship or temple or Christian center. This is probably healthy, given people's distrust of bureaucracies and institutions in general. For the many people who think of a church as dry and boring, a fellowship is surely more inviting. The Spirit can surely function through denominations *and* independent fellowships.

809. the 1970 United Presbyterian report

Like most mainline denominations, the United Presbyterians (now known as the Presbyterian Church in the U.S.A.) struggled with how to deal with the emerging renewal. Most Presbyterian churches have not been receptive to the movement, but in 1968 the United Presbyterians, the largest Presbyterian body in the U.S., commissioned a study of the movement. The study—which was thorough, and which became a model for other mainline denominations to follow—produced in 1970 a *Report on the Work of the Holy Spirit*. It generally had a positive view of the movement, setting a trend for mainline denominations to take a "live and let live" approach to renewal.

810. *Whitaker* v. *the Synod of Arizona,* 1968

Robert Whitaker was pastor of First Presbyterian Church in Chandler, Arizona, near Phoenix. Baptized in the Spirit in 1962, he witnessed several of his members having the same experience. Proceeding cautiously, he allowed tongues speaking and laying on of hands at the church's home prayer meetings (though not in Sunday morning worship), and revival broke out. In 1967 some elders who opposed what Whitaker was doing took their case to the presbytery, which asked Whitaker to stop speaking in tongues and casting out demons. He refused and was ousted from his pulpit.

Whitaker appealed to the synod of Arizona, claiming that the ouster was contrary to Scripture. The synod ruled against him. Aided by charismatic Presbyterian pastor Brick

Bradford (who had been a lawyer), Whitaker appealed to the church's highest court, which agreed with Bradford's argument that the synod of Arizona could not impose such anticharismatic restrictions on Whitaker. The decision gave hope to other charismatic Presbyterian pastors.

811. United Evangelical Churches

More than a few mainline and even evangelical pastors have been ousted from their pulpits because they professed to having a baptism in the Spirit. Some have been allowed to remain but made to feel uncomfortable. As a result of denominational disapproval, many Spirit-filled ministers chose to form their own denomination, the United Evangelical Churches, which (true to the name evangelical) emphasizes traditional Christian beliefs but also emphasizes empowerment through the Holy Spirit. (A more appropriate name would have been the Evangelical Charismatic Church.)

812. crypto-charismatics

Most renewed Christians are happy to identify themselves as such, but not all do. Some are pleased with their own baptism in the Spirit, but they remain in their mainline churches and choose not to connect with other charismatics. They may want to avoid any stigma attaching to themselves or their families. Another type of crypto-charismatic exists in countries (and there are many) actively persecuting Christians in general and charismatics in particular.

813. Episcopal Renewal Ministries

Dennis Bennett (see 573) helped organize a 1973 gathering of Episcopal ministers interested in charismatic renewal. They gathered in St. Matthew's Cathedral in Dallas, marking the beginning of the Episcopal Charismatic Fellowship, later known as Episcopal Renewal Ministries (ERM). The group sponsored charismatic conferences around the nation involving hundreds of clergy and laymen. The group published a newsletter, *Acts 29*, taking its name from the fact that the Bible's book of Acts has only twenty-eight chapters (meaning that the work of the Spirit today is Acts 29).

Lighthouse churches are Episcopal churches open to charismatic renewal. Even so, many charismatic Episcopalians have moved on to other denominations. In a denomination that has traditionally emphasized ritual and solemnity (and, in recent years, political liberalism) over the deeper Christian life, the ERM definitely has an important role to play.

814. Blessed Trinity Society

Jean Stone Willans had been active at St. Mark's Episcopal Church in Van Nuys, California, under the pastorship of Dennis Bennett (see 573). After her baptism in the Holy Spirit, she founded the Blessed Trinity Society in 1960 to encourage charismatic renewal in the mainline denominations. The society began a quarterly magazine, *Trinity*, and also distributed books and pamphlets on the charismatic movement. The group sponsored speakers and meetings to teach people about spiritual gifts and assisted pastors who lost their positions because of their involvement in the charismatic movement. The society's position on speaking in tongues is this: when done in public, there should be an interpreter.

815. the FCC in the UCC

The United Church of Christ (UCC) has a reputation for liberalism, yet within the denomination are evangelicals and charismatics who have no wish to leave their church. Several of them organized after attending the 1977 Kansas City Conference on Charismatic Renewal. The new Fellowship of Charismatic Christians (FCC) in the UCC launched such programs as Acts Alive (lay witness missions), Ekklesia (building on the foundations laid by Acts Alive), and a newsletter for news and networking. But given the UCC's coolness toward the renewal movement, many UCC charismatics have moved on to other denominations or independent churches.

SOME MAINLINE MOVERS

816. Michael Scanlan (b. 1931)

A former lawyer, Scanlan became a Catholic priest in 1964 and is now a key figure in the Catholic charismatic renewal. While serving as head of a Catholic seminary in 1969, he was baptized in the Spirit. Afterward he became head of the small College of Steubenville, a Catholic school that he developed into the larger University of Steubenville with a vibrant spiritual life. The college is a frequent meeting place for conferences on spiritual renewal, for both clergy and laity. In 1983 he joined with three other popular Catholic speakers to form F.I.R.E. (faith, intercession, repentance, and evangelism), holding evangelistic rallies in major cities. His books include *Inner Healing, Deliverance from Evil,* and his autobiography, *Let the Fire Fall.*

817. Brick Bradford (b. 1923)

George Crain Bradford, born in Texas, is a leader in the renewal movement among mainline Presbyterians. In 1967 he was booted out of his pastorate after admitting to speaking in tongues. Bradford became an itinerant speaker and eventually head of the Presbyterian Charismatic Communion (PCC), the renewal group of the Presbyterian Church in the U.S.A. He played an active role in the church trial of Robert Whitaker when the presbytery of Phoenix ousted Whitaker because of speaking in tongues and casting out demons (see 810 [*Whitaker*]). Whitaker won the case, much to the pleasure of the PCC.

818. William Graham Pulkingham (1926–93)

An Episcopalian, he went to pastor the Church of the Redeemer in Houston in 1963. The church was in a run-down district, and Pulkingham sought the power of the Spirit in rejuvenating the church and its neighborhood. The church became a model of parish renewal. He moved to England in 1972 and founded the Community of Celebration.

819. C. Donald Pfotenhauer (b. 1930)

The Lutheran Church—Missouri Synod (LCMS) has not been receptive to the renewal movement, one example being its expulsion of Pfotenhauer. He received the baptism in the Spirit and reported it to the LCMS congregation he pastored in a Minneapolis suburb. The LCMS suspended him from the ministry in 1964 and completely expelled him in 1970. He has not been idle since that time, ministering to nondenominational pastors and congregations in both the U.S. and Germany.

820. Peter Hocken (b. 1932)

Reared in the Church of England, Hocken converted to Catholicism in 1954 and became a priest. He is a respected theologian and historian, known for his involvement in the charismatic movement. He has written several notable books, including *The Church Is Charismatic* and *One Lord, One Spirit, One Body*. He places particular emphasis on the transdenominational flavor of the renewal movement.

821. Ann Elizabeth Shields (b. 1939)

A nun and a leader among Catholic charismatics, Sister Ann was baptized in the Spirit in 1971. She left her order of nuns and went to serve as head of an interdenominational group of women, Servants of God's Love, part of the Word of God community in Ann Arbor, Michigan.

822. George T. Montague (b. 1929)

He is a notable scholar and leader in the Catholic renewal movement. The author of such books as *The Spirit and His Gifts, Maturing in Christ,* and *Building Christ's Body,* Montague was baptized in the Spirit in 1970. He has served as a seminary professor and a speaker at charismatic conferences.

823. Stephen B. Clark (b. 1940)

Along with Ralph Martin, another noted leader in Catholic renewal, Clark was baptized in the Spirit in 1967 and helped to found the Word of God community in Ann Arbor, Michigan. Clark became a noted teacher and author, with such books as *Building Christian Communities, Growing in Faith, Baptized in the Spirit,* and *Spiritual Gifts.*

824. Larry Christenson (b. 1928)

Christenson, a leader among Lutheran charismatics, was pastoring a Lutheran church in California when he became interested in the work of the Spirit. He was baptized in the Spirit and spoke in tongues at a Foursquare Gospel church in 1961. Afterward he led his own church in a charismatic revival. He has published several books, including *The Renewed Mind* and *The Charismatic Renewal Among Lutherans.* He left his pastorate to direct the International Lutheran Renewal Center.

825. Kevin Ranaghan (b. 1940) and Dorothy Ranaghan (b. 1942)

The charismatic movement is alive and well in the Catholic church. The Ranaghans have been active in the movement since its beginning in 1967, and their 1969 book *Catholic Pentecostals* drew attention to the growing movement. They have published several books, including *A Day in Thy Courts, Renew the Face of the Earth,* and *The Lord, the Spirit, and the Church.*

826. Delbert Rossin (b. 1932)

There are charismatics in the Lutheran Church—Missouri Synod (LCMS), despite the denomination's coolness toward the movement. Rossin graduated from Concordia, the LCMS seminary, and experienced the baptism of the Spirit, which his congregation, Faith Lutheran in Geneva, Illinois, accepted. The church grew into a vibrant charismatic church, and Rossin became a noted spokesman for the movement. He helped found the International Lutheran Conference on the Holy Spirit in 1972.

827. J. Rodman Williams (b. 1918)

Educated at Columbia University and Union Theological Seminary, Williams is proof that the charismatic renewal can attract scholars from the mainline denominations (Presbyterian, in his case). Williams linked up with Presbyterian charismatics early on and became president of the International Presbyterian Charismatic Communion. He was professor of theology at California's Melodyland School of Theology and at Regent (formerly CBN) University in Virginia Beach. Williams has published several books on the renewal movement, including *The Era of the Spirit*, *The Gift of the Holy Spirit Today*, and *Renewal Theology: God, the World, and Redemption*, which has become a basic theology text for charismatics.

828. Richard E. Winkler (b. 1916)

Winkler was a pastor at Trinity Episcopal Church in Wheaton, Illinois, in the 1950s when a prayer group experienced miraculous healings and speaking in tongues. Soon Trinity was home to prayer and praise meetings, healing services, prophesyings, and tongues with interpretation. These events occurred in the earliest stages of renewal in the mainline denominations. The Episcopal diocese of Chicago felt compelled to issue a statement saying that tongues speaking should not be permitted to divide the church.

829. Charles J. Clarke (1903–84)

A minister in the Methodist church in England, Clarke was baptized in the Spirit in 1963. He published a quarterly magazine of charismatic renewal, *The Quest*, and later published *Dunamis*, a newsletter for Methodist charismatics.

830. Jean Stone Willans (b. 1924)

She might qualify as the charismatic movement's first public relations person. She was a member of Dennis Bennett's

St. Mark's Episcopal Church in Van Nuys, California, and one of the first in the church to speak in tongues. When Bennett resigned after announcing his baptism in the Spirit, she helped the event gain national publicity in summer 1960 by notifying *Time* and *Newsweek*. She founded the Blessed Trinity Society (see 814) and helped organize Christian Advance conferences on the West Coast. She was a key mover in renewal in the mainline churches, the Episcopalians in particular.

831. Robert Faricy (b. 1926)

An American Catholic theologian, Faricy taught at the Gregorian University in Rome and became involved in a charismatic prayer group there. Since then he has become a key figure in the Catholic charismatic renewal, for a time editing the newsletter *Renewal in the Spirit*.

832. Donald L. Gelpi (b. 1934)

Gelpi had been a Catholic priest for several years when, in 1969, he was baptized in the Spirit. This influenced the writing of his book *Discerning the Spirit: Foundations and Futures of Religious Life*. He later published *Pentecostalism: A Theological Viewpoint* and *Pentecostal Piety*. A teacher at the Jesuit School of Theology in California, Gelpi is one of the most prominent Catholic theologians in the renewal movement.

833. John Gunstone (b. 1927)

The Church of England has a wing known as Anglo-Catholics, very traditional in their beliefs and style of worship. Gunstone is a leader in the charismatic movement among the Anglo-Catholics. Serving a parish near London, Gunstone was baptized in the Spirit in 1964. He has written several popular books, including *Greater Things Than These*, *Pentecostal Anglicans*, and *The Lord Is Our Healer*.

834. Robert Hawn (b. 1928)

A former army chaplain, Hawn is noted for his involvement with Episcopal Renewal Ministries. It became a nationwide organization under his leadership, which included launching the newsletter *Acts 29*. He was one of the planners of the 1977 charismatic conference "Jesus Is Lord" in Kansas City.

835. Theodore Jungkuntz (b. 1932)

A Lutheran born in Germany, Jungkuntz is a theologian and noted author on the charismatic movement, particularly the direction it has taken among the Lutheran churches. Although he received his education in his native Germany, it was while teaching theology at Valparaiso University in Indiana that he became involved with the charismatic movement. He currently resides in Ann Arbor, Michigan.

836. Francis Martin (b. 1930)

He was a noted Catholic teacher of the Bible as well as a priest. He was baptized in the Spirit in 1968 and has since been a leader in the Catholic charismatic renewal. He taught Bible at the University of Steubenville in Ohio and is the author of such books as *The Feminist Question, Baptism in the Holy Spirit, Touching God, Footprints of God,* and *The Songs of God's People.*

837. Ralph Martin (b. 1942)

Martin was converted through a Cursillo and became active in that movement. In 1967 he was baptized in the Spirit, and he and some colleagues began a prayer meeting that evolved into the Word of God community (see 157). Since then he has become a leading figure in Catholic renewal. He hosted a weekly television program, *The Choices We Make,* and he is the author of *Hungry for God, Fire on the Earth, A Crisis of Truth,* and other books. He is a popular speaker at conferences.

838. Eusebius Stephanou (b. 1924)

He is a Greek who was born in Wisconsin. Both his father and his grandfather were Greek Orthodox priests, as he is. He served several Orthodox churches in the Midwest and taught theology at an Orthodox seminary. He was intro-duced to the Orthodox renewal movement by another priest, and in 1972 he was baptized in the Spirit. He pub-lished *Logos,* a monthly magazine of the Orthodox renewal, and has worked to convince the Orthodox churches that the charismatic movement is a fulfillment of all that is best in the Orthodox tradition. The Orthodox officials have not always been receptive, however, and he was threatened with losing his credentials as a priest. He has written several books, some in Greek, some in English, including *The Worldwide Outpouring of the Holy Spirit* and (an appropriate title) *Renewal Pains in the Orthodox Church*.

839. Kilian McDonnell (b. 1921)

McDonnell is not only a Catholic but also a Benedictine monk. He expanded his interests to include charismatic and Pentecostal believers and founded the Institute for Ecumenical and Cultural Research, a center for bringing people together for interfaith dialogue. Several noted renewal leaders have participated at the center's activities. With David du Plessis (see 577) he has pursued the vision of cooperation among Catholics and Pentecostals. He has published several notable books, including *Charismatic Renewal and the Churches* and the three-volume *Presence, Power, Praise*.

840. Briege McKenna (b. 1946)

She is a Catholic nun of the Poor Clares order, known for her healing ministry. Afflicted with rheumatoid arthritis, she was dramatically healed and baptized in the Spirit at a charismatic retreat. On Pentecost 1970 she received the divine message to share her gift of healing. She has become noted as a leader of retreats for clergy and is author of *Miracles Do Happen.*

841. Francis McNutt (b. 1925)

A noted healer, he was a Catholic priest and theologian when he received the baptism of the Spirit at a retreat in 1967. He became active in the Catholic renewal movement and was particularly active among Catholics in Latin America. In 1980 he shocked his church by marrying, which led to his excommunication, which was later lifted. He left the Catholic church and continued his ministry through the Institute of Christian Healing. He has written the books *Healing, Power to Heal,* and *The Prayer That Heals.*

842. Terry Fullam (b. 1930)

Everett L. Fullam is a key figure in the renewal movement among Episcopalians. Under his pastorate, St. Paul's Church in Darien, Connecticut, grew amazingly, becoming one of the most dynamic Episcopal churches in America. Fullam has been a leader in the nationwide Episcopal Renewal Ministries, and he is also author of such books as *Living the Lord's Prayer, Riding the Wind,* and *How to Walk with God.* He left his pastorate in 1989 to become a full-time speaker for Episcopal Renewal Ministries.

843. Ross Whetstone (b. 1919)

A leader in the United Methodist renewal, Whetstone was baptized in the Spirit in 1937 and worked with the Salvation Army for several years before being ordained as a Methodist pastor and served several churches before becoming a staffer with the Methodists' Board of Evangelism. In 1977 he helped organize the United Methodist Renewal Services Fellowship (now generally called Aldersgate Renewal Ministries) and served as its head until retiring in 1989.

844. Dick Denny (b. 1923)

Dick and Betty Denny have been familiar faces among Lutheran charismatics, both being licensed lay ministers in the Lutheran church. Both experienced baptism in the Spirit after a son was killed in Vietnam. Dick began working with Lutheran Youth Encounter, ministering on college campuses. He sponsored the first International Lutheran Conference on the Spirit (1972), which became an annual event.

16

The Faith Abroad

845. missions

Christianity has been an evangelistic faith since its beginning (see 27 [evangelist]), following the example of the apostles who could not keep the gospel (meaning "good news") to themselves. The book of Acts shows the faith spreading beyond its birthplace to the Samaritans, to the Roman province of Asia (what we today call Turkey), then jumping into another continent, to Macedonia and Greece, the gospel's introduction to Europe. Paul, the greatest missionary in the Bible, referred to himself and his coworkers as "ambassadors for Christ" (2 Cor. 5:20). Spirit-led believers have been some of the most ardent missionaries in the world.

846. Reinhard Bonnke (b. 1940)

"I am a soul harvester," says this internationally known evangelist, who felt the call to be a missionary in Africa. He conducted a mass healing crusade there in 1975, which packed a stadium with more than 10,000 people. Shortly afterward he purchased a 10,000-seat tent but found himself preaching to crowds of more than 40,000. He later purchased a tent that would accommodate 34,000, the largest gospel tent ever made. One crusade in 1986 in Nigeria drew a crowd of 250,000. The Africans love Bonnke. His crusades are accompanied by exorcisms and healings, speaking in tongues, and even bonfires into which converts throw their charms and amulets, connected with occult practices. Many converts are Muslims, who are traditionally very resistant to Christianity. In 1994 in Ethiopia more than 100,000 conversions were reported.

847. the China revival

One of the big surprises that began in the 1990s was the revival of Christianity in China. The Communist Party has always worked to turn young people on to Marxism and to make religion out to be a relic of the past. But one Communist official in China was quoted in 1998 as saying, "If God had the face of a seventy-year-old man, we couldn't care less. But He has the face of millions of twenty-year-olds, so we are very worried."

848. Nicholas Bhengu (1909–86)

He was known in Africa as the black Billy Graham. Bhengu was the grandson of a Zulu chieftain, but his father had been an evangelist. Young Nicholas had flirted with Marxism but returned to Christianity and studied at the South African General Mission Bible Training School, graduating in 1937. He became a full-time evangelist in 1938 and conducted Back to God Crusades, having been told in a dream that "Africa must get back to God." Bhengu had helped establish more than 1,700 assemblies, with 250,000 members and 450 ministers. Touched by his preaching, people would lay their knives, brass knuckles, and other weapons at his feet. He said he wanted to see the crime rate in Johannesburg drop by 25 percent, and indeed, crime rates did drop in areas where he preached.

849. the Smorodintsy

The message of baptism in the Spirit travels through strange routes. Andrew Urshan was born in Iran, settled in America, and preached in Finland, where his message was heard by N. P. Smorodin, who took the message to his native Russia. There a Pentecostal group formed, naming itself after him. This occurred sometime around 1911. It is one of many examples of the global nature of the renewal movement.

850. Daniel Mark Buntain (1923–89)

Canadian-born Buntain was best known as a missionary to the starving people of India. He went there in 1953 with a wife and infant in tow and established the Calcutta Mission of Mercy, believing that he could not feed the people spiritually unless they were also fed physically. The mission came to feed more than twenty thousand people daily as well as operate a hospital, village clinics, a nursing school, and schools for children. Through the Assemblies of God radio network, Buntain addressed huge audiences in northern India. His widow, Huldeh, continues the ministry there.

851. Aril Edvardsen (b. 1938)

Some of the best missionaries simply stay at home. Born in Norway, Edvardsen was baptized in the Spirit in 1958 and has traveled worldwide as a Pentecostal evangelist, but he has concentrated on the unreached people in his native Norway. There he published a widely read charismatic magazine, *Evidences of Faith*. He sponsors the Valley of Sharon summer retreats.

852. Ted Vassar (1909–75)

Theodore Roosevelt Vassar and his wife were both Assemblies of God missionaries to India, where they supervised an orphanage and school and encouraged Indian converts to minister to their own people. Many did, leading not only to more converts but also to the growth of the Assemblies of God in India.

853. John Herbert Walker Jr. (1928–88)

The troubled land of Haiti, with its poverty and voodoo religion, has witnessed the work of Spirit-filled missionaries. Walker and his wife were missionaries there for several years, sent by the Church of God (Cleveland, Tennessee). Walker wrote a book on the country and later served as a professor at the CG's Lee College.

854. C. Austin Chawner (1903–64)

Missionaries often have to be jacks-of-all-trades in the churches they minister. Chawner was one. He started Pentecostal Bible schools in Mozambique and South Africa, and he also wrote and published gospel songs, tracts, correspondence courses, and other literature in more than forty African languages. His Emmanuel Press was a Pentecostal fountain in southern Africa during the 1940s and 1950s.

855. Christian Schoonmaker (1881–1919)

An Assemblies of God missionary to India, Schoonmaker received the baptism of the Spirit in 1908. He had a healing ministry and also had the gift of discernment of spirits. He died of smallpox because for faith reasons he had refused to be vaccinated. His wife published a biography of her husband, *A Man Who Loved the Will of God*.

856. Hans R. Waldvogel (1893–1969)

Son of German-speaking Swiss parents, Waldvogel began to pastor a small German Pentecostal mission in New York in 1925. It grew into the Ridgewood Pentecostal Church, supported evangelists, added services in English, and opened branch churches. Hans handed over his pastorate to his brother and nephew and traveled as a tent evangelist in German-speaking Europe, where he drew immense crowds.

857. Emilien Tardif (b. 1928)

A French-Canadian Catholic, Tardif was in the mission field when he was stricken with tuberculosis. A charismatic prayer group prayed over him, and he was healed. He returned to his mission in the Dominican Republic, and many healings took place under his ministry. As an evangelist in Spanish- and French-speaking nations he draws huge crowds.

858. Douglas Scott (1900–1967)

For a country that is reputedly so secular, France has had some amazing revivals. One noted revival figure in this century was Englishman Douglas Scott. Converted in 1925 and baptized in the Spirit shortly afterward, Scott was healed of a speech disability and believed the Lord had empowered him to evangelism. He planned to go to Africa as a missionary but found a spiritual need much closer to home—in France. Healings occurred under his ministry at the Ruban Bleu (Blue Ribbon) mission in Le Havre, and he evangelized in Normandy, southern Belgium, and Switzerland.

859. Mel Tari (b. 1946)

Born in Indonesia, Melchior Tari has seen dramatic events in his native land, notably a 1965 revival in the Soe Reformed Church, during which the sound of a mighty wind was experienced. The church reported many miracles, and in 1970 Tari toured the U.S. to publicize the revival in Indonesia, which he also did in his book *Like a Mighty Wind*.

860. J. H. Ingram (1893–1981)

James Henry Ingram was still traveling as a missionary well into his eighties. A well-respected figure in the Church of God (Cleveland, Tennessee), Ingram undertook a Golden Jubilee World Tour in 1936 to mark the fiftieth anniversary of the Church of God. This led to numerous conversions and new churches around the world, notably in India and China. His many writings were collected in the book *Around the World with the Gospel Light*.

861. David Pytches (b. 1931)

A minister in the Church of England, he and his wife went as missionaries to Chile in 1959. His wife was baptized in the Spirit in 1969, and he had the experience a few months later. The Church of England made him bishop of Chile, Bolivia, and Peru in 1972. He witnessed many miracles in his years in Latin America and went on to write *Spiritual Gifts in the Local Church* and *Some Say It Thundered*.

862. Cecil H. Polhill (1860–1938)

A group known as the Cambridge Seven were missionaries with the China Inland Mission in 1885, and Polhill was one of them, ministering on the China-Tibet border. He was baptized in the Spirit in Los Angeles in 1908 and, being from a wealthy family, decided to use his social pull to promote the Pentecostal movement. He was still zealous for missionary work, and he helped found the Pentecostal Missionary Union. He is to be commended for his zeal for the Pentecostal movement at a time when other upper-class British people mocked the movement.

863. Bernhard Johnson (1931–95)

He was born in California, but was best known in Brazil, where his Good News Crusades drew incredible crowds. Johnson had evangelized in Brazil since 1957, and at his crusades people not only accepted Christ but also were baptized in the Spirit and healed of illnesses. At some of the gatherings as many as 175,000 people were in attendance. The Brazilian connection went back to his childhood. At age nine, he was taken there by his parents, Assemblies of God missionaries.

864. Wesley Robinson Hurst (1922–87)

Wesley Hurst, son of a pastor, was for many years an Assemblies of God (AG) missionary in Africa, but his chief claim to fame is his work with the AG's Asian missions. He worked with the Far East Advanced School of Theology (FEAST) to spread the gospel in the Orient.

865. Everett L. Phillips (1905–88)

With his wife, Dorothy, he was a pioneer missionary in Nigeria. There they opened what became the Assemblies of God Divinity School. The call to mission work there had come in 1940 from some Spirit-filled Nigerians. Everett was superintendent of the AG in Nigeria and oversaw the founding of churches.

866. J. Philip Hogan (b. 1915)

Hogan and his wife, Virginia, were Assemblies of God missionaries in China when the Communists took over in the late 1940s. He has since become a missions executive for the denomination, watching as the AG—and its army of missionaries—has grown steadily.

867. Luigi Francescon (1866–1964)

An Italian Presbyterian? Yes, there are some. Francescon moved from Italy to Chicago in 1890 and had been raised Catholic, but came under the influence of the Waldensians (see 367) and joined the Italian Presbyterian Church. That was just a way station, for he later experienced baptism in the Spirit and speaking in tongues at the North Avenue Mission and afterward helped form the first Italian-American Pentecostal church, Assemblea Cristiana. He traveled throughout the U.S. to establish Pentecostal churches among Italian communities. He also helped the movement spread in Argentina, which has its own large Italian community.

868. William F. P. Burton (1886–1971)

Burton was known as Africa's tramp preacher, and he became field director of the Congo Evangelistic Mission in 1919. The Liverpool-born Burton had been educated at the Pentecostal Missionary Union's Bible School. He became a respected pioneer missionary and author of more than twenty books.

869. Andrew Murray (1828–1917)

A South African, Murray was a noted devotional writer and evangelist. Active in the Dutch Reformed Church, he was a speaker at Holiness conventions and a prime mover in his church's missions. Murray's most famous devotional book was *Abide in Christ,* but he also wrote *Divine Healing,* in which he assured readers that, yes, miracles of healing do still occur, as he himself had witnessed. Murray had a severe throat condition that would have stopped his preaching for more than a year, but he was divinely healed of it. In his book he wrote that "the pardon of sin and the healing of sickness complete one another."

870. Abraham Kuyper (1837–1920)

Kuyper, a Dutchman, was a rarity: political head of his country and also a theologian. He served as prime minister of the Netherlands but is remembered today as a Calvinist theologian. One of his many books was *The Work of the Holy Spirit*, in which he looked at the Spirit's work in the ministry of Christ and in the church today.

871. Robert Phair (1837–1931)

The vast and rugged Canadian Shield was the scene of Phair's missionary work. Born in Ireland and trained in England, Phair lived in primitive conditions as he ministered to the natives in the bleak region. He was baptized in the Spirit in 1907 but kept his credentials as minister in the Anglican church.

872. Victor Guy Plymire (1881–1956)

Tibet was the scene of Plymire's missionary work. Born in Pennsylvania, he became a pastor with the Christian and Missionary Alliance and served churches in the U.S. before he felt God calling him to missions. He and his wife endured a hard life in Tibet, laboring there sixteen years before he baptized his first convert. At home on a mission furlough in 1920, he was baptized in the Spirit, afterward affiliating with the Assemblies of God and returning to serve in Tibet.

873. P. C. Nelson (1868–1942)

Born in Denmark, Nelson came to the U.S. while a small boy and eventually entered the Baptist ministry. After his Pentecostal experience, he found himself unwelcome at his congregation in Detroit. He became an evangelist, settling in Oklahoma and founding Southwestern Bible School. He affiliated with the Assemblies of God and continued as an evangelist, being a widely respected preacher.

874. Nicholas Nikoloff (1900–1964)

He was from Eastern Europe—Bulgaria, to be specific. Converted while reading the Bible, Nikoloff received the baptism in the Spirit while living in New York City and attending the Glad Tidings Tabernacle (see 54). God called him back to evangelize in Bulgaria, where he also served as head of a Bible school for training young people to preach in Eastern Europe. He left Bulgaria at the beginning of World War II and finished graduate school in the U.S., but will always be remembered as a key figure in the growth of Pentecostal churches in Eastern Europe, particularly in his native Bulgaria.

875. Francisco Olzabal (1886–1937)

Born in Mexico, he was in San Francisco when converted under the ministry of Carrie Judd Montgomery (see 518). He pastored Hispanic churches in California, and when he later met Montgomery, found she had become Pentecostal, as did he, affiliating with the Assemblies of God. But he left it and, with other Hispanic pastors, formed the Latin American Council of Christian Churches. More important, he became a renowned evangelist, with crusades in Puerto Rico, California, Texas, and the Midwest. The beloved evangelist known as El Azteca died in an auto accident.

876. Alice Luce (1873–1955)

From England to India to the Hispanic quarters of Los Angeles—such were the travels of missionary-educator Alice Luce. She was a Church of England missionary in India when she met two women who had received the baptism in the Holy Spirit. Afterward she prayed for the baptism and received it. After a few years she became affiliated with the Assemblies of God in the U.S., where she became a tireless worker among the Hispanic population in Los Angeles. She founded the Berean Bible Institute in 1926 to train pastors and evangelists for Hispanics, believing that the best way to evangelize Hispanics was to have ministers among their own people.

877. Herman Lauster (1901–64)

The Church of God in Nazi Germany? Indeed. Born into a Lutheran family in Germany, Lauster and his wife moved to the U.S., where he was converted, then later received the baptism of the Spirit. He joined the Church of God (Cleveland, Tennessee) and returned to Germany in 1936 as a CG missionary. He managed to establish three churches, but the Nazis frowned on Pentecostals, and they sent

Lauster to prison. Even so, new churches were founded in Germany through World War II.

878. Otto Keller (1888–1942) and Marian Keller (1889–1953)

The African nation of Kenya was the Kellers' mission field, their affiliation being with the Pentecostal Assemblies of Canada. Their missionary society in Kenya, known as the Pentecostal Assemblies of God, led to the training of hundreds of native pastors in the country.

879. Melvin Hodges (1909–88)

This great missionary to Latin America was ordained in the Assemblies of God and began his first mission in 1936 in El Salvador. He became a respected authority in the area of missions and was professor of missions at the Assemblies of God Theological Seminary. He wrote numerous books on missions and church planting.

880. Willis C. Hoover (1856–1936)

South America, South America, South America were words that Hoover kept hearing inwardly, leading him in time to Chile to work at a Methodist mission. Hoover had a medical degree but no formal religious training, but he studied while he worked and was ordained. Many Chilean converts were made, and Hoover harnessed their energy, making them into the equivalent of circuit-riding preachers. Hoover was deeply moved after reading *The Baptism of the*

Holy Ghost. He left the Methodists, along with some of the churches he had established. This new body, the Iglesia Methodista Nacional, soon outgrew its parent body. Eventually, Hoover headed the Iglesia Evangelical Pentecostal de Chile. Both denominations are now the first and second largest Protestant denominations in Chile, with more than 300,000 members.

881. William Wallace Simpson (1869–1961)

Tibet has received a lot of attention in recent years, and Simpson was a missionary there, as well as in China and other Asian nations. Born in Tennessee, he trained with the Christian and Missionary Alliance (CMA) and went to China in 1891. At a missionary convention in China in 1912 he received the baptism of the Spirit and spoke in tongues, causing some conflict with his CMA supervisors. He affiliated with the Assemblies of God and evangelized throughout China, Tibet, and Mongolia, most often traveling on foot. He was known for training the locals to minister to their own people. He left China following the Communist takeover in 1949.

882. Tommy Hicks (1909–73)

In the 1950s Hicks was a well-known evangelist abroad, notably in Argentina. When he arrived there in 1954, he asked to see Juan Peron, the president. Peron's aides were amused at this total stranger expecting to see the president, but after Hicks healed an aide's ailing knee, he was ushered in to meet Peron. The president granted Hicks's request for the use of a large arena and free access to government radio. Hicks drew such crowds that his revival was held in a stadium seating 110,000 people. During the fifty-two-day revival, at which many healings were reported, two million were said to have attended.

883. Esther Bragg Harvey (1891–1986)

She had been healed of a supposedly incurable illness after Pentecostal friends prayed over her. After receiving the baptism of the Holy Spirit, she went with a band of missionaries to India to assist James Harvey, whom she later married. Both were ordained in the Assemblies of God and established Sharannagar Mission for widows and orphans. Following James's death in 1922, Esther stayed at the mission for many years.

884. H. A. Baker (1881–1971)

Tibet has received a lot of media attention in recent years, but H. A. Baker was there many years ago. He left his pastorate in Buffalo, New York, in 1912 to minister in Tibet with his wife, Josephine. While on a furlough in the U.S., both received the baptism in the Holy Spirit. They returned to China as independent Pentecostal missionaries, opening an orphanage and witnessing outpourings of the Spirit among the tribal peoples. The couple returned to the U.S. after the Communist takeover of China and ministered to the Navajo of New Mexico.

885. Henry Cleophas Ball (1896–1989)

Ball was already a bilingual evangelist before he had really mastered Spanish. Living in Ricardo, Texas, near the Mexican border, he ministered to Mexican families, beginning an outreach to Hispanics that took him to all parts of Latin America.

After receiving the baptism of the Spirit, Ball split from his denomination (Methodist) and affiliated with the Assemblies of God. He became the denomination's first superintendent of the Latin American Conference. Ball wrote many books and articles, along with a Spanish songbook called *Hymns of Glory*. He established the Latin American Bible Institute in San Antonio, Texas, in 1926, with the school sending its alumni to preach in Mexico, Nicaragua, Puerto Rico, Spain, and Cuba.

886. Thomas Barratt (1862–1940)

An Englishman and a Pentecostal in Norway? That's what Barratt was. Barratt's English father, a miner, had moved to Norway when Thomas was small, and Thomas studied music under the famous composer Edvard Grieg. He was ordained a pastor and established the Oslo City Mission in 1902. Visiting the U.S., he came in contact with the Pentecostal movement and helped spread the movement to Norway. His Pentecostal magazine appeared in Norwegian and also in editions in Swedish, Finnish, German, and Spanish.

887. Andrew D. Urshan (1884–1967)

He was the Persian evangelist. A native of Iran (called Persia at the time of his birth), Urshan immigrated to the U.S. in 1902 and was baptized in the Spirit in 1908. He established an Iranian mission in Chicago, then in 1914 returned to his homeland as a missionary. He fled to Russia during World War I and established Pentecostal churches there.

888. Robert Semple (1881–1910)

He stands in the shadow of his more famous wife, Aimee Semple (McPherson), but he was a noted evangelist in his own right. Born near Belfast, he immigrated to the U.S. in his teens and encountered the Pentecostals at a storefront church in Chicago. He became an evangelist in Ontario, where he met and married Aimee Kennedy. He worked in a factory by day and was an evangelist in his off hours.

Returning to Chicago, he worked with the North Avenue Mission, then held a crusade in Belfast, where the mayor gave him the key to the city. He and Aimee sailed to the Far East, with plans to be missionaries in China. Before arriving, Robert contracted malaria and died in an English sanatarium. Their daughter, Roberta, was born after his death. The tall (six-foot-six), handsome Semple was a gifted speaker who was dedicated to the gospel.

889. Minnie Abrams (1859–1912)

Minnie was truly a transnational figure. From the U.S. she went as a missionary to India. A Pentecostal revival occurred at her mission in 1906, and Minnie was baptized in the Spirit. In her book *The Baptism of the Holy Ghost and Fire* (1906), she described the revival, and the book influenced the beginnings of a Pentecostal revival in Chile.

890. G. H. Schmidt (1891–1958)

Gustav Herbert Schmidt, born in Russia, was converted to Christ in 1908 and a few years later was baptized in the Spirit. He immigrated to the U.S., trained as a missionary, and was sent by the Assemblies of God to Poland in 1920. Europe was still recovering from World War I, and Schmidt spent his time in both evangelism and relief work. He won many converts, and in 1927 he and Paul Peterson organized the Russian and Eastern European Mission.

He returned to Poland in 1929 and opened his Bible institute in Danzig. It was the first Pentecostal Bible institute in eastern Europe. When World War II broke out, Schmidt was imprisoned by the Nazis and would have been sent to a concentration camp had he not been an American citizen. He managed to escape from Nazi-occupied Danzig, a story he told in *Songs in the Night*.

891. Albert Norton (d. 1923)

A missionary to India, Norton worked with famine relief alongside Pandita Ramabai (see 935) in 1899 and observed the great outpouring of the Spirit at her Mukti Mission in 1905. He ministered to the Kurkus of central India and witnessed another outpouring of the Spirit at the boys' home he founded for the Kurkus.

892. Lewi Pethrus (1884–1974)

Born in Sweden, Pethrus was a Baptist pastor who became interested in a Pentecostal revival in Norway. He traveled there, became a Pentecostal, and took the message back to his home church. His home church accepted it, although the Swedish Baptist Convention did not, so it expelled him and his congregation. Pethrus became the leader of Swedish Pentecostals. He was a dynamic figure, working to establish a rescue mission, publishing house, Bible school, daily newspaper, and worldwide radio network. At the time of his death his Filadelfia Church in Stockholm was the largest Pentecostal congregation in the world.

893. Daniel Berg (1884–1963)

Born in Sweden, Berg came to the U.S. in 1902 and began a long association with Adolf Gunnar Vingren (see 894). He met Vingren at a Swedish Pentecostal conference in Chicago, and a prophet told both men that they would go as missionaries to Brazil. They arrived in Brazil in 1910 and worked to build the nation's first Pentecostal church, with Berg helping to pay for Vingren to learn Portuguese, the language of Brazil. Their church, an Assembly of God, grew into Brazil's largest Protestant denomination.

894. Adolf Gunnar Vingren (1879–1933)

Born in Sweden, Vingren pastored a Swedish Baptist church in Michigan. After his conversion to Pentecostalism, he began fellowshipping with Swedish Pentecostals in Chicago.

Accepting a Pentecostal pastorate in Indiana, he received from one of his church members a prophecy that he would go to Para in Brazil. He and fellow Swede Daniel Berg traveled there in 1910. They organized the Apostolic Faith Mission in a home, and the small group grew into the largest Protestant body in Brazil.

895. Paul Peter Waldenstrom (1838–1917)

He was a pastor in the established Lutheran church of Sweden, but he disliked its emphasis on creeds as opposed to a vibrant spiritual life. He preached the importance of a deep fellowship with the loving God. Eventually, he left the state church and joined a renewal movement, the Evangelical National Association. Waldenstrom's devotional writings were much loved by Swedish evangelicals.

896. Alfred Lewer (d. 1924)

"Brother Alf" was a British missionary to the area of China bordering on Tibet. After his baptism in the Spirit in 1913, he served with the Pentecostal Missionary Union, taking time to learn Chinese to minister to the people of that nation. The Lisu people of southwestern China came to love him. He drowned while crossing the Mekong River.

897. Thomas Hezmalhalch (1848–1934)

"Brother Tom" was a noted Pentecostal evangelist in the U.S. and South Africa. Born in England, Tom came to the U.S. in the 1880s and became a Holiness preacher, later experiencing baptism in the Holy Spirit. With John Lake he preached widely in South Africa, leading to the formation of the Apostolic Faith Mission in that country.

898. Ivan Voronaev (1886–?)

Russian-born Voronaev had been a Cossack, but after his conversion he pastored Baptist churches in Siberia. When the Russian Orthodox Church began one of its persecutions of Protestants, he fled to the U.S. and pastored a Russian Baptist church in New York City. There he had a Pentecostal experience, which led him to establish the city's first Russian Pentecostal congregation. Feeling a burden for his homeland, he returned there in 1920 to build the Pentecostal movement, but the Communists passed antireligious laws that led to Voronaev's imprisonment.

899. Ralph Darby Williams (1902–82)

Born in England and educated at a U.S. Bible college, Williams went with his wife as missionaries to El Salvador in 1929. He planted several Assemblies of God congregations, which grew to more than four hundred in a few years. He also established a Bible institute there for training the locals to minister to their own people.

900. Paul Bettex (1864–1916)

Some mystery surrounds the murder of missionary Paul Bettex in China. Bettex was somewhat controversial during his lifetime, being regarded as a dedicated missionary but also considered a fanatic by some. He was born in France and converted through the Salvation Army ministry. He received the baptism of the Spirit and spoke in tongues while a student at Princeton Seminary. He went as a missionary to South America and, after the Azusa Street revival in 1906, identified with the Pentecostal movement.

901. Praying Hyde

John Hyde (1865–1912) was one of several college classmates in Illinois who felt called to be missionaries. He went to India in 1902 and experienced the baptism of the Spirit. For almost twenty years he was an evangelist in Indian villages. He watched a revival break out at a girls' school, and he saw an amazing outpouring of the Spirit at a 1904 missionary conference. In 1908 he prayed that he would win one soul per day: he won four hundred in a year. He then prayed to win two a day, and eight hundred converts were made. He was called "Praying Hyde" because he prayed so often that he sometimes went without sleep.

902. Juan Carlos Ortiz (b. 1934)

Ortiz is a well-known evangelist in Latin America and has been a key figure in the charismatic renewal in that region. A native of Argentina, he assisted the evangelistic crusade of Tommy Hicks (see 882) and later became a noted preacher in his own right. He made an impression at the Lausanne Congress on World Evangelization in 1974. In 1991 he joined the staff of Robert Schuller's Crystal Cathedral to minister to Hispanics.

903. Pavel Bochian (b. 1918)

Christians can be persecuted by Communists and by other Christians—sometimes in the same country at the same time. Pavel Bochian faced that situation in Romania, where as a Pentecostal pastor he faced harassment from both the government and the Romanian Orthodox church. Through the power of the Spirit, the Pentecostal church in Romania grew anyway and even established its own seminary in 1976.

904. R. Kenneth Ware (b. 1917)

At a revival led by Smith Wigglesworth, he had been healed of a speech disability and told by Wigglesworth that "this tongue will preach the gospel." He and his wife evangelized in France and Switzerland and were noted for producing Christian literature in French.

905. A. C. Valdez Sr. (1896–1988)

From a Catholic family, he was caught up in the famous Azusa Street revival in Los Angeles and afterward became an evangelist with a ministry lasting more than seventy years. He and his son, A. C. Jr., led revivals in the South Seas, Australia, New Zealand, India, Japan, and South America. He wrote the book *Fire on Azusa Street*.

906. Thomas Roberts (1902–83)

A Pentecostal Welshman in France? Roberts was. He was sent to France in 1902 by the Apostolic Church, and he became pastor of an independent Paris church in 1936. He was deeply involved with the Union de Prière (Prayer Union) and was excited at hearing of the charismatic renewal taking place in America. Throughout his ministry, he worked to build bridges among Christians and to see a Pentecost over Europe.

907. Noel Perkin (1893–1979)

Born in England, Perkin was a banker in Canada when he became interested in the ministry and missions. He ministered in Argentina and later joined the Assemblies of God (AG), becoming its missionary secretary. In that office he helped the AG's foreign missions expand greatly, adding not only many foreign converts but also more missionaries and more foreign Bible schools. He was the first Pentecostal elected president of the Evangelical Foreign Missions Association.

908. Peter Kuzmic (b. 1946)

Growing up in the Communist nation of Yugoslavia, Kuzmic has been an authority on Christianity's relation to Marxism. His father was a Pentecostal pastor in Slovenia, then part of Yugoslavia, and Peter studied in Germany and the U.S. as well as in his native country. He directed a biblical and theological institute in Yugoslavia and pastored a

Pentecostal church. He has been deeply involved in dialogue between Catholics and Pentecostals.

909. Paul Peterson (1895–1978)

While a young man, Peterson chose to devote his life to evangelism in Russia and Eastern Europe. Under the auspices of the Russian Missionary Society, he and his wife went in 1924 as missionaries to Poland and Latvia. He later returned to the U.S. and, with G. H. Schmidt, formed the Russian and Eastern European Mission, which he headed until his death. He traveled worldwide to familiarize people with the spiritual needs of the Slavic peoples, and during World War II, he urged people to send food and clothing to Russia and Eastern Europe.

910. Louis Dallière (1897–1976)

France is a very secular nation now, but in recent years there have been stirrings of the Spirit. Dallière was a Protestant pastor who in 1930 received the baptism of the Spirit and, later, the gift of tongues. He wrote a brief book on the Pentecostal movement and began a monthly periodical, *Esprit et Vie* (*Spirit and Life*), to promote the movement. He founded the Union de Prière (Prayer Union) in the hope of Pentecostals banding together.

911. Bill Burnett (b. 1917)

Born in South Africa, Burnett was ordained in the Anglican church and became bishop of the city of Bloemfontein in

1957. He was baptized in the Spirit in 1957, and he used his authority as a bishop (he later became archbishop of Cape Town) to increase awareness of charismatic renewal. Under his influence, several South African bishops were baptized in the Spirit. He retired in 1981 and has continued as a popular speaker and a leader in the worldwide charismatic renewal in the Anglican churches.

912. Christendom, also known as Korea

The word *Christendom* used to refer to Europe (since it was all theoretically Christian). As the Europeans settled America, the term expanded to include the New World. But now (since the Spirit moves where He will) the world's largest churches are in Korea. The Asian nation is not only home to David Cho's church, the largest church in the world, but also to the world's largest Southern Baptist church (40,000) and the world's largest Methodist churches (30,000 and 20,000). These megachurches are charismatic in their ministries even if not officially charismatic. Along with the megachurches are hundreds of smaller Korean churches, which are proving that Christendom is wherever Christ is being worshiped.

17

Works of Compassion

913. Teen Challenge

David Wilkerson started this remarkable evangelistic program to help troubled teens, particularly gang members. It began in 1958 as Teen Age Evangelism and grew when churches in the New York City area gave generously to support the ministry. (Wilkerson began modestly, saying he needed only twenty churches to pledge five dollars each per week.) Street teens, even drug addicts, were converted and went on to convert others.

News of the rehabilitation of former druggies brought Wilkerson invitations to speak everywhere. Teen Challenge branched out to Chicago, Los Angeles, and other major cities, and young people from colleges and Bible schools were eager to join the ministry. Finding his expanding ministries to be a lot to manage, he handed over Teen Challenge to the supervision of the Assemblies of God in 1963. The ministry is still transdenominational and operates centers in forty-three states and sixty nations.

914. Lillian Trasher (1887–1961)

"Mamma Lillian" was a much-loved figure in Egypt, where she founded an orphanage at the town of Assiout. Aided by friends in Egypt and the U.S., and also by the Egyptian government, Mamma saw the orphanage grow from 50 children in 1916 to more than 1,000 in 1955. Today the Lillian Trasher Memorial Orphanage sits on 12 acres and houses 650 children and widows. Trasher's background was interesting. Becoming a committed Catholic at a young age, Trasher was ordained in the Church of God (Cleveland, Tennessee) but later affiliated with the Assemblies of God. Living in a strongly Muslim country, she managed to keep the respect of the locals.

915. Youth with a Mission (YWAM)

Loren Cunningham (b. 1935) founded this interdenominational group in his parents' home in 1960. He had a vision of sending out young evangelists to every continent in the world. YWAM began with a bang, making six thousand converts in the Bahamas during one summer. The young people with YWAM raise their own funds for their short-term missions. As many as fifty thousand short-term people per year are involved. YWAM has opened the Pacific and Asia Christian University in Hawaii to train missionaries to Asia, a School of Urban Missions in Europe, two mercy ships providing medical relief, and other ministries that touch many nations.

916. Union de Prière (UP)

The UP (its French name means "prayer union") began in 1946 as Louis Dallière helped organize renewed Christians in the French Reformed churches. The UP has emphasized baptism in the Spirit and exercise of spiritual gifts, as well as evangelistic work, particularly outreach to Jews.

917. faith homes

These were hospices, open for people seeking healing and also for sick people with nowhere to go. They arose out of the Holiness movement in the late 1800s with its emphasis on divine healing. Earlier, J. C. Blumhardt of Germany (see 939) opened a faith home where people studied the Bible and prayed for the sick. The home became the center of his healing ministry. Charles Cullis, a Boston doctor, opened America's first faith home in 1864. One woman with an inoperable brain tumor was healed while there. Healing evangelist John Alexander Dowie opened his Divine Healing Home in Chicago. Charles Parham opened Bethel Healing Home in Topeka, Kansas. Not every person at these faith homes was healed, though many were. The homes provided comfort, spiritual nourishment, and fellowship for every person.

918. Upper Room Mission

A Baptist minister, Elmer Kirk Fisher, formed this Los Angeles mission in 1906 with aid from people from the Azusa Street Mission. Consisting of a three-hundred-seat auditorium and a few rooms on the second floor of an office building, the mission had the slogan "Exalt Jesus Christ, Honor the Holy Ghost." The mission held three Sunday services, Bible studies, evening worship, and baptisms—not in the mission but on an island in Los Angeles harbor. People from the mission did street evangelism in the seedy districts nearby.

919. the 10/40 window

No, this has nothing to do with the IRS. The "window" is the section of the earth between 10 degrees and 40 degrees latitude north of the equator. In the 1990s, evangelists and missionaries made it a priority to spread the gospel to this section, which has the lion's share of the world's unreached people. Some missionaries call it the Resistance Belt because of the anti-Christian bias of the Islamic nations and the more passive resistance of Buddhists and Hindus. Spirit-led missionaries, sometimes risking persecution or even death, continue to labor in the 10/40 window.

920. Gospel to the Unreached Millions

Born into a Hindu family in India, K. A. Paul has been beaten and left for dead as he has spread the gospel to the people of his native land. He and other missionaries to

India in recent years have found that many Hindus treat Christianity as a Western religion, a product of America and Europe that no Hindu should accept. Violence against Christian missionaries is fairly common in India. Nonetheless, K. A. Paul founded Gospel to the Unreached Millions, based in Houston, Texas, and focused on the 10/40 window, the sections of the world that have been so resistant to Christianity (see 919 [10/40 window]).

921. Pisgah Home

Finis Yoakum (see 491), a former doctor and healing evangelist, was widely loved for his outreach to the destitute in the Los Angeles area. Divinely healed after a near fatal accident, Yoakum founded the Pisgah Home in 1895 to provide 9,000 clean beds and 18,000 meals per month to homeless people, drug addicts, alcoholics, and prostitutes. He sent his workers out to the streets to distribute nickels that the outcasts could use as trolley fare to the Pisgah Home.

Yoakum's Pisgah Store, staffed by volunteers, distributed food and clothing that people had donated. A large open area named Pisgah Gardens gave ailing people a place for exercise and fresh air, and it also grew fruits and vegetables used in the Pisgah charities. The Pisgah Ark was a home for recovering drug and alcohol addicts and prostitutes. The Pisgah complex continued for several years after Yoakum's death in 1920.

922. Divine Healer

Charles F. Parham was often called this in the years following the outpouring of the Spirit at his Bible school in Kansas (1901). As he traveled about and preached, many people were healed at his meetings. Though many newspapermen scoffed, they couldn't help noticing that the healings weren't just among the lower classes but among "respectable" and educated people. The Spirit was moving among the poor, but moving beyond them as well.

923. City of Faith

Adjoining Oral Roberts University in Tulsa, Oklahoma, was this eighty-acre medical and research center, affiliated with the ORU School of Medicine and Nursing School. The hospital opened in 1981, and the City of Faith had a thirty-story hospital, sixty-story clinic tower, and twenty-story research tower, all ultramodern in design. Roberts, known as a faith-healer, drew some criticism for this complex that, by its very nature, emphasized the scientific art of healing. Roberts claimed that God had led him to open the City of Faith, and that the City of Faith combined under one roof the physical, emotional, and spiritual sources of healing. The complex experienced serious financial crises and was sold in 1989.

924. Elizabeth Baker (1849–1915)

A Methodist pastor's daughter, Baker and her four sisters founded the Elim Tabernacle, Elim Publishing House, Elim

Home, and Rochester Bible Training School. Baker's second husband, a doctor, had no luck treating her severe throat ailment, but she was healed after being anointed and prayed over by a Methodist pastor who believed in faith-healing. Baker embraced divine healing, and she and her sisters opened the Elim Faith Home in Rochester, New York, in 1895 to meet the needs of those seeking healing. Learning about the tongues phenomenon in the Azusa Street revival in California, Baker and her sisters studied it closely and believed it was valid.

The sisters received criticism because of the issue of women in leadership roles. They prayed for the right man to lead their Elim Tabernacle, but none appeared, so they continued in their leadership.

925. generous to missions

Pentecostals did and do have a strong interest in world missions, taking seriously Jesus' Great Commission (Matt. 28:19–20). This is reflected not only in the number of missionaries sent but also in the amount of giving. In most Pentecostal denominations in the U.S., missions receives the largest amount of funds.

926. partners

Praying and sending funds to support faraway missionaries are nothing new. In the television age a new word has gained currency to describe the person who makes contributions and (presumably) prays for the television ministry: *prayer partner* or sometimes just *partner*. Critics of televangelism claim that financial giving to a TV ministry means the person is not contributing to a local congregation, but surveys show this is usually not the case. Many partners contribute financially to their local churches *and* to their favorite TV ministries.

927. *Voice of Healing*

Gordon Lindsay (see 638) was the founder and for many years the editor of this nondenominational magazine designed to publicize the work of healing evangelists around the world, including documentation of healings that occurred. The magazine helped unite Christians who had an interest in the Spirit's healing work. It also helped unite evangelists into a kind of Voice of Healing fellowship. The magazine sponsored Christian radio programs around the world and gave encouragement to missions and evangelists everywhere. Begun in 1948, the magazine changed its name in 1967 to *Christ for the Nations*.

928. *Christian Healing*

There are many books *about* Christian healing, but this 1990 book by Episcopal pastor Mark A. Pearson is a genuine how-to book about introducing a healing ministry into the church. Pearson founded the Institute for Christian Renewal.

929. *Acts of the Holy Ghost*

Noted healing evangelist Maria Woodworth-Etter (see 492) published this testimonial book in 1922. In it are testimonies of people healed through her nationwide crusades, with a multitude of disabled, blind, deaf, and other sick people whose ailments had never responded to medical treatment but who had responded to the healing power of the Spirit. In the days before TV and radio, such testimonial volumes publicized healing evangelists.

930. Russian and Eastern European Mission

Long known as the Eastern European Mission (EEM), the group was founded in 1927 to evangelize the Slavic nations. With Russia and, later, the Eastern European nations being officially atheist, it was only a matter of time before evangelism would be prohibited. That occurred in Russia in 1929, and by 1930 all the EEM missionaries had been arrested and either exiled or imprisoned. In the following decade the mission had better success in the other Slavic countries, but World War II forced the return of many missionaries to America. During the 1950s, as the cold war became a continuing reality, the EEM concentrated on missions in Western Europe. Since 1987 the group has been named Eurovision. Now that communism no longer dominates most of Eastern Europe (Bulgaria being a glaring exception), it will be interesting to watch the direction of missions.

931. David Nunn (b. 1921)

Feeding the hungry is important, both materially and spiritually. Nunn, a healing evangelist, emphasizes both. His Bible Revival Evangelistic Association operates Free Food Kitchens in India, China, Africa, and the Philippines, feeding 500,000 people per month. The agency also operates an orphanage, a hospital, and three Bible schools. Nunn has witnessed many healings at his services, including people who were totally blind.

932. John L. Meares (b. 1920)

A Church of God (Cleveland, Tennessee) pastor, Meares is known for his work with inner-city residents. He began a tent meeting ministry in Washington, D.C., in 1955, settling his congregation in a theater that became the Washington Revival Center. In time his ministry of healing and evangelism led to the founding of the Evangel Temple. He has been a leader in racial reconciliation between black and white believers. The city council of Washington, D.C., honored his work with a proclamation of John Meares Week in 1985.

933. "Mother" Wheaton (1844–1923)

Widowed at an early age, Elizabeth Wheaton turned to the Lord in her distress. She received sanctification at a Holiness service and had a vision of Jesus that led to her starting a prison ministry. She traveled so often in her prison ministry that many railroads, familiar with her face, allowed her to travel for free. In 1906 she attended one of the revival meetings at Azusa Street in Los Angeles. She had gone there "tarrying for the Pentecost," but it was several months before she was baptized in the Spirit and spoke in tongues. Mother Wheaton died at a faith home she had founded.

934. Florence Steidel (1897–1962)

Prophecy and visions definitely did *not* end with the age of the apostles—nor did the loathsome disease known as leprosy. In 1924 Florence Steidel had a vision calling her to minister to the sick people of Africa. In the vision she saw the home in Liberia where she would later live. Before going there, she trained as a nurse and, in 1934, received the baptism in the Spirit. She established a girls' school in Liberia and saw the home that she had seen in the vision years before. She established New Hope Town, a leper colony built by people with leprosy. Hundreds of people with the disease were cured, and most of them were converted to Christ.

935. Pandita Ramabai (1858–1922)

We use the word *pundit* to mean "expert." The word comes from the Indian *pandit* (wise one) or, for a woman, *pandita*. Sarasvati Ramabai was known for her ability in reciting the Hindu scriptures, so she was titled *pandita*. She met Christians in Bengal, began to read the Bible, and became a Christian, convinced that her mission was to minister to India's women. After training in England and the

U.S. she returned to India to open a girls' school and a home for widows who had been treated badly by their husbands' families. She made no attempt at first to convert her pupils, though some of them did convert, drawn to her quality of life. She named her school the Mukti Mission and in 1897 began instructing pupils in religion. The mission (*Mukti* means "salvation") grew into a community of more than 1,300 and also became a revival center. After a severe famine in 1896 she was ardent in her relief work. Pandita Ramabai was a combination evangelist and social worker.

936. David Wesley Myland (1858–1943)

Having been healed several times while close to death, evangelist Myland naturally preached healing. His denomination, the Methodists, disapproved, so Myland transferred to the Christian and Missionary Alliance (CMA). He pastored a church, wrote hymns, and ran El Shaddai, a faith home. His newspaper, *Christian Messenger*, taught the fourfold gospel of salvation, sanctification, healing, and the Second Coming. He experienced the baptism of the Spirit and left the CMA because of the denomination's break with Pentecostalism over the issue of speaking in tongues. Though associated with the Pentecostal movement the rest of his life, and though he knew and influenced many of the founders of the Assemblies of God (AG), he never joined the AG. He opened another El Shaddai home in Ohio and throughout his long life wrote numerous hymns still widely used in Pentecostal churches.

937. Divine Healing Home Number One

Healing evangelist John Alexander Dowie often generated controversy. In 1894 he opened his Divine Healing Home Number One in Chicago. The city's health commissioner ruled that such faith homes (see 917) had to have a medical doctor on staff. Dowie did not believe in medical science, and more than once he was arrested for violating the city rule. Since any publicity is good publicity, Dowie's arrest called attention to his faith home. He opened two others in Chicago, drawing hundreds of people who wanted healing prayer. So great was his renown as a healer that in 1896 he purchased the luxurious Imperial Hotel and made it his Zion Divine Healing Home.

938. Charles Cullis (1833–92)

More Faith Cures, published in 1881, was subtitled *Answers to Prayers in the Healing of the Sick.* Its author was Cullis, a Boston doctor who had undergone a spiritual crisis in 1862 and vowed to use his talents to serve sick and neglected people. In the 1880s he opened various charities, including faith homes for poor people dying of tuberculosis. He conducted camp meetings that emphasized divine healing, and went as a healing evangelist to major cities in the U.S. Cullis did more than anyone else to make divine healing a key part of the Holiness movement.

939. Johann Christoph Blumhardt (1805–80)

The gift of divine healing has often been neglected. Blumhardt was a German pastor who, beginning in 1838, led a revival movement notable for the many people healed of physical and mental diseases. Many claimed to be freed from demon possession. Ministering at a time when many Germans practiced a dry "head" Christianity focused on theology, Blumhardt eventually opened a healing center for people wanting freedom from illness of any kind. Blumhardt's motto was "Jesus Is Victor."

940. George Müller (1805–98)

Born in Germany and trained as a Lutheran minister, Müller was not actually converted until 1825, when he attended a prayer meeting in a home. He moved to England where he pastored at Bethesda Chapel in Bristol. He founded the Scriptural Knowledge Institution for Home and Abroad to stimulate education on scriptural principles and to aid in missions. But he is most remembered for the orphanage he founded, which grew from one house to a large complex of buildings in Bristol. Ahead of his time in many ways, he emphasized believer's baptism and the practice of having laymen speak at church meetings. He adopted the principle—still followed by some ministries today—of never asking for funds but waiting on the Lord to move people to provide.

941. Bethel Institutions

A German pastor with the cumbersome name of Friedrich von Bodelschwingh was involved with a revival in Germany in the 1860s. Near Bielefeld, Germany, he helped establish the Bethel Institution for epileptic boys, a ministry later expanded to mental patients, homeless people, refugees, and troubled youths. The Bethel administrators emphasized the spiritual gift of healing, which they interpreted to refer to any relief of physical or mental distress.

18

Getting Wisdom and Knowledge

942. *Scofield Reference Bible*

C. I. Scofield (1843–1921) published his *Scofield Reference Bible* in 1909, and it would be an understatement to say that it became a classic. Its explanatory notes set forth the view known as dispensationalism (see 38), although not everyone who has owned a *Scofield* is necessarily a dispensationalist (or even knows what it means). Many Pentecostals have owned and loved the *Scofield Bible* even though it bluntly declares that spiritual gifts no longer operate. The note on 1 Corinthians 14 states that "tongues and the sign gifts are to cease," which is the dispensationalist view. In many Pentecostal-run Bible schools the *Scofield Bible* was the Bible of choice.

943. *The Spirit-Filled Bible*

Bibles geared toward charismatics and Pentecostals are old hat by now, but the first and still one of the most successful is this study Bible, edited by Jack Hayford (see 48 [Church on the Way]) and published in 1991.

944. L.I.F.E.

This occurs in many names related to the International Church of the Foursquare Gospel (ICFG). L.I.F.E. stands for Lighthouse of International Foursquare Evangelism. ICFG founder Aimee Semple McPherson founded the L.I.F.E. Bible College in 1923, and its graduates went forth to establish branch churches known as Lighthouse churches. The college had a three-year degree program leading to the Bachelor of Theology (Th.B.), and for several years it offered the Doctor of Theology program (which, since it required only four years of study after high school, did not measure up academically to Th.D. programs in traditional seminaries). McPherson deserves credit for taking an interest in higher education for Pentecostal church workers.

945. ORU

Oral Roberts University, opened in Tulsa, Oklahoma, in 1963 was the first Pentecostal university in America. It signaled a change from an earlier time when Pentecostals were highly suspicious of higher education and "intellectual" clergy. ORU's school of theology opened in 1965 but closed in 1969. The school reopened in 1975, describing itself as "catholic, evangelical, reformed, and charismatic," attempting (obviously) to attract a wide range of students who adhere to basic Christian beliefs.

946. CBN / Regent University

Oral Roberts was the first televangelist to open a university (see 945 [ORU]). Pat Robertson followed suit in 1977 with his CBN University in Virginia Beach. Named for its parent organization, the Christian Broadcasting Network, the school is now Regent University. Regent is a graduate school, with programs in law, theology, ministry, and biblical studies.

947. Assemblies of God Graduate School

Over the years churches have been supplied with seminary graduates—some of them deeply spiritual, but some who seem to be just doing a job without much conviction. Pentecostals have, for good reason, been suspicious of seminary-trained clergy and have often filled their pulpits with Spirit-led men and women who had little or no formal education. In recent years the larger Pentecostal denominations have been more open to college and seminary training for their ministers, although the idea of seminary still bothers many people. For this reason the Assemblies of God chose to call its graduate theology school the Assemblies of God Graduate School instead of a seminary. Opened in 1973, the school *was* a seminary, but its name paid its respects to that old suspicion of seminaries. In 1984 it became the Assemblies of God Theological Seminary.

948. teaching by prophecy

Pentecostals were long suspicious of higher education, but young pastors often trained under more experienced pastors or evangelists. Sometimes informal, sometimes set up as short-term Bible schools, the teaching sessions might involve teaching via the usual methods of lecture and discussion. But some instructors taught via prophecy or interpretation of tongues, which might involve quietly waiting upon God to give direction to the class.

949. the *Voice*

After a long career in journalism, Thomas Roy Nickel attended a 1953 meeting of the new Full Gospel Business Men's Fellowship International (FGBMFI). Impressed with the group, he offered his services to founder Demos Shakarian and for many years edited the group's magazine, the FGBMFI *Voice*. The magazine's circulation expanded to 250,000 and greatly increased awareness of the FGBMFI.

950. the *Charisma* family

Strang Communications, with offices near Orlando, Florida, is probably the best-known publisher of magazines for the charismatic/Pentecostal market in the U.S., publishing *Ministries Today, Christian Retailing,* and *Charisma* (which absorbed the long-running *Christian Life*). It is also home to Creation House, a charismatic book publishing firm.

951. Gallup polls

The Gallup organization has been polling America on thousands of topics for decades. In the area of religion, polls show that Americans by and large define themselves as religious people, and the majority identify themselves as Christian. Quite a few consider themselves Pentecostals or charismatics. But polls also show that people (including those who consider themselves Christian) are amazingly ignorant of the Bible and unfamiliar with Christianity's basic teachings.

This contrast has been apparent in the polls for decades. Yes, Americans are (or claim to be) religious. No, they do not know much about the Bible and beliefs. For all the laudable growth in churches, much needs to be done in the way of helping believers know and apply the basics of the faith.

952. Rochester Bible Training School

This two-year school was founded by Elizabeth Baker and her four sisters in 1906 and was an early example of Bible training for missionaries and other church workers. The only textbook was the Bible, which students studied book by book. Students who could pay little or nothing were urged to pray in their fees, which happened quite often. (Being run on the faith basis, the school did not solicit funds.)

953. Holmes Theological Seminary

Based in Greeneville, South Carolina, the school had been supported by Holiness churches since 1898, and when the supporting churches accepted Pentecostalism around 1907, the school became a training ground for future Pentecostal missionaries.

954. alternative schools

In the interest of "separation of church and state," public schools in the U.S. have become more and more secular and even (many would say) downright anti-Christian. Not surprisingly, private Christian schools have sprouted up like mushrooms, and home schooling has likewise grown. In the past, private religious schools were the domain of Catholics, Jews, and Missouri Synod Lutherans, but in recent years Assemblies of God, Baptists, and hundreds of independent churches have moved into private schooling. The Association of Christian Schools International has developed a program to certify graduates of Christian colleges as teachers in private schools. This ensures a measure of quality control among teachers who should (parents hope) be academically qualified *and* genuine Christians.

955. "Professional Use Only"

Pentecostals and charismatics have learned to "do theology" in seminaries and in writing theological books. We can hope that what they produce will not be like the lion's share of theology in the past century. One secular critic pointed out that most contemporary theology has little or nothing to say to the man in the street, and that it all might as well be labeled "For Professional Use Only." Surely the grassroots nature of the renewal movement will prevent this from happening.

956. Life in the Spirit seminars

Jesus told Nicodemus that the Spirit, like the wind, "blows where [He] wishes" (John 3:8), meaning that the Spirit of God is not under human control. Even so, there is nothing wrong with praying to be filled with the Spirit. And many charismatics, Catholics in particular, have helped prepare candidates for the baptism of the Spirit by courses known as Life in the Spirit seminars. Recognizing that a person can't be trained into the baptism of the Spirit (any more than the Spirit can be trained), the seminars work on the assumption that a person can be made more open to the working of God.

957. "Dumb Dogs"

In the past Pentecostals had a suspicion of theological training, since (as is still true) people with theological degrees are not necessarily spiritual people. The Doctor of Divinity degree, abbreviated D.D., was said by some critics to mean "Dumb Dogs," and seminaries were referred to as "cemeteries." The attitude has changed, and Pentecostals today operate not only Bible training schools but also accredited seminaries.

958. Pathway Press

This is the publishing house for the Church of God (Cleveland, Tennessee), launched in 1910 when it began a weekly journal, *Church of God Evangel,* still being published. The firm purchased its own printing plant to produce its Sunday school curriculum and is today one of the largest Christian publishing firms in the U.S.

959. Logos International

Logos, until it filed for bankruptcy in 1981, was a major publisher of charismatic and Pentecostal books and magazines. The company had limited success with its charismatic magazines, *National Courier* and *Logos Journal,* but it published books that were runaway best-sellers. Nicky Cruz's *Run, Baby, Run,* written with Jamie Buckingham, sold more than eight million copies. Merlin Carothers's *Prison to Praise* was also popular, as was *The Holy Spirit and You* by Dennis and Rita Bennett. Logos was founded in 1966 by Dan Malachuk, who watched the company soar through the 1970s, then drop with a thud. After Logos filed for bankruptcy, some of its titles were taken over by Bridge Publishing.

960. Gospel Publishing House

Since 1918, Springfield, Missouri, has been home to the large publishing wing of the Assemblies of God (AG). As the AG has grown phenomenally, so has Gospel Publishing House. It is one of the few religious publishers still operating its own printing plant. The company produces not only books but also the Radiant Life curriculum series, used by the AG and by many independent Spirit-led churches.

961. Calvinists

Many people would admit to being both evangelical and Pentecostal, but in the past there was some mutual suspicion between the two. Many evangelicals, especially the more educated ones, looked down on Pentecostals as being too, well, emotional. And many Pentecostals looked upon the more intellectual of the evangelicals as being Calvinists, too concerned with correct belief and not concerned enough with feeling the power of the Spirit. As time goes on there is healthy dialogue between the two groups, but Spirit-filled Christians are right to be wary of an overintellectualized faith.

19

Odds and Ends

962. one of *Life's* biggies

In its October 1997 issue, *Life* magazine listed the 1906 Azusa Street revival as one of the top one hundred events in the last one thousand years. (See 674 [Azusa Street revival].)

963. Hammer

How many stars are big enough to get by with just one name? Hammer, also known as M. C. Hammer (born Stanley Burrell), is one. One of the megastars of pop music, Hammer accepted Christ in 1984 and had a gospel group known as the Holy Ghost Boys. After a period of backsliding, Hammer rededicated himself to the Lord in 1998.

964. *Newsweek* and Pentecostals

A quote from *Newsweek*, April 13, 1998: "When Pente-costal Christians read the Bible, they find the Holy Spirit in action everywhere—something modern theologians often miss."

965. Miss America, 1990

Debbye Turner, a member of Maranatha Christian Church in Columbia, Missouri, was crowned Miss America, 1990. She claimed her church's prayer warriors had prayed for her to win the title.

966. televangelists in Britain?

Televangelists have been a fixture of American TV for many years, but in 1992 Morris Cerullo became the first televangelist on British TV.

967. the raising of Olive Mills

Can Christians literally raise the dead? No one has dupli-cated Jesus' feat in raising Lazarus (who had been buried for four days), but there are valid accounts of people being clinically dead for minutes or even hours, then coming back to life. In 1899 the controversial Frank Sandford, head of the Shiloh community in Maine, brought about the resur-rection of Olive Mills, who had just died of meningitis. Sandford and two other men prayed over her, and Sandford shouted, "Olive Mills, come back! In the name of Jesus of

Nazareth, come back!" She opened her eyes and within a few hours was up and dressed. More than once, Jesus told His followers that they would heal people and raise the dead (Matt. 10:8; Luke 7:22; Acts 20:9–11).

968. what founder?

Who started the renewal movement? So many religions and movements begin with one person, a dominating figure, or perhaps a small group. Martin Luther was one, as were John Calvin, John Wesley, and Francis of Assisi. But although there have been many notable figures in the renewal movement, there is no one individual who dominates the consciousness of Spirit-filled believers. That is as it should be—the glory goes to God. The movement has been for the most part grassroots, people responding to the working of the Spirit.

969. "these evils on television"

The 1955 Manual of the United Pentecostal Church referred to "the display of all these evils on television" and disapproved of any members owning televisions. Consider how evil television today is compared to 1955 (but also consider how many religious programs now air).

970. Bette Davis, Pentecostal?

The 1976 TV movie *The Disappearance of Aimee* delved into the mysterious 1926 disappearance of renowned preacher Aimee Semple McPherson. The movie suggested that her alleged "kidnapping" was in fact a brief fling with a male companion. Aimee's mother, the formidable Minnie Kennedy, was portrayed by the formidable Bette Davis, with Faye Dunaway as Aimee.

971. TBN

The Trinity Broadcasting Network (TBN) is the brainchild of Paul Crouch, its founder and head. He graduated from Bible college and worked in radio and TV, then in 1961 began directing film and TV productions for the Assemblies of God. With Jim and Tammy Bakker (before the days of scandal), Paul and his wife, Jan, founded a station in Santa Ana, California, that was to be TBN's foundation station. Not long after that, TBN began broadcasting via satellite, bringing its programs to millions worldwide.

972. Fields of the Wood

A Pentecostal theme park? Not exactly, but a *biblical* theme park, operated by a Pentecostal denomination, the Church of God of Prophecy. The site in Cherokee County, North Carolina, was purchased by the denomination for historic reasons and named Fields of the Wood by evangelist A. J. Tomlinson. On the site the church has staged Easter pageants, Thanksgiving reenactments, tent revivals, and other activities. The tract of land has on it a mountain slope with the Ten Commandments in huge letters (each about six feet tall), plus a huge Bible (more than thirty feet wide) open to Matthew 22:37–40. Other features on the site are the Lord's Prayer, the Beatitudes, Psalm 23, a huge cross, and a replica of Jesus' tomb.

973. "men-made creeds"

When the Church of God (Cleveland, Tennessee) was in its formative stages in the 1880s, its founders had issued a statement calling on all Christians "desirous to be free of men-made creeds and traditions." This reflects an ongoing theme in Christian renewal: a desire to get back to the Bible and bypass all the unbiblical traditions of denominations. Of course, every group that does this ends up forming a denomination.

974. Campus Farthest Out (CFO)

The CFO conferences were begun in 1930 by Glenn Clark to help Christians become athletes of the Spirit. The CFO gatherings usually lasted a week and featured many speakers who had experienced the baptism of the Holy Spirit. Many of the attendees received the baptism of the Spirit. For many people in the mainline denominations, the CFOs were their first exposure to the charismatic movement.

975. Warren Badenoch Straton (1907-66)

Pentecostal and *the arts* are not words that people usually connect, but Straton was an Assemblies of God (AG) pastor *and* a noted artist. A gifted painter from an early age, he sold his sculptures at Tiffany's in New York and designed the Chrysler Building, the eagles on the Memorial Bridge to Arlington, and the Department of Justice building. He taught art at the AG's Evangel College and at Oral Roberts University.

976. *Jesus and the Kingdom*

George Eldon Ladd, a professor at Fuller Theological Seminary in California, published this book in 1964. He concluded after intense study of the New Testament that Jesus is the King and Christians are His subjects, and that the King equips His subjects with power to preach, drive out demons, and heal the sick. The gospel is a call to be part of this kingdom, with Christ as King. The book was a key influence on John Wimber, his Vineyard Christian Fellowship, and the broad renewal movement.

977. territorial demons

Are demons attached to certain locations? The question is not a silly one. C. Peter Wagner (see 574) researched the subject at length and concluded that some evil spirits are apparently tied to certain locations, as evidenced by missionaries' encounters with them. Wagner's views have not been accepted by everyone, but he made a good case for them in his 1991 book *Engaging the Enemy: How to Fight and Defeat Territorial Spirits*.

978. church growth movement

A missionary to India, Donald McGavran, observed that though missionaries were doing many works of compassion abroad, most of their churches were not growing. Curious about why some churches grew and others stagnated, he traveled to Africa, Thailand, Mexico, and other locales to study church growth. In 1961, after years of study he established the Institute of Church Growth in Eugene, Oregon. In a few years he left to start a School of World Mission at Fuller Theological Seminary. This graduate school requires its degree candidates to produce a thesis based on original fieldwork in a particular locale. The theses, when published, have been valuable tools for present and future missionaries. The church growth movement was not founded for the specific purpose of helping the Pentecostal and charismatic movements, but it has certainly had that effect.

979. radio Pentecostals

Hard as it is to believe, there are people in regions of the world whose only contact with Spirit-led Christianity is the radio. In the Communist world (dwindling though it may be), the broadcasts received are usually foreign in origin.

980. "the source is from the skies"

William J. Seymour, pastor of the Azusa Street Mission, made this statement about the amazing revival that occurred there in 1906. Seymour was definitely a key leader in the revival, but also a very humble man, and his statement does credit to him. Most of the early Pentecostal leaders were not egomaniacs, and most were emphatic in giving credit to the Spirit, not to themselves.

981. Tomlinson and the apostles

A. J. Tomlinson, founder and first head of the Church of God (Cleveland, Tennessee), had no doubts about the historical roots of his denomination: it sprang from Jesus and the apostles. In one sense he was right: the same Spirit who empowered the first Christians also empowered the Pentecostal renewal that gave birth to the Church of God and other denominations. Tomlinson was in the tradition of restorationism (see 782), the desire to restore the church to what it was in the New Testament. Of course, the Church of God did not directly descend from the apostles, for there were centuries in between and many people and movements that led to the founding of the Church of God. But he was correct in giving credit to the chief mover, the Spirit.

982. "independent" evangelists?

Some of the greatest evangelists have been affiliated with a major denomination (Billy Graham is a Southern Baptist, for example), but all have worked across denominational lines, putting the conversion of the individual before any concern for a denomination. Many church authorities criticize this, saying that evangelists are basically antichurch— outside the control of any denomination, and making converts who have no ties to any fellowship. But the criticism is unfair. Almost all reputable evangelists work to bring converts into fellowship with local churches. Indeed, the most successful evangelists could not have succeeded without the cooperation of local churches in the areas being evangelized.

983. Stone's Folly

Charles F. Parham, one of the prominent names in the early renewal movement, opened his Bethel Bible School at a home in Topeka, Kansas, in October 1900. The home was a fifteen-room, three-story mansion, built by a man named Stone but never completed inside. Stone had made the home look castlelike on the outside (including towers and battlements), and the first two floors had beautiful carved staircases and general opulence. But since he ran out of funds, the third floor was left unfinished. The home was known as Stone's Folly.

Parham hoped to make it the center of a Christian community like Frank Sandford's Shiloh in Maine. Stone's Folly became briefly famous after the amazing outpouring of the Spirit there in January 1901, drawing visitors from around the country. Facing a financial crunch, Parham had to sell Stone's Folly with its famous Prayer Tower. The buyer was a local bootlegger, and (probably to Parham's satisfaction) the mansion burned to the ground that same year. The site has a secure place in the history of the renewal movement. (See 476 [Parham]; 477 [Agnes Ozman].)

984. *Kol Kare Bombidbar*

It's Hebrew for a "voice crying in the wilderness," quoted in Matthew 3:3. It was the title of Charles F. Parham's first book, published in 1902 after the amazing outpouring of the Spirit at his Bible school in Kansas. Parham saw himself as leader of a new renewal movement, a "voice crying in the wilderness" to draw together God's faithful remnant of committed believers.

985. Azusa anniversaries

Renewal Christians focus on the present work of the Spirit (and rightly so), but some are also interested in the historical roots of the renewal movement. Looking back to the historic Azusa Street revival in 1906, Thomas Nickel of California has worked for Azusa Street anniversary celebrations, the first in 1991, and one every five years until Jesus returns.

986. presidential clout

Billy Graham has achieved a reputation as the presidents' preacher, having hobnobbed with many. In an earlier age, healing evangelist John Alexander Dowie was granted personal audiences with two presidents, William McKinley and Theodore Roosevelt.

987. *Bridal Call*

This was the name of a magazine published by Aimee Semple McPherson's ministry, and it is one of many publications in the renewal movement that mention "bride." Which bride are they referring to? The church, of course— or more specifically, the church in heaven, eternally pure and suitable for the "groom," Christ: "I, John, saw the holy city, New Jerusalem, coming down out of heaven from God, prepared as a bride adorned for her husband" (Rev. 21:2).

988. *Life,* June 9, 1958

Liberal Christians have been less than kind to the renewal movement, but there are exceptions. Henry Van Dusen, president of the liberal Union Theological Seminary in New York, was complimentary toward the growth of Pentecostal and Holiness groups in the U.S. His favorable comments appeared in a *Life* magazine article, "The Third Force in Christendom."

989. Mormons

The Latter-day Saints, better known as the Mormons, encouraged spiritual gifts, at least in their earlier days. The seventh Article of Faith stated that Mormons "believe in the gift of tongues, prophecy, revelation, visions, healing, interpretation of tongues, etc."

990. "baptism of burning love"

Wesleyan theologian John Fletcher (see 420) used this phrase in the 1700s to describe what some call the baptism in the Spirit. It sounds similar to the fire baptism that some Pentecostal denominations teach.

991. Wesley's Aldersgate experience

The United Methodist Renewal Services Fellowship has been an active organization for many years. In 1979 it began hosting annual Aldersgate Conferences for Methodist charismatics, and the fellowship is now generally called

Aldersgate Renewal Ministries. The name comes from a life-changing experience in the life of Methodist founder John Wesley. In May 1738 Wesley attended a Christian meeting in Aldersgate Street in London, and during the meeting he felt his heart "strangely warmed . . . Then it pleased God to kindle a fire which I trust shall never be extinguished."

992. "heart-religion"

John Wesley, founder of Methodism, was criticized by the Church of England for his followers' *enthusiasm* (the slur word then for emotion in religion). Wesley defended it as being "heart-religion; in other words, righteousness, peace, and joy in the Holy Ghost. These must be felt, or they have no being." (See 415 [Wesley]; 707 [enthusiasm].)

993. the Pawnee in Galena

Charles F. Parham (see 476) was privileged to behold the modern Pentecost break out at his Kansas Bible school in 1901. Afterward he took the message on the road and saw many new converts and baptisms in the Spirit. In Galena, Kansas, in 1904, during one of his meetings, a woman arose and spoke for ten minutes in a language no one understood—except for a Pawnee from a nearby reservation. He claimed that the woman spoke in his tribal language, and that he understood her perfectly. (See 31 [xenolalia].)

994. "heavenly chorus"

At the Azusa Street revival in Los Angeles (1906), some people attending the packed church broke into "heavenly chorus," spontaneous song utterly unknown to them but quite harmonious. Some of the people who sang so "heavenly" had been those who had never sang well before.

995. Professor Cox, admirer

Perhaps the poster child for liberal Christianity in the 1960s was Harvey Cox, famed for *The Secular City*. In 1995 Cox published *Fire from Heaven*, an admiring look at the Spirit-led renewal around the world. Cox had come to believe that spirituality, not secularity, was winning the battle.

996. "the Hallelujahs"

Mexico, still predominantly Catholic, has seen phenomenal growth in its Pentecostal churches. Many of the Mexicans are impressed with the joyous worship of the Pentecostals and refer to them as "the Hallelujahs."

997. the word (and Spirit) man

Peter Funk has for years produced "It Pays to Increase Your Word Power," a popular feature in *Reader's Digest*. A grandson of the Funk of *Funk & Wagnalls Encyclopedia* fame, he is a lay evangelist in the Episcopal church and known for laying hands on the sick and praying for healing.

998. Pentecostal on celluloid

Academy Award–winning actor Robert Duvall could find no one to produce a story about a Pentecostal preacher, so he did it himself, spending $5 million out of his own pocket. Duvall produced, wrote, directed, and starred in *The Apostle,* his 1997 movie about a flawed but genuine Pentecostal preacher. He was nominated for another Academy Award. Many Christians who saw the film were pleased that (contrary to Hollywood tradition) it did not show the man as a buffoon or a shyster, but as a three-dimensional human being.

999. grow, grow, grow

It has been estimated at the end of the century that Pentecostal/charismatic churches are growing at the rate of thirty-five thousand people per day.

1,000. accountable evangelists

Are there crooked evangelists and ministries? A few—but enough to give Christianity a bad name. In 1979, Billy Graham helped establish the Evangelical Council for Financial Accountability to make evangelists more accountable to the public. It has a Donors Bill of Rights, with tips on making sure the organization is guided by the Spirit and not by greed.

1,001. S. Lee Braxton (1905–82)

The rich have never embraced the gospel in such large numbers as the poor have, yet more than a few wealthy Christians have made great contributions to the faith, not only in money but in energy. One was Braxton, a millionaire in North Carolina and adviser and contributor to Oral Roberts. Braxton also assisted Demos Shakarian in building the Full Gospel Business Men's Fellowship into a dynamic part of the worldwide renewal movement.

Index

Numbers refer to the 1,001 entry numbers, not to page numbers. The main entry for each topic is set in boldface.

References to certain key topics (such as speaking in tongues, baptism of the Spirit, gifts of the Spirit, laying on of hands, healing, Pentecostals, and charismatics) are so numerous that to list them all would be of little help to the reader. In such cases only the numbers of the main entries are given.

Index

healing, gift of, **14**
Helper and Comforter, Spirit as, **276**
helpers, gift of, **15**
Hezmalhalch, Thomas, **897**
Hickey, Marilyn, **557**
Hicks, Tommy, **882**
"high praise," **84**
Hilary, **351**
Hildegard, **368**
Hinn, Benny, **562**
Hippolytus, 40, **343**
Hocken, Peter, **920**
Hodge, Charles, **706**
Hodges, Melvin, **879**
Hodgson, Teddi, **721**
Hogan, J. Philip, **866**
holiness, concept of, 344, 445, 738, 739
Holiness Baptists, **452**
Holiness movement, 192, 210, **449**, 455, 457, 469, 476, 702, 917
Hollenweger, Walter J., **661**
Holmes Theological Seminary, **953**
holy laughter, **81**
Holy Rollers, **685**
Holy Spirit Teaching Mission, **152**, 153, 201
home schooling, 954
Hoover, Willis C., **880**
Hopkins, Gerard Manley, **465**
Horton, Stanley M., **662**
Household of God, The, 776
hovering Spirit, **234**
Hughes, Ray H., **596**
Huguenots, 392, 404
Humbard, Rex, **566**
Hume, David, **711**
Hurst, Wesley Robinson, **864**

Ignatius of Antioch, **332**
IHS, **103**
illumination, **306**, 421

In the Power of the Spirit, **455**
"indisputable proof," **33**
indwelling of the Spirit, **304**
infant exorcism, **366**
Ingram, J. H., **860**
"initial evidence," **35**, 476, 500, 530
Integrity Communications, **153**, 201
International Church of the Foursquare Gospel, 52, **151**, 474, 616, 620, 944
interpretation of tongues, gift of, **26**
Irvingites, **436**
Isaiah, 249–251, 268, 738

Jansenists, **399**
Jefferson, Thomas, **710**
Jeffreys, George, 193, **512**
Jeffreys, Stephen, **513**
Jenkins, Leroy, 207
Jeremiah, **252**
Jericho march, **78**
Jesus and the Kingdom, **976**
Jesus '78, **679**
"Jesus Is Lord" (confession of faith), **311**
"Jesus Only," 87, 163, 502, 525, 736
Jesus People, 69, **143**, 582
Jesus' ascension, **282**
Jesus' baptism, 119, **265**
Joachim of Fiore, **371**
Joel, 255, 256, 741, 771
John "in the Spirit," **326**
John Paul II, Pope, **584**
John the Baptist, 89, **261**, 265, 286
Johnson, Bernhard, **863**
Jones, Bob, 554, **698**
Joshua, 78, **240**
judges of Israel, 241
Jungkutz, Theodore, **835**
Justin Martyr, **338**

About the Author

J. Stephen Lang is the author of fifteen books, including *1,001 Things You Always Wanted to Know About the Bible But Never Thought to Ask*, *The Complete Book of Bible Trivia* (which has sold more than 500,000 copies), and *The Complete Book of Bible Promises*.

Lang has a B.A. in religion from Vanderbilt University and an M.A. in communications from Wheaton College, and he is a former book editor for Tyndale House Publishers. He is also a regular contributor to *Moody*, *Discipleship Journal*, *Christian History*, and other periodicals.

Also by
J. Stephen Lang

1,001 Things You Always Wanted to Know About the Bible
But Never Thought to Ask

In this book, you'll discover how the Bible has impacted
language, U.S. history, worship, music, art, literature,
movies, and theater; how the Bible was passed down to us;
plus every key person, place, event, and idea in the Bible.
Best-selling Bible trivia author J. Stephen Lang's intriguing
tidbits will leave you yearning to know more about the
world's most fascinating book.